JOURNAL FOR THEOLOGY AND THE CHURCH

2

TRANSLATING THEOLOGY INTO THE MODERN AGE

hαrper ✝ torchbooks

A reference-list of Harper Torchbooks, classified by subjects, is printed at the end of this volume.

JOURNAL FOR THEOLOGY AND THE CHURCH

2

TRANSLATING THEOLOGY
INTO THE MODERN AGE

J. C. B. MOHR (PAUL SIEBECK) TÜBINGEN
HARPER & ROW, PUBLISHERS, INC. NEW YORK
1965

JOURNAL FOR THEOLOGY AND THE CHURCH

In association with the

ZEITSCHRIFT FÜR THEOLOGIE UND KIRCHE

In Gemeinschaft mit

Erich Dinkler / Hartmut Gese / Ernst Käsemann
Gerhard Rosenkranz / Hanns Rückert / Ernst Steinbach

herausgegeben von

Gerhard Ebeling

Printed in the United States of America

©

1965
J. C. B. Mohr (Paul Siebeck) Tübingen
Harper & Row, Publishers, Inc. New York
First edition: HARPER TORCHBOOKS, published 1965 by
Harper & Row, Publishers, Incorporated
49 East 33rd Street
New York, N. Y. 10016

CONTENTS

AUTHORS

BIZER, ERNST, University of Bonn
   Lutfridstraße 8, Bonn, Germany

BULTMANN, RUDOLF, University of Marburg
   Calvinstraße 14, Marburg/Lahn, Germany

EBELING, GERHARD, University of Zurich
   Nägelistraße 5, Zurich, Switzerland

MEZGER, MANFRED, University of Mainz
   Nerotalstraße 39, Mainz-Gonsenheim, Germany

VON OPPEN, DIETRICH, University of Marburg
   Am Kornacker 8, Wehrda bei Marburg, Germany

RÜCKERT, HANNS, University of Tübingen
   Am Apfelberg 15, Tübingen, Germany

TRANSLATORS

CARLSTON, CHARLES E., State University of Iowa
    Iowa City, Iowa

FUNK, ROBERT W., The Theological School, Drew University
    Madison, New Jersey

KRAFT, ROBERT A., University of Pennsylvania
    Philadelphia, Pennsylvania

LEITCH, JAMES W., Pastor
    High Manse, Bathgate, Scotland

MACCORMICK, CHALMERS, Wells College
    Aurora, New York

SATROM, MERLYN E., Campus Minister, Portland State College
    Portland, Oregon

ABBREVIATIONS

BETh	Beiträge zur Evangelischen Theologie
BHTh	Beiträge zur Historischen Theologie
ExpT	Expository Times
HNT	Handbuch zum Neuen Testament
HTR	Harvard Theological Review
ICC	International Critical Commentary
JR	Journal of Religion
NTS	New Testament Studies
RE	Realencyclopädie für Protestantische Theologie und Kirche
RGG	Die Religion in Geschichte und Gegenwart
ThLZ	Theologische Literaturzeitung
ThR	Theologische Rundschau (NF = Neue Folge)
ThW	Theologisches Wörterbuch zum Neuen Testament
TU	Texte und Untersuchungen zur Geschichte der Altchristlichen Literatur
WA	Martin Luther, Werke: Weimarer Ausgabe
ZAW	Zeitschrift für die Alttestamentliche Wissenschaft
ZDPV	Zeitschrift des Deutschen Palästina-Vereins (NF = Neue Folge)
ZNW	Zeitschrift für die Neutestamentliche Wissenschaft (und die Kunde der Älteren Kirche)
ZThK	Zeitschrift für Theologie und Kirche

FOREWORD

JOURNAL FOR THEOLOGY AND THE CHURCH was conceived in a late night conversation with Gerhard Ebeling during the First Drew Consultation on Hermeneutics in 1962. Looking back on the road that has been traversed since that first talk, now that the first two numbers are ready for the press, it seems short and troublefree indeed. To be sure, many obstacles had to be overcome, but the support and encouragement received by the board helped smooth the way as well as buttress the conviction that the undertaking was worthwhile.

That JOURNAL FOR THEOLOGY AND THE CHURCH 1 and 2 are to appear simultaneously in 1965 is to be credited, above all, to Gerhard Ebeling and the board of ZEITSCHRIFT FÜR THEOLOGIE UND KIRCHE. This distinguished circle agreed, in the course of conversations with members of the *JThC* board, than an English affiliate of *ZThK* would not only serve to broadcast current (in distinction from recent) Continental theology, but to enter into its formulation and testing as well. A sister organ in English, moreover, might be of some benefit to English language theology in and of itself. They were disposed, as a consequence, to lend themselves to the effort of launching a comparable English language journal. They did not propose to help create their own echo, but to help precipitate, if it were desired, a theological dialogue native to the English language world. Such a journal, to be sure, ought to maintain a lively tension with its counterpart in the interests of both Continental and American theology. The board of *JThC* is acutely aware of the trust that has been vested in it by virtue of this invitation to enter into association.

Hans Georg Siebeck, the *Inhaber* of the J.C.B. Mohr *Verlag* and publisher of *ZThK*, was no less sensitive to the possibilities of such a move. He opened the way by agreeing to publish the JOURNAL under his own imprint if necessary. Harper & Row subsequently entered the picture, with the joint result now before the reader. Vindication of the courage of both publishers and of the generosity of the editor and board of *ZThK* now rests with the editorial circle of *JThC* – which will endeavor to merit the attention of all those concerned with theology for the church and for our time – and with the reader – who will perhaps find something in these pages worthy of his sustained consideration.

It should also be said that others gave unstintingly of their time and effort in helping us analyze innumerable problems and proposals. In addition, we should like to acknowledge the special contribution of Professor Raymond P. Morris of the Yale Divinity School, whose keen insight and sound judgment have proved invaluable.

Beyond those who helped bring JOURNAL FOR THEOLOGY AND THE CHURCH into existence, there are those who shared in the production of the first two numbers. For that something extra which makes translation an art rather than a science, thanks are due my colleague, Karlfried Froehlich, who masterfully edited the translations. He is also responsible in part for formal matters. And finally, notice must be taken of the translators who worked industriously and imaginatively at a difficult task. While such quality as has been achieved would not have been easily possible without such assistance, the board and editor must take responsibility for the final form of the material and such blemishes as the JOURNAL may have.

A word is in order regarding format. It may seem odd that a journal should take the form of a paperback book. On the other hand, when one reflects on it, it seems odder still that it is not the rule rather than the exception. The paperback is a more convenient size than the standard journal, comes already bound for the benefit of those who find preserving issues a headache, and is readily available on the bookrack at the local bookseller. Building and maintaining a subscription list, and the expense of mailing, moreover, are formidable overhead items which drive the subscription rates of journals up. The paperback journal, by contrast, is distributed through regular channels, thus making it possible to offer it at a substantially lower price. It is to be hoped that our readers will appreciate this difference and will find it possible to acquire the JOURNAL regularly, either through a local bookseller or by standing order at one of the mail-order houses.

JOURNAL FOR THEOLOGY AND THE CHURCH 1 and 2 reflect the initial stage of the JOURNAL as conceived by the board – one in which we are leaning exclusively or heavily on our affiliate, the *ZThK*. There are two reasons for this. First, we wish to make available some of the significant material published in *ZThK* since it was reorganized under the editorship of Gerhard Ebeling. Early numbers of the JOURNAL will therefore be devoted largely to what has been going on in the pages of *ZThK* between 1950 and the present. And second, the flow of English language contributions will require some time – hopefully no more than a few issues – to develop and to create its own focus. As quickly as the latter materializes, the initial stage will give way to one in which original contributions in English take their place alongside the most significant essays from *ZThK*. For it is the concern of the board of *JThC* to cultivate an indigenous English language theological conversation no less than to foster an international dialogue. In fact, if the former does not emerge, both aims of the JOURNAL will have been frustrated. James M. Robinson has set out this ground plan, together with its underlying rationale, in his introductory essay in the first number.

JOURNAL FOR THEOLOGY AND THE CHURCH 1 presents eight provocative essays from the biblical field, all taken from *ZThK*. In the judgment of the board, each of these essays is significant both for the special discipline from which it emanates and for theology as a whole. It is these two criteria which governed the selection of items to be included. *JThC* 2 offers six stimulating essays in historical, systematic and pastoral theology. These essays likewise reach deep into and far beyond their particular domains. If we have succeeded in forging an inseparable unity between sound scientific scholarship and theological relevance in these numbers, we will have established the character we intend the JOURNAL to have throughout its existence. And we are rash enough to think that English language theologians, theological students, ecclesiastical officials, pastors, and even, or perhaps especially, laymen will welcome the confluence of the two and will profit by it.

Second Sunday in Advent, 1964   ROBERT W. FUNK, Editor
                                        The Theological School
                                        Drew University

The Reformation – Medieval or Modern? *

by

Hanns Rückert

Translated by Charles E. Carlston

How is the Reformation to be classified in intellectual history? This first became problematical in our generation. From the standpoint of the nineteenth-century view of history the answer seemed to be obvious: It was assumed as demonstrated fact that in the Reformation the conquest of the Middle Ages and the birth of the modern period took place. With this *communis opinio*, however, two quite different, even antithetical, evaluations of the Reformation, the Middle Ages, and modern times were associated. Their divergence may be sketched by the contrasting of the idealistic and the romantic understanding of history which H. Bornkamm worked out in his book, *Luther im Spiegel der deutschen Geistesgeschichte*,[1] and which is illustrated by Hegel on the one hand and Novalis on the other.

For Hegel the achievements of the Reformation, as he sees them, not only stand under that auspicious omen which his philosophy of history presumes to place over *all* advances in historical development; they also receive at his hand a special emphasis as epoch-making events. He includes them all in the concept of "subjectivity" in order to render what Luther meant by "faith," which must be brought into being by each individual for himself. "*His* feeling, *his* faith, *his* subjectivity – in short, what is *his*, his *own* inner certainty is demanded of him; in relation to God this alone is truly of any moment." Where subjectivity appropriates the Spirit of truth and | grants it lodging, it comes to itself in its own truth, i. e., it becomes free. "This is the essential content of the Reformation: man is determined by himself to be free." Since Hegel interprets the message of the Reformation in this sense, he makes the Reformation responsible for the discovery of Idealism's central truth; in so doing he makes it a new and final step in the self-unfolding in history of the absolute Spirit. In the

---

* "Die geistesgeschichtliche Einordnung der Reformation," ZThK, 52, 1955, pp. 43–64. – A lecture given in Tübingen on University Day, December 7, 1954.
[1] Gütersloh, 1954. – It is from the second part of this book ("Texte") that the citations from HEGEL, NOVALIS, HARNACK and TROELTSCH in what follows have been taken. Using this section of BORNKAMM's book, one can easily check the citations in the original works.

Reformation the curve of historical development ascends sharply to its zenith, and Hegel understands himself and his philosophical enterprise within the development initiated by it. With the Reformation "the new and final standard has been raised around which the nations gather, the banner of the free Spirit, which is self-subsistent, subsisting in the truth and self-subsistent only in the truth. This is the banner under which we serve and which we bear. The period from then until now has had no other task than to inculcate this principle into the world."

Novalis also understands the roots of his own modern world to lie in the Reformation. But he is bitterly opposed both to this modern world and to the movement that has brought it about. The great error of Protestantism consists in the fact that it destroyed the unity of Christendom, in which the unity of Europe and the dominance of the sense of the Unseen – and hence the salvation of western man – had been conceived. "They separated the inseparable, divided the indivisible Church and tore themselves sacrilegiously out of the common Christian society through which and in which alone true and lasting rebirth was possible." "The Reformation spelled the end for Christendom. From now on it simply ceased to exist." There were – and are – only mutually exclusive sectarian confessions, of which the Protestant confessions in particular are characterized by the establishment of state churches, which "sacrilegiously confined religion within state boundaries and laid the groundwork for the gradual undermining of cosmopolitan concerns based on religion."

At the same time, however, Novalis draws a direct line from the Reformation to the Enlightenment, that arch-enemy of Romanticism, which he charges with having murdered Europe's soul. Luther's biblicism is "a denial of the Christian spirit" and by it is introduced a new "letter" – in spite of the fact that "nothing desensitizes the religious outlook like the letter" and through the letter it is made "immeasurably more difficult for the Holy Spirit to bring new life, inspiration, and revelation." This biblicism is the beginning of the "impoverishing | influence" of philological science in religious matters, a "scientism" of the Spirit, which had an even more devastating effect in the role to which philosophy degenerated as a consequence of having taken over the Reformation's separation of faith and knowledge. "The nearer the history of European humanity came to the period of all-conquering pedantry" the more "men sought the cause of the general stagnation in faith and hoped to relieve it through the advance of knowledge." "The result of this modern mode of thinking was called philosophy; under it was subsumed everything that was opposed to what was ancient, of which this anti-religious conceit was a prime example." Further, "this hatred of religion naturally and consistently was extended to include all objects of 'enthusiasm'; it calumniated imagination and feeling, morality and love of art, antiquity and the future; it classified man

only with difficulty at the top of the scale of 'natural' beings; and it
transformed the eternally creative celestial music into the monotonous
clatter of a monstrous mill, a mill driven by and floating in a stream of
circumstance, self-contained, built by no one and used by no one, a true
perpetuum mobile that even does its own grinding." Hence for Novalis the
Reformation stands at the beginning of the history of modern unbelief; it
is "the key" to "all the monstrous phenomena of modern times."

The differing views of history represented by Hegel and Novalis are a
prefiguration of the divergence between Protestant and Catholic historical
consciousness in the nineteenth century. In the process of divergence both
conceptions were forced to submit to the vulgarizing and over-simplifying
that are inevitable in such popularizations. Novalis' *Die Christenheit oder
Europa* necessarily had quite a different effect from what he intended, if
for no other reason than that twenty-seven years elapsed between its
composition in 1799 and its publication by Friedrich Schlegel. During this
period the romantic movement had grown old and the whole world sur-
rounding it had fundamentally changed. Otherwise the writing could not
have been misunderstood as it was. Its view of history was intended to
support the vision of a new future Christianity, born of the romantic spirit
and transconfessional in nature; it was understood in the sense of the
catholicizing tendency evidenced by the numerous conversions among the
late romantics. It was also understood as programmatic for a romanticizing
Catholicism of a distinct ultramontane stamp which had opted for a
restoration of the Middle Ages and the exclusion of everything that
smacked of the Enlightenment or Idealism, a Catholicism for which the
word "Modernism" | became the equivalent of "heresy" and which
simultaneously became acutely conscious once more of its irreconcilable
opposition to Protestantism.

I do not profess to have given an exhaustive characterization of nineteenth-century Catholicism by emphasizing its yearning for the restoration
of the Middle Ages and its conscious antipathy to the modern spirit. But it
will hardly be disputed that these two tendencies were imbibed as thoroughly and as early as maternal milk, or that from them came the power
for the highly impressive movement of consolidation which was the
hallmark of nineteenth-century Catholic development, or that they
remained a basic ingredient in the picture which Catholicism presented at
least until 1914. Even in our day the Catholic historical consciousness, at
least, is formed by them. The Middle Ages, with its ecclesiastical and
cultural unity, its large and powerful social organizations giving security
to the individual, with its organically developed and firmly fixed orders, its
unassailable authorities and its tradition, rich enough to allow for freedom
and unambiguous enough to allow for genuine obligations – this was the
classical period of both the Church and the West. Its end coincided with the

beginning of the great Apostasy, the rebellion of man against God, which has led increasingly to chaos and disorder. Salvation for man and his derailed world is possible only if medieval values and traditions can be made binding once more. This historical consciousness stood and stands in a relationship of mutual support with the Catholic Church's dogmatic judgment on the Reformation, at least as long and as far as the proposition is valid that the Reformation is the end of the Middle Ages and the beginning of the modern period. If this historical classification of the Reformation be right, then it is no wonder that in the Catholic view the great calamity of modern times grew out of the great Heresy. In the context of this view the proposition that the Reformation should be understood as the birth-hour of modern times implies the condemnation of *both* the Reformation *and* modern times.

German Idealism also had to disintegrate, as it did in the latter third of the nineteenth century, before Hegel's view of history could level off into a self-justification of that kind of Protestantism which is rightly characterized as "culture-Protestantism." What Hegel called subjectivity – which is simply indefinable without the complementary concept of substantial content, i.e., objectivity – dissolved | into a subjectivism that recognized as the criterion of truth only the sincerity of the seeker, and showed itself incapable of expressing a truth that puts man under obligation. Precisely for this purpose appeal was made to Luther's teaching on faith, conscience, and Christian freedom. In doing so – and for many other reasons besides – this kind of Protestantism was emphatically and self-consciously "modern," a force for modern intellectual life, in which in any case it was also deeply involved through its acquiescence in the Enlightenment, in Idealism and Romanticism. It shared the faith in the upward movement of humanity which began in the Enlightenment and set as its goal the widest possible extension of this movement into all areas of human life, taking the lead wherever possible. From this exalted vantage point it looked down with contempt on the benighted Middle Ages, with its blind faith in authority, its silencing of the individual by the Church, its slavery to tradition. In all this, this kind of Protestantism knew itself to be the true heir of the Reformation; for it was the Reformation that brought about the conquest of the Middle Ages and the birth of modern thought.

Again I should not like to be misunderstood, as if this kind of culture-Protestantism were the whole of Protestantism in the nineteenth century. Perhaps the evangelical church up until 1914 is even less accurately characterized by it – especially if the whole of Protestantism and its genuine substance is taken into account – than Catholicism during this period is by the element of nostalgia for the Middle Ages described above. Nevertheless, the existence of this culture-Protestantism is a prominent trait in the historical picture, and the historical consciousness which developed along these lines is a potent force across the broad spread of the Protestant intellectual spectrum. Or should one say that it *was?* It is the context within which again two things gave mutual support to one another: a basic assent to the inheritance of the Reformation and a similar assent, however qualified, to the onset of modern thought — at least as long as the proposition remained valid that the Reformation represents the birth of the modern period.

But this proposition, which lay at the bottom of both portrayals of history, has for some time now — at least since the end of the nineteenth century and the beginning of the twentieth — come to be doubted and even disputed. Hence the classification of the Reformation in intellectual history has now become a problem.

Naturally, long before this, even within the context of the traditional view, it was clear that the advent of the modern period did not preclude historical continuity with the medieval world, and the connecting lines between the two epochs had occasionally been pointed out. In the work of A. Harnack and W. Dilthey this awareness crystallizes into the judgment that, | while much that was medieval remained in the Reformation, its central emphasis lay unambiguously on what was non-medieval. In this judgment, to be sure, Harnack looks not so much forward to modern times as backward to the renewal of Paulinism and the completion of the legacy of Augustine. Hence his reference to the connection between the Reformation and the Middle Ages is characteristically sonorous: "It is a totally one-sided, even reprehensibly abstract, way of looking at Luther to herald him as a man of modern times, as the hero of a period of ascendancy or the creator of the modern spirit. He who wants heroes like this should look to Erasmus and his colleagues, or to men like Denck, Franck, Servetus and Bruno. Not only around the periphery of his existence but also in some respects in the depths of his being Luther was a Catholic-medieval phenomenon." Yet it was E. Troeltsch who first took the decisive step along this line of historical research with his masterly formulation: "Protestantism in its essential characteristics and manifestations is *above all* a reshaping of the medieval idea, and the non-medieval or modern elements that undeniably lie within it in a significant way can only be thought of as 'modern' after the first, classical form of Protestantism has collapsed or been destroyed." This proposition was characterized as basic by Troeltsch, as the presupposition of any truly historical understanding of Protestantism. Hence it became a pressing question whether the break in intellectual history at the birth of the Enlightenment was not far more profound than that which occurred about a century and a half earlier in 1520, whether the men and the world of this 150-year interval, which Troeltsch called the Confessional Period and, with reference to the history of Protestantism, named the Old Protestant era — whether these men and their world were not much more akin to the men and the world of pre-Reformation times than to the men of the eighteenth century and the world of Neoprotestantism.

Before we discuss the truth or falsity of Troeltsch's thesis, it should be clearly pointed out that the scholars just named – Harnack, Dilthey, and Troeltsch – feel themselves spiritually distant from the Reformation in exactly the same measure as they assign it to the Middle Ages. This in spite of the fact that they were Protestants, two of them even theologians. Their objection to making the Enlightenment the direct heir of the Reformation does not come from any intention of absolving the Reformation from responsibility | for an illegitimate development. As far as the alternatives, Reformation *or* modern times, become real for them they personally choose unequivocally and unhesitatingly for modern times and against the Reformation. Their intention is, in Troeltsch's terminology, to be Neoprotestants, and they distinguish themselves from the Protestants of the nineteenth century, who were also "Neo"-protestants, only by virtue of the fact that their better scientific insight prohibits them from claiming the authority of the Reformation for their Neoprotestantism. With the sobriety that comes from historical training they are well aware – and they confess that fact to themselves and others – how thin the thread is that still binds them and their Protestant contemporaries to the Reformation. When the Reformation is thus classified with the Middle Ages it is an expression of the inner estrangement of Protestantism from its historical origin.

Evangelical theology and the Evangelical church today no longer share this feeling of estrangement vis-à-vis the Reformation. On the contrary, they know themselves to have been conditioned by an extremely vital encounter with it, an encounter that began immediately after the first World War, and the fruitfulness of which is even today, in my opinion, by no means exhausted. Nevertheless it is not difficult for us to recognize and hold to the element of truth in the thesis represented by Troeltsch and even to expand it.

For there is simply no question in our minds that the Protestantism of the confessional period bears a much more medieval than modern stamp. This is especially clear if one looks at it from the sociological standpoint which was also decisive for Troeltsch. What modern tendencies he sees within it and elaborates, as, e.g., the peculiar connection, so strongly emphasized by Novalis, between Church and State as it is reflected in the development of state churches, administered along territorial lines – on closer examination this is seen to be not specifically a part of the Reformation but simply the legacy of the late Middle Ages. It is merely the elaboration of the *advocatura ecclesiae* which the late medieval national state and the contemporary territorial and municipal powers had long claimed for themselves and widely practiced. It is not really modern either;

for in the meantime it has turned out that the course of modern development has been, not to tie church and state more closely together, but to separate these two partners as clearly as possible from one another.

| At this point we come upon a commonly-noted function of the Reformation in intellectual history which was also emphasized by Harnack and Troeltsch. Regardless of whether this development is conceived positively or negatively, as the dissolution of the Middle Ages in the fourteenth and fifteenth centuries or as the birth of modern thought, in either case it is clear that the Reformation acted more as a retarding than as an accelerating force. This is perhaps most obvious with respect to the concept and configuration of the State. Of course here matters are especially complicated by the fact that in this area the development in Reformed territory bears an entirely different character from that in the predominantly Lutheran regions. In Reformed lands the concept of the state has a distinctly progressive stamp. But at least for Lutheranism it is true that under the influence of the Reformation a civil life comes into being which is very much closer to the old Augustinian ideal of the Christian state than anything else to be found in Western Europe.[2] In the patriarchal form it comes to assume it seems simply archaic, not only in comparison with what had already developed in the thought of Machiavelli and in the states of the Italian Renaissance, but also in comparison with the image presented by the Catholic national state in the seventeenth century. This reversion to Augustine is all the more remarkable in the light of the fact that Luther's own political thought, as the formula of the two realms shows, includes every conceivable criticism of Augustine's scheme and specifically and decisively rejects the ideal of the Christian state – however much Luther may have remained indebted to Augustine and to his great conception of the *duae civitates*. In fact, the state is so excluded from the area in which a *lex christiana* might be applicable and so consigned as a "worldly thing" to the realm under the dominance of reason, that many interpreters believe that he establishes the state as a realm of self-contained laws, and consequently class him almost with Machiavelli. How far afield this interpretation goes is shown by the German Lutheran territorial states of the sixteenth and seventeenth centuries. They are more medieval than the late Middle Ages, and I rather doubt that their highly potent connection with the Christian norm, which was taken with utter seriousness by the princes and municipal magistrates, is rightly interpreted when it is one-sidedly understood as a negative reaction to the teaching of the two realms. Luther, to be sure, did not bind the princes to the Word of God *qua* official office-holders; | but he did so bind them as Christian *persons* and emphasized all

---

[2] Cf. G. RITTER, Die Neugestaltung Europas im sechzehnten Jahrhundert, Berlin, 1950, pp. 302 ff.

the more strongly how in the use of reason civil authority is dependent upon the instruction of the conscience through the office of Christian preaching. It seems to me that this very theory is reflected in the patriarchal structure which was characteristic of the Lutheran state in the period of orthodoxy. But if that is so, it is a confirmation of our thesis about the retarding effect of the Reformation on the course of historical development – a confirmation at the place where modern forms in other circumstances made themselves felt earliest and most speedily became established. There is much to be said for Troeltsch's conception, according to which the Reformation is in general assigned the role of having detained a late-medieval process of disintegration which was just about to take place in the Renaissance and in Humanism, and in which the Western spirit was already longing for emancipation from Christian-ecclesiastical authority, and of having subjected Europe for no less than two hundred additional years to the Christian norm.

This picture is not essentially different if one shifts his attention from the State to the Church which arose out of the Reformation. Naturally as far as content is concerned a very great deal – one can even go so far as to say everything – is entirely different. The effort to work out what is medieval in the basic characteristics of early Protestantism ought never to be misinterpreted, of course, so as to minimize the Reformation's substantial opposition to Catholicism and its significance for *church* history. But our concern is with the intellectual rather than the ecclesiastical aspects of the Reformation and with its thought-forms and the forms of its sociological phenomena rather than its Christian content. From this point of view the church of the Reformation is also much more like the medieval church than is the spiritualist-Baptist movement in the ideals and forms of community which it created. Contrasted with these aspects of that movement the Reformation again represents a pronounced conservative posture. It preserves those formal elements of ecclesiastical life which had been carved out in early Catholicism and accepted as basic in the Middle Ages as well: the authority of Scripture, preaching, the sacraments, the ministry – however much these things, viewed from a different standpoint, had been decisively reinterpreted and re-formed. It is especially important in this connection to note that Luther held firmly to that form of the church in which church and community were co-extensive *(Volkskirche)* and hence to the 1200-year-old tradition of the Constantinian era – and this in spite of the fact that, as a famous passage in the | preface to the German Mass (1526) shows, he clearly understood and seriously considered the alternative possibility, namely, the forming of small communities of "those who earnestly desire to be Christians." In this point, too, then, the whole Reformation is medieval in comparison with the Baptists and Spiritualists, who represent the concept of a "community of believers" and hence show themselves in this regard as well to be the conveyers of progressive-modern thought.

The institutional character of the church similarly remained unchanged. It is true that one must ask how far the institutional development in the realm of the Reformation corresponded to Luther's original intention which certainly had, at least on occasion, a strong inclination toward the communal principle. But the final decision was coincident with that for the *Volkskirche*, and this decision too had Luther's sanction. Here, to be sure, as in other areas of ecclesiastical re-formation, there was a discrepancy, a difference between what was willed and what became historical reality. It is for this reason that some have spoken of a "miscarrying" of the Reformation – an overly pointed formula for a situation in which the facts are very complex but one which requires mentioning because it is important for our theme. The historical form of the church that came from the Reformation is in one respect more medieval than the Reformation itself, if by "reformation" one understands the evangelical focus and starting-point of Luther's theology.

It is well known how conservative and medieval a liturgical order the Reformation gave to its churches as it developed. In the Lutheran territories, in fact, the liturgy was externally only a slightly altered form of the Mass. Here too the comparison with the development among the Reformed churches is instructive: the stronger humanistic influence forced Zwingli and Calvin in a progressive direction and toward more radical solutions in their services of worship. So here too it was really humanism that was the conveyer of progress; the Reformation conveyed it only insofar as it was open to humanism's influence.

Finally, in the realm of theology the connection between the Reformation and medieval tradition is patent. Harnack's judgment about the medieval elements in Luther rested on the observations which his training as a historian of dogma enabled him to make in this area. He described Luther as the restorer of dogma, and this assertion is all the more important because it really fits very badly with Harnack's scheme of the development of the history of dogma and with his own theological and ecclesiastical preferences. Moreover, it is only the most recent research on the history of the Reformation that has taught us how | far the dissolution of the unity of the church's teaching had proceeded in the development of the late Middle Ages and has demonstrated that the elaboration of binding dogmatic formulations at the Council of Trent represented a retrogressive movement brought forth only by the antecedent of the Reformation. A look at the Spiritualist and Humanist movements also shows that it was by no means a self-explanatory fact that Luther took over without modification the trinitarian and Christological dogma and hence the basic conclusions of ecclesiastical dogmatic development, and that he laid the greatest possible emphasis on this basic agreement as a proof of the catholicity of his Reformation. Among the left-wing fanatics and in the great antitrinitarian movement that developed out of humanism this dogma was contested and rejected, and as early as the sixteenth century the groundwork was laid for the concepts that recur repeatedly later in the Enlightenment's criticism of it. Luther, to be sure, offered a unique interpretation of this dogma in connection with his new theological starting-point and focus, but it never transgressed the limits of orthodoxy. Yet one may, with Harnack, point to this very inclusion in the recoining process which went on during the Reformation and to the elaboration of dogma that resulted from it as evidence that Luther was far more involved in it than had ever been the case in the Middle Ages, in which the final product of the development in the ancient church was simply transmitted unchanged.

Above all, Protestant theology in the period of Orthodoxy is a purely medieval phenomenon and shares certain essential characteristics with Scholasticism: the re-acceptance of Aristotelianism; the distinction, of such enormous consequence for theology, between natural and revealed theology; and the strong tendency toward system-building.

How convincingly the Reformation's connection with the traditions of the ancient church and of the Middle Ages has come to the fore in recent Luther research can also be seen in the fact that under its influence Catholicism has begun to revise its image of the Reformation and of the great Reformer. J. Lortz,[3] the outstanding example of this process of revision, has coined the formula that Luther is to be understood, at least from one point of view, as an early contender *for* essential Catholic truth against the thoroughly non-Catholic, even anti-Catholic, teaching of late medieval Nominalism. This is the Catholic variant of our thesis that Luther was in many ways | more medieval than the late Middle Ages and that he was more responsible for restricting and retarding the impact of the disintegrative phenomena of the late Middle Ages than for aiding and abetting them. In this connection Lortz drops the charge, recurrent since Novalis, that there is a direct line from the Reformation to the Enlightenment and its falling away from God. Even the formula about Luther's subjectivism, which is much more firmly rooted in Catholic polemic, occurs in Lortz' work only in a very altered and sublimated form. He shows that humanism and the Spiritualist movement that developed out of the mysticism of the Middle Ages were the true precursors and pioneers of the Enlightenment and of subjectivism, and that Luther was their greatest opponent, that they represented in fact the second front against which Luther did battle as fiercely as against the Roman papal forces. This absolves him in Lortz' eyes and also prevents him from naming Luther in the same breath as the Enlightenment.

---

[3] Die Reformation in Deutschland, vol. I-II, Freiburg, 1939-40; 3rd ed., 1948.

Now, of course, the story is not complete with the establishing of what the Reformation and the Middle Ages had in common. To halt here would be inexcusably one-sided, a distortion of historical reality, and a retrogression back beyond Harnack, Dilthey, and Troeltsch. They are all aware of another side to the Reformation, one which seemed to them more basic. Even Troeltsch speaks of the "non-medieval, modern elements that undeniably lie significantly within Protestantism" and which "can only be thought of as 'modern' after the first, classical form of Protestantism has collapsed or been destroyed." It would be disastrous if the evangelical church and its theology were to get into the habit of overlooking this other side of the Reformation, since its understanding of the Reformation and its understanding of itself are inseparable. If future developments were to take this course the encounter with the Reformation which, as we saw above, has taken root so deeply in very recent Protestant history, would become an encounter with a part of the Middle Ages. The movement toward inner reflection and concentration which has been under way in the evangelical church since the end of the first World War would then appear to be a parallel phenomenon to the Catholic movement toward inner concentration which took place 125 years ago; it would seem to be a romantic restoration, an attempt to turn its back on its own times and shift the gears of history into reverse. Its result, as in all such attempts at restoration, could only be failure and sterility. I confess that this seems to me to be a danger hovering over | the evangelical church and its theology today. It is thus all the more urgent a task to see clearly that side of the Reformation that is directed toward the present and that points beyond the present to the future.

The fact that the Reformation breaks through to insights in which it anticipates the peculiarities of modern thought is, to be sure, not superficially obvious. The tendencies in this direction do not crystallize into theories and programmatic assertions; they do not precipitate out into the institutions created by the Reformation or into the dogmatic structure which it erects. In fact they are to be seen in Luther alone; even his immediate disciples hardly understand them, and what little they do accept of them becomes almost unrecognizable in the traditional forms into which they reshape it. Even in Luther himself these tendencies are deeply embedded in the legacy of tradition. They exist in a rather submerged stratum which he seldom brings forth into his consciousness and from which they never emerge in a pure and abstract form. He does not pursue them consistently, nor does he ever put them to polemic use against the tradition. Yet, for all their hiddenness, they show themselves to be remarkably effective. They are the only adequate basis of certain phenomena that come clearly to light in Luther's thought. Anyone who seeks them and tries to name them in abstraction from their effects leaves himself open to the charge of over-interpretation; but anyone who does not take them into consideration is really renouncing the quest for any ultimate understanding of Luther's thought as whole. One can call them "modern" thought-forms only with reserve. They are in any case completely non-medieval elements that coincide with certain perspectives in modern thought. But they do not recur in modern times in the same form as in Luther. They are absolutely original and remain unique.

The surprising, even astonishing thing about all this is that these developments do not take place in the sphere where current influences affected Luther. He did indeed receive various stimuli from mysticism and humanism, but they did not basically lead him beyond the realm of the medieval. I allude here to what did not come from outside him but rather developed in the innermost reaches of Luther's theology, where he was alone with himself and with his God, and where he spoke what was most truly his. It is consequently always in the most intimate association with matters of central basic content, with the content of his teaching on justification, his Christology and exegetical | method, and it remains embedded within them. From this indissoluble association two things follow: On the one hand a man may repeat the formulae of Lutheran theology ever so correctly and still fail to grasp the whole if he fails to consider the unique thought-structure in which that whole stands. On the other hand, one would really have to elaborate the entire content of Luther's theology in order to portray those non-medieval elements and make them at least partially visible. For isolated from that content they do not really exist; they become something different from what they are in Luther. All this makes it difficult if not impossible to speak of them with even tolerable appropriateness within the confines of a single essay. If I nevertheless undertake the task, it is only in the form of some propositional suggestions which not only need to be expanded and completed but also, as I am all too conscious, need to be much more fully thought through.[4]

1. One must begin with the catchword which came up as early as Hegel and which we meet again in Lortz, the catchword "subjectivity" and "subjectivism." Neither term is univocal in itself; both need inter-

---

[4] I am here merely setting forth ideas that have been frequently discussed in recent Luther interpretation. In addition to the two names given below (pp. 18f.) I refer to the works of G. EBELING, especially his essay: "The Significance of the Critical Historical Method For Church and Theology in Protestantism," in: Word and Faith, Philadelphia, 1963, pp. 17–61, and also to E. METZKE, "Lutherforschung und deutsche Philosophiegeschichte," Blätter für deutsche Philosophie, 8, 1934/5, pp. 355 ff. The section on temptation makes use of formulations by Pastor Dr. H. BUHR (Pfrondorf near Tübingen) which were contributed in a discussion of an earlier draft of this essay. Finally, I can no longer sort out my own contribution to my way of looking at the matter from what I owe to a continuing conversation with G. EBELING and E. FUCHS.

pretation. I have already indicated that Hegel's "subjectivity" has little in common with modern subjectivism, insofar as the latter is understood to refer to the freedom from restraint of the individual who establishes himself as his norm. And even where Lortz speaks of Luther's "subjectivism" he must, as we already saw, distort the concept almost to the point of unrecognizability. And yet these terms are always supposed to point to an affinity between Luther and modern thought. As far as Luther is concerned, they refer to a structure in his theology, one which he constantly emphasizes, e. g., in his definition of faith: faith is only justifying faith if it involves "me," "mine," "for me," etc. Not the fact that God is, that Christ died and rose again, that he died for the sins of men – these are not the declarations of the faith that justifies. All this "the demons also believe and | tremble" (James 2: 19). To believe means to believe that God is *my* God, that Christ died and rose again *for me*, that in him *my* sins are forgiven. This is the sense in which Luther exegetes the first and third articles: "I believe" – not that the world was created by God but – "that He created *me* together with all creatures," "that *I* cannot of my own reason or strength believe in Jesus Christ or come to him, but the Holy Spirit has called *me* through the Gospel," etc. By this structuring of faith the Reformation breaks through the ontological thought-pattern of the Middle Ages, which takes as the starting-point a world of that which exists in itself, a structure in which the knower participates by the very act of knowing. In this opposition to the Middle Ages the Reformation has an affinity with the great change in the view of the world that took place in the seventeenth and eighteenth centuries, in which – as represented in Descartes – the thinking and knowing I stands at the origin in the system of coordinates and the world becomes a bundle of relationships.

Of course the pointing out of this structural affinity is instantly distorted if it is vulgarized into an identity of statement. Historically and essentially Meister Eckhardt stands incomparably nearer to Hegel's "subjectivity" than Luther does, and so does Erasmus to modern subjectivism. If one is trying to express simultaneously both what is held in common and the *differentiae specificae* between the Reformation and modern subjectivity, it turns out that all terms which are connected with the subject-object scheme are inappropriate for rendering the thought of the Reformation. I am well aware that we constantly lapse back into this scheme, and perhaps it can never be entirely dispensed with in the language of philosophy and theology. But if it is used one should be fully conscious of the fact that it is hardly appropriate for the interpretation of Luther and that it is as much a hindrance as a help in illuminating theological data for anyone who wishes to see them in the light of the outlook of the Reformation. The believer who comprehends the personal pronouns – "my," "to me," "for me," etc. – is not a subject because what he refers to in using them is not an object. God and Christ are never, for Luther, "objects" *(Gegenstände)* simply because they are persons, and being a person and being an object are mutually exclusive. For Luther God and Christ are simply not the object of faith because they are its subject instead. How else is one to understand Luther's statement that faith is the work of the Holy Spirit? It does not mean that in my faith God believes on himself, but it does mean that | in my faith the very same saving act of God that happened once and for all in Christ happens here and now to me. In view of this fact, it becomes rather pointless for anyone in the realm of evangelical Christianity to try to play off "objectivity" against the influx of modern subjectivist thought into theology and the church. It is just as perverse as adducing the supposed rights of "subjectivity" in opposition to a tendency toward ontology and objectification – and citing passages from Luther as proof-texts. The terms should be changed: "person" should be used for "subject" – and "object," – and "personality" should be used instead of "subjectivity." In this way the sterile – because inappropriate – antithesis inherent in the subject-object scheme would be avoided. At the same time, it would become evident just wherein the relative right of modern subjectivism over against medieval ontology consists. And it would show that this right does not imply the necessity of countering subjectivist distortions by lapsing back into objectivity, which would mean, at least in the matter under discussion, a leaping over the Reformation back into the Middle Ages. This would be using Beelzebub to drive out the devil!

2. There is a unique line running from the Reformation's exegesis of Scripture to the modern historical consciousness. Ultimately, of course, it goes back beyond the Reformation to the New Testament itself. It begins with the statement that God's revelation in Christ is a revelation in history, that in Christ God entered history. In this line the historical thinking of the Old Testament is taken up, and from it a new historical consciousness, fundamentally different from the Greek historical consciousness, arises in the West.

In addition to this, however, several questions arise from the historical character of revelation which have always played a central part in the Christian church, the differing answers to which have again made possible very basic variations within the common Christian relationship to history. Everyone who studies the development of the early and medieval church cannot help being struck by the relatively restricted role – measured by contemporary standards – history plays during these periods. The historicity of the figure of Jesus Christ is discussed within the framework of christological dogma under the superscription, "the human nature of Christ." The historical category is replaced here by an ontological category: an immutable human nature. The other side of the Christian paradox of revelation, namely, that it is God who has | entered history in Christ, is put into dogmatic form by speaking of the divine nature of Christ. The christological dogma of the church developed, to be sure, in conscious opposition to the docetism of the Gnostics. But it never quite succeeded in conquering the enemy; a docetic nimbus hovers over the entire construct. For it is simply not complete humanity, our humanity, that Christ assumed. It is better predisposed toward the divine nature than ours is, and it becomes further different from ours through the co-inherence of the divine nature. Where this Christology, thought out in physical-metaphysical categories, is projected onto the problem of history and historical revelation, a meta-history results which is usually called "redemptive history" *(Heilsgeschichte)*. This term is used to express the fact that in the history of Jesus Christ and the apostolic period of revelation defined by it genuine history is present, and yet that this history does not share in the relativity of the historical; rather – unlike all other history – it expresses what is eternal and unconditioned. But the result of this latter formulation is that the "historicity" of "redemptive history" becomes a purely formal structure which it has in common with all other history, while its essence consists specifically in the fact that it is beyond history, timeless, eternal – and thus, in short, unhistorical.

The same phenomenon appears again in connection with the other problem that arises out of the historicity of revelation. Since the common Christian profession is that the absolutely decisive and basic act for the salvation of mankind occurred at a very distant historical moment, under the Roman rulers Augustus and Tiberius, and in a remote corner in Palestine, the Christian church has been called on again and again to answer two questions: "How does this far-off event become present here and now in such a way as to become a saving event for me?" and "How can one be sure that what happens here and now to me and in my presence is identical with what happened then?" The questions of re-presentation and re-assurance must be answered wherever revelation is historical revelation.

The answer of medieval Catholicism corresponds exactly to its Christology in the categories used in its construction. It refers, for one thing, to the sacraments. In the metaphysical qualification of their elements, effected once for all, and in their consequent elevation beyond all historical change they bring about the re-presentation of what happened in Christ and at the same time guarantee the identity between that event and what happens here and now. This happens | most clearly in the sacrifice of the Mass, which in its identity with the sacrifice of Golgotha is the source, ever being renewed, of all the other sacraments. A further guarantee is the Church itself, which as the mystical body of Christ is the extension throughout all history of the Incarnation, established *in perpetuum*. It is historical only in its formal structure; according to its essence it is metahistorical, removed from the process of historical change and from the relativity of the historical.

Now let us look at Luther. We have already pointed out in connection
with Christology the conservative element in Luther's relationship to the
dogma of the two natures of Christ. Now it is time to speak of the beginnings made in the direction of a new development. Those beginnings take
as their point of departure an estimate of Christ's humanity, i.e., of the
full historicity of Jesus Christ, that is simply unique in the history of
Christian thought, one that for the first time avoids even the slightest trace
of docetism. The humility of his birth, the elements of weakness in the
Gospel portraits, Hebrews' "tempted in all points like as we are," the suf-
fering, the pain, the dereliction of the final moment, when the Crucified
cries out, "My God! My God! Why hast Thou forsaken me?" –these are the
pillars on which Luther's teaching about Christ's person and work are built.
In all this there is of course no intention of minimizing the deity of Christ,
nor does any such depotentiation actually result. The modalistic element in
Luther's trinitarian doctrine has often been pointed out; it is reflected in
the fact that the second person of the Trinity can be simply identified with
the first, as happens in the well-known passage in "A Mighty Fortress":
"Christ Jesus, It is He – Lord Sabaoth His Name." So it is not only from the
side of the humanity, i.e., of the historicity of the Redeemer, but also from
the side of his deity that Luther heightens the dogmatic propositions right
to the very edge of heterodoxy. But it is this fact that points to a structure of
christological thought in which God's deity and his full historicity are not
mutually limiting concepts; they stand side by side, mutually absolute.
Just as in the Old Testament, God shows himself as God in Luther's
thought not *in spite of* the fact but *because* of the fact that he reveals
himself in genuine, actual history.

The same thing is true of the problem of re-presentation and re-assurance. Luther answers this problem by pointing to the Word of God. This
Word of God re-presents the revelation and re-assures us of the identity
between what happened in Christ and what is proclaimed here and now.
But since the Word of God | is nothing but Christ and Christ nothing but
the Word of God one can also put it this way: No one but Christ himself
makes himself present to us in the Word, and in the faith effected by the
Word, and makes himself certain to us. And just as he was completely and
actually historical long ago under Augustus and Tiberius, so he is completely and actually historical in his present form. As he then took on the form
of man, even the form of a servant, so today he comes to us in the servant-
form of the word of man, written down by men in the biblical books and
proclaimed in the church by men. There are no assurances to be provided
by the church and the sacrament, whose metaphysical and metahistorical
character, once accepted, then guarantee the presence of Christ. It is just
the other way around: Church and sacrament are constituted only by the
presence of Christ in the Word and in faith. There is no way of knowing from

the outside whether the word is the Word of God or the word of man, a word from a history that has fallen away from God or a Word of the God who reveals himself within history. This is always learned only in the act and decision of belief or unbelief.

It is only when the conception of a metahistorical redemptive history, separated off from all other history, is thus overcome that the fundamental Christian assertion about the historical character of revelation is *genuinely* expressed, i.e., without being refracted by the ontological categories which come from ancient Greece and from which the historical element is absent. Consequently Luther points in a unique way beyond the Enlightenment to the nineteenth century, which came to understand the world as history. He is much more "modern" than humanism, not only the humanism of his own time but also that of the next three centuries, which in its relationship to history never got beyond the concepts of *memoria (ἀνάμνησις)*, and *exemplum* or the relationship to the past expressed by these terms. In Luther's consciousness of history there is contained – long before its redis-covery in the past half-century – an element by means of which he is able to know that true historicity consists not only in being irrevocably past, but also and equally in being immediately present.

3. In this renunciation of metaphysical and metahistorical supports for faith rest the possibility and constant actuality of temptation *(Anfechtung)* in Luther. It plays a central role in his life and in his theology. Both the concept and the reality of temptation come, to be sure, from medieval mysticism. But Luther made something new out of what was transmitted from the Middle Ages, in | connection with his theology of the Cross. It is in his thought for the first time that temptation belongs to faith as the shadow belongs to the light. Faith always exists only as the concrete overcoming of temptation. The significance of this for the question under discussion in this essay can be made particularly clear in connection with the temptation involved in Luther's consciousness of his reforming mission. This con-sciousness of mission was no more a perpetual certainty for him, at his disposal in any and all circumstances, than his assurance of pardon was. On the contrary, he saw his mission repeatedly threatened by the thought that he in his teaching stood alone in opposition to so many others, to so ancient a tradition, to a church endowed with so much power and authority. In such moments mere recourse, theologically unreflecting re-course, to the Scripture offered no or at least no enduring help. Luther's historical situation is of course different from ours specifically in the fact that for him and his time the divine origin of the Scriptures still belongs axiomatically to their outlook. But, as his teaching about Law and Gospel and his famous formula, "the Scripture, insofar as it teaches Christ" *(soweit sie Christum treibet)*, show, he had thought through the her-meneutical problem to the point where the indissoluble connection between

the question of the authority of the Scripture and the question of its right understanding becomes visible. This connection provides the Devil a foothold when he denies in that moment of temptation that the appeal to the Scripture is conclusive and expresses the opinion that Luther really appeals only to his own exegesis. At least in this form the historicity of revelation – devoid of assurance, always capable of being confused with the word of man, sharing the relativity of everything historical – was immediately and existentially real for Luther. And consequently, in spite of the difference between his intellectual situation and ours, temptation acquires for Luther a striking similarity to what in our post-Cartesian spiritual world has come to be recognized as belonging, like the shadow to the light, to faith and to all knowledge: a resemblance to doubt.

4. After the continual effort F. Gogarten has devoted to the problem of secularization I need indicate only briefly the final point of contact between the Reformation and modern forms of thought and life. It concerns the relationship of the Christian to the world and the world's relationship to Christianity. In Luther, particularly in his battle with monasticism, his view of the Christian's worldly calling, and in his much-discussed teaching of the two realms, | there are sharp antitheses to *both* of the solutions to this problem which are combined into a *complexio oppositorum* in the definition of this relationship set forth in the early church and the Middle Ages: against both the demarcation from secular life of a special "Christian" sphere and the Constantinian-Augustinian conception of a totally Christian world as well. Luther coined the formula: the world must be allowed to be the world; only thus will the spiritual again be truly spiritual. And just as surely as the Christian is snatched by God out of the world and all that belongs to it in the *punctum mathematicum* of faith, where he stands entirely alone before God as a *person* – and no longer as man or woman, slave or free, Greek or Jew – so surely is he again sent back by the same God to the very place in the world, determined by birth and destiny, in which he formerly stood, so that in that place he might live out his Christian profession. And if he does not live it out there, he does not live it at all. The question naturally arises whether all of this does not have a very basic and even thoroughly positive relationship to the de-christianization and secularization of the world which the Enlightenment brought about. Gogarten contends, with good reason, for the thesis that the secularized world of modern times is a genuine Christian possibility in the Reformation sense, better than either the Constantinian façade of a "Christian" world or its modern offshoot, the "sphere of the Church." It is quite possible that evangelical theology and the evangelical church have been called to the full elaboration of the truth of the Reformation by grasping *this* possibility, and it is possible that only thus will they fulfill the task incumbent upon them in all circumstances to proclaim salvation to an era disintegrating in

"secularism." D. Bonhoeffer's thought also revolved around the conception of a new, total worldliness of the Christian life.

We have now arrived at the end of our deliberations and look back at the two-sided results to which they have led. Are we to see in these results only the characteristics of a transitional epoch which, like all such epochs, is partially turned toward the past and partially preparatory of the future? I do not believe that this formula represents an adequate understanding of the relationship we have sketched here. It leaves unexplained the peculiar phenomenon that on the one hand the Reformation portrays in its medieval elements a retrogressive movement as compared with the late Middle Ages and, on the other, it is in one distinct substratum more modern than the humanist and spiritualist movements of the sixteenth century which are the immediate predecessors of the | modern world, even more modern than anything yet to have come forth from those movements. This paradoxical relationship of the Reformation to the past and the future points to the mystery that lies at its heart, a mystery by virtue of which in a deeper sense it transcends the current pattern of the historical distinction between the "Middle Ages" and the "modern period." This mystery is the mystery of that truth that Luther saw facing him in the *punctum mathematicum* of his faith. Just as it is itself older than the old and newer than the new, so it stamps with a two-sided mold the spirit of him who is called to reflect on and express it: it has an eminently conservative effect over against the whims of the spirit of the age, but at the same time it gives birth to a transition into the future which requires the passing of many centuries before its radicality can be fully grasped.

Reformed Orthodoxy and Cartesianism[*]

by

Ernst Bizer

Translated by Chalmers MacCormick

Reformed orthodoxy successfully asserted itself at the Synod of Dort against Arminianism and gave itself its basic law. The unity achieved was, to be sure, not without tensions. The opposition between the supralapsarians and infralapsarians persisted; the German Reformed theologians appear thereafter to have settled all the more on infralapsarianism. A little later, the secretary to Synodal President Bogerman, the Englishman William Amesius,[1] developed the program of Reformed Pietism which, as a matter of fact, was well received by the acknowledged leader of orthodoxy in the following generation, Gisbert Voetius, who in 1634 became a professor at Utrecht | and dominated the faculty there for more than forty years. But then the "halcyon days" of the Church[2] were disturbed by the new movement associated with the name of John Coccelus, who in 1636 became a professor at Franeker, and in 1650 at Leiden, where he died in 1669. The "Federal Theology" which he founded came into clear and more and more keenly felt tension *vis-à-vis* the scholasticism which had hitherto been cultivated. This opposition not only split the theological schools, but rent the whole Church asunder. As is well known, it concerned the unity of the Old and New Testaments, the validity of the sabbath-commandment, typological exegesis, and finally, indeed, the right of a historical approach to revelation. The peculiarities of Coccelus, at first scarcely noticed, appeared gradually to be a threat to orthodoxy as a whole.

On top of this situation, there now arose the discussion with the new philosophy of Descartes. This philosophy, with its demand for radical doubt and its specific alliance of philosophy and natural science, placed everything in question, in order to reconstruct it on a new foundation. The history of

---

[*] "Die reformierte Orthodoxie und der Cartesianismus," ZThK, 55, 1958, pp. 306–372.

[1] For the names I refer for brevity's sake to my "Historische Einleitung" in: HEINRICH HEPPE, Die Dogmatik der Evangelisch-Reformierten Kirche, 2nd ed., edited by E. BIZER, Neukirchen Kr. Moers, 1958.

[2] FR. SPANHEIM the younger, Opera, II, Leiden, 1703, col. 949; see below p. 40, and p. 58 note 188.

this discussion has not yet been written in detail. Otto Ritschl[3] devoted no attention to it; Emanuel Hirsch[4] limits himself to Balthasar Bekker, the most conspicuous exponent of Cartesianism, but does not even touch upon the discussion within theology. The following is a first attempt; it is limited to the Netherlands.[5]

I. Descartes and Voetius – the Question of Theological Method

In the first period the discussion consisted merely of fending off Descartes with traditional means.[6] It ended with | a victory for the orthodox theologians – a victory which, to be sure, did not rest on their intellectual superiority. It consequently did the opposition scarcely any damage, and therefore could also not be of lasting import.

1. The Course of the Discussion

Descartes had resided since 1628 in the Netherlands, where he composed the "Meditations" (on the first philosophy, the existence of God, and the immortality of the soul). They were published on August 28, 1641; the second edition, published in May 1642 by Elzevier in Amsterdam, was supplemented by the letter to the provincial of the French Jesuits, Father Dinant. In this writing the philosopher defends himself against the attacks of P. Bourdin, S. J., professor at the Collège de Clermont in Paris. The immediate purpose of the letter was to convince the Jesuits of the author's orthodoxy. Incidentally, however, and probably not unintentionally, Descartes recounts the beginning of his conflict with the Reformed orthodox theologians in Utrecht. His account[7] of the events is as follows:

---

[3] O. RITSCHL, Dogmengeschichte des Protestantismus, III, Leipzig, 1926.

[4] E. HIRSCH, Geschichte der neueren evangelischen Theologie, I, Gütersloh, 1949.

[5] The material is in every respect so difficult of access that I believe I am doing the reader a service by citing it in as much detail as possible.

[6] Cf. GUSTAVE COHEN, Les écrivains français en Hollande pendant la première moitié du XVIIème siècle, Paris, 1921; and the two essays by C. LOUISE THIJSSEN-SCHOUTE and PAUL DIBON in the volume: Descartes et le cartésianisme hollandais, Etudes et documents, Paris-Amsterdam, 1950. See also C. L. THIJSSEN-SCHOUTE, Nederlands Cartesianisme, Amsterdam, 1954 (Verhandelingen der Koninklijke Akademie van Wetenschappen, Afdeeling Letterkunde, Nieuwe reeks, Deel LX). – The standard work for VOETIUS is still A. C. DUKER, Gisbertus Voetius, Leiden, I 1897, II 1910, III 1914. DUKER's earlier book: School-gezag en eigen-onderzoek. Historisch-kritische studie van den strijd tusschen Voetius and Descartes, Leiden, 1861, has thereby been replaced and corrected.

[7] See the standard edition by CH. E. ADAM and P. TANNERY, Paris, 1897ff., vol. III, pp. 563ff. – I shall cite the works of DESCARTES simply according to the volume and page number of this edition.

Gisbert Voetius, the leading theologian at Utrecht, had, in 1639, taken the funeral oration for the Cartesian Henri Régnier (Reneri) as the occasion to raise the charge of atheism against the new philosophical movement, without, however, mentioning names.[8] Voetius sought already at that time to incite Father Mersenne in Paris to come forward publicly against Descartes,[9] not suspecting that he had thereby landed on the advocate and most intimate friend of the philosopher, a man who kept in close contact with Descartes. New provocation to interfere was given to Voetius by a disputation of the professor of medicine and physics, Regius, in December 1641. The cause lay this time (according to the report of Descartes) in the thesis "*ex mente et corpore non fieri unum ens per se, sed per accidens.*" Especially the term *ens per accidens* was regarded by Voetius as an unpardonable sin and a danger for science, including theology. Connected with it was the | question of the *formae substantiales*, i. e., the doctrine of the soul.[10] The name of Descartes was drawn into the debate by both sides. Regius composed a writing against Voetius' attack (February 16, 1642); it was suppressed by Voetius, in his capacity at the time as Rector, by having it confiscated by the city council.[11] This measure was subsequently endorsed by a decree of the university senate of March 16, 1642,[12] in which the new philosophy was accused of being bound up "*cum verborum insolentia,*" serving as an affront to all those who had previously represented the universally accepted truth.[13] One felt the new philosophy to be a revolution in the whole academic procedure which could only be injurious to the interest of young scholars. One saw the danger for theology in particular in this, that conclusions could be drawn which contradicted orthodox doctrine. To be sure, these conclusions are not specified in the senate's decree.[14]

---

[8] VOETIUS' theses may be found in his *Disputationes Selectae*, I, pp. 114–226 (De atheismo; June/July 1639). Cf. F. SASSEN, Henricus Renerius, de eerste 'Cartesiaansche' hoogleeraar te Utrecht, Amsterdam, 1941 (Mededelingen der Nederlandsche Akademie van Wetenschappen, Afd. Letterkunde, N. r., Deel IV, no. 20). DESCARTES recounts the story in VIII, 2, pp. 203 ff.

[9] III 230 and 602; Letters of DESCARTES to MERSENNE, dated Nov. 11, 1640, and MERSENNE to VOETIUS, dated Dec. 13, 1642. At least five letters of VOETIUS are involved but unfortunately they have been lost. Cf. III 604.

[10] VII 587, line 12: quas omnes, excepta anima rationali, medicus negarat.

[11] VII 589, 8: quo facta est, ut reliqua cupidius emerentur ac curiosius legerentur. Cumque nihil in iis appareret, de quo theologus juste queri posset, praeter solam vim rationum, quas declinare non poterat, omnes eum irriserunt.

[12] For the text see III 551–53; cf. 557 f., VII 590 ff.

[13] VII 11 ff.: se improbare eam propugnandi pro nova et praesumpta philosophia rationem, quae in praedicto libello frequentatur; utpote cum verborum insolentia coniunctam, in eorum opprobrium, qui hic et alibi contrariam et vulgarem, omnibusque in academiis receptam philosophiam ut veriorem profitentur.

[14] VII 25: Tertio, se reiicere novam istam philosophiam: primo quia veteri

Descartes now came to the support of his partisan, Regius, by publishing the aforementioned letter to Dinant. In doing this, he perhaps also intended to commend himself to the Netherlanders as one who was persecuted by the Jesuits. If this was his intent, he did not, in any case, attain his objective; rather, the council of Utrecht resolved to give him a public reply. Paul Voet, Gisberts' son, was commissioned to draft it. The document was not, however, completed before March 1643 and was printed in October of the same year.[15] | Gisbert Voetius did not want to wait that long. In the summer of 1642 he persuaded one of his students, the Groningen professor Martin Schoock, to write against Descartes. Schoock had intended to enter into discussion with the new philosophy anyhow. With the material that Voetius and his Utrecht friends furnished, the writing he had planned now became an outspoken polemic, printed anonymously in Utrecht but with a preface signed by Schoock. The title "*Admiranda Methodus novae philosophiae Renati Des Cartes*"[16] – and, even more, the page headings, "*Philosophia Cartesiana*" – gave the impression of a philosophical investigation, indeed perhaps an (already announced) writing by Descartes himself; and they were perhaps intentionally so chosen. In reality, however, it is a defamatory writing of the worst kind. The philosopher is represented as an ignoramus and adventurer, who has not even mastered the rudiments of philosophy[17] and who now seeks to hide his slovenliness in a foreign land. Descartes says of this writing that it presented no reasons, but simply added new slanders to the old. In it was again raised the charge of atheism, sharpened by the reference comparing Descartes to Vanini, who had recently been burned in Toulouse on account of his atheism.[18] To be sure, Descartes proves the existence of God, the document avers, but only in order, through the inadequacy of his proof, to undermine faith more than

---

philosophiae, quam academiae toto orbe terrarum hactenus optimo consilio docuere, adversatur, eiusque fundamenta subvertit; deinde quia iuventutem a vetere et sana philosophia avertit, impeditque quominus ad culmen eruditionis provehatur, eo quod, istius praesumptae philosophiae adminiculo, technologemata in auctorum libris professorumque lectionibus et disputationibus usitata percipere nequit; postremo, quod ex eadem variae, falsae et absurdae opiniones partim consequantur, partim ab improvida iuventute deduci possint, pugnantes cum ceteris disciplinis et facultatibus, atque in primis cum orthodoxa theologia. – In VIII, 2 p. 4, line 15, DESCARTES says that the reproach was that he advanced "varias, falsas et absurdas opiniones . . . pugnantes cum orthodoxa theologia."

[15] Testimonium Academiae Ultrajectinae et Narratio historica qua defensae, qua exterminatae novae philosophiae. – The text of the council's resolution is found in III 568.

[16] VIII, 2 p. 5, note.

[17] quem certo possum probare ne quidem terminos philosophiae peripateticae intelligere (VIII, 2 p. 15).

[18] Cf. E. LENOIR, Au seuil du grand siècle: Trois novateurs, trois martyrs: Vanini, Campanella, Giordano Bruno, Paris, 1939.

ever. This charge is supported only by pointing out possible consequences;[19] the authors admit that it cannot be proved from the words of Descartes.[20] | Schoock's book is therefore a complete disappointment if one hopes to learn the motives for opposing Descartes or the reasons for rejecting his philosophy.[21] There is no word, in any case, about the fact that the Cartesian proof of God does not lead to the Christian concept of God and is therefore beside the point! No word at all of a christologically based doctrine of God! What Voetius and his followers actually defend is Aristotelianism and the validity of the traditional proof of God, but not the biblical concept of God.

Descartes regularly received, as they came from the press, the proof-sheets of the Schoockian *"Methodus"* from the printer (doubtless through the latter's indiscretion) and wrote his rebuttal, the *"Epistola ad Voetium,"* while the printing was in progress.[22] The printing was interrupted, however, because Voetius became entangled in the dispute about a Marian brotherhood which still existed in Hertogenbosch – a brotherhood whose cause was represented by Samuel Maresius (at that time still pastor in Hertogenbosch, and a man just as orthodox as he was disputatious) – and Voetius had to make room for a polemic on this matter. Thereupon Descartes also took up the theme, because it seemed to him especially suited to expose the malice and pious untruthfulness of Voetius. Thus, the *"Epistola"* – a book of over 200 pages – is in the first and last thirds a

---

[19] VIII, 2 p. 171: In secundo capite pag. 225 meam Methodum recta ad enthusiasmum ducere dicitis, hoc nullo alio probantes argumento, quam quod scripserim mentem abducendam esse a sensibus ut Deum contemplemur. – VIII, 2 p. 172: Deinde pag. 258 sic loquimini: Deum sibi inexistentem Cartesianus quis deprehendit per ideam; cur non ergo instar enthusiastae sic etiam concludet: 'Deus in me est, et ego in Deo, ergo per Deum inexistentem omnia ago et consequenter neque fallo neque pecco neque peccare possum.' Quas consequentias fateor a solis enthusiastis, deliris et vestri similibus elici posse. In tertio capite pag. 261 affirmatis me Atheismum docere et propagare. Additis quidem, si prae ignorantia id faciam, me esse commiseratione dignum; si vero prae malitia puniendum. Sed non vultis dubitari quin faciam; imo omni arte, omni industria, id persuadere conamini; ac postquam multa ea de re verba fecistis, serio concluditis pag. 265, me in imperitorum animis thronum erigere laborare ... Atque ad hoc unum confirmandum et hominibus persuadendum, totum vestrum librum composuisse videmini; nam in praefatione pag. 13 promittitis vos in reliquo tractatu ostensuros: me subdole ac admodum occulte atheismi venenum aliis affricare.

[20] VIII, 2 p. 174, line 12: 'Unicum invenio totius probationis vestrae fundamentum, quod, ut loquimini pag. 261,' si verba virtutem arguerent, iisque tuto fides adhiberi deberet, ab atheismi levissima etiam suspicione essem alienissimus. – For the comparison with Vanini see 174, line 23 ff.

[21] Even the testimony of the academic senate of March 1, 1643, prefixed to the Narratio, (text: VIII, 2 p. 325 ff.), only says: quippe cum res ipsa clamaret, non posse non veterem philosophandi rationem magno cum academiae detrimento mutari.

[22] VIII, 2 p. 1: Epistola ad Celeberrimum Virum D. Gisbertum Voetium, in qua examinantur duo libri, nuper pro Voetio Ultrajecti simul editi, unus de Confraternitate Mariana alter de Philosophia Cartesiana, Amsterodami, 1643.

rebuttal of the "*Methodus*," while the middle part is devoted to the affair in Hertogenbosch – and here Descartes appears on the side of his incontestably orthodox countryman, Maresius. From afar, i. e., from the viewpoint of his French friends, the former pupil of La Flèche could, as his biographer notes, thus appear at the same time as a fighter for the honor of the Holy Virgin, to whom, a few years earlier, Louis XIII had dedicated his kingdom.

In the "*Epistola*" Descartes does not treat his opponent in a way that is exactly gentle. He deals with the "*Methodus*" first of all as a work of Voetius, then becomes aware of the fact that another author is speaking; | but to the end he insists that Voetius is his real opponent, and to that effect cites a series of scarcely flattering reasons.[23] Over and above that, he characterizes Voetius as a liar and slanderer, caricatures the manner of his erudition,[24] his demagogical way of preaching, and the scholastic method of his disputations; he accuses him of false documentation, adding that Voetius does not even note when a citation contradicts his own opinion; he misuses Scripture and therefore is neither a scholar whose method is to be taken seriously, nor a priest who is worthy to wear the robe of his Lord.[25]

The Utrechters, to whom Descartes sent the book, arrayed themselves behind Voetius, their famed professor. On June 13, 1643,[26] Descartes was summoned with fanfare – "avec grand bruit, au son de la cloche, comme si j'eusse été criminel,[27] ... d'une façon plus célèbre que l'ordinaire, avec plus grande convocation de peuple,[28] ... et par des affiches, qui furent mesmes envoyées avec soin de tous costés en ces provinces, comme si j'eusse été un vagabond ou un fugitif qui aurait commis le plus grand et le plus odieux de tous les crimes"[29] – to appear before the council. He did not appear, but instead sent a letter (July 6, 1643),[30] in which he challenged the competence of the council. With far less display and almost to the exclusion of the public, a judgment[31] was delivered on September 13, 1643 which designated

---

[23] VIII, 2 p. 55.

[24] VIII, 2 p. 41, line 21: Te autem in locis communibus et commentariis et lexicis talibusque evolvendis esse valde exercitatum, manifestum est ex tuis scriptis, in quibus saepissime illos citas. Sed non ita possum deprehendere cum libris illis primariis, a quibus omnis vera eruditio, quae legendo acquiri potest, dependet, magnam consuetudinem habere. VIII, 2 p. 42, 8: multa legi ex scriptis tuis, atque nullam unquam in iis reperi ratiocinationem, nullamque cogitationem, quae non humilis aut vulgaris, nullam, quae virum ingeniosum vel eruditum redoleret. Cf. 46, 14 ff.; 27, 26 ff.; 50, 11 ff.; 62, 25 ff., among other places.

[25] VIII, 2 p. 180, line 24.

[26] III 696 f.

[27] VIII, 2 p. 214, line 27.

[28] VIII, 2 p. 218, lines 3 ff.

[29] VIII, 2 p. 269, line 17.

[30] IV 9–12.

[31] IV 20–23; latin text VIII, 2 p. 320.

both of his writings as "*diffamatoria*" and "*famosi libelli*," by which not only Voetius, but also the academy and the administration had been insulted. The production and distribution of the writings within the territory of Utrecht were forbidden, "idque sub poena arbitraria, pro re nata, servato Domini praetoris huius urbis . . . iure actionis." The charge of atheism stood. Descartes complains[32] about the fact that he did not even receive a copy of the judgment, but learned about it only through confidential and (for caution's sake) anonymous letters. For protection he turned to influential friends; the French embassy in the Hague, the Prince of Orange, even | the estates of the Province of Utrecht interceded for him, so that at the year's end the danger for him and his books was removed.

But Descartes did not rest satisfied with that. Since there was nothing to hope for in Utrecht, he turned (Feb. 17, 1645), again supported by a letter from the French ambassador, to the estates of Zeeland, in order to demand an inquiry in Groningen against Schoock.[33] The estates commissioned the University of Groningen to undertake the investigation; Schoock had just become the Rector there and, since January 1643, Maresius also belonged to its faculty. In Groningen they first let Schoock's year as Rector terminate and handled the matter under the new Rector, Maresius. On April 10, 1644,[34] the decision was rendered. Schoock backed down completely from the "*Methodus*" and explained that he had undertaken to write the book at the instigation of Voetius, and that the latter had furnished him with the material. He maintained that the book was not, however, printed in the form in which he had written it, many things having been inserted by an unauthorized hand, and the whole having gone out, with his name attached to it, against his will. To his knowledge the changes were to be traced back to Voetius, who used the services of a student for that purpose. Schoock admitted that the book was unduly caustic. He retracted the charge of atheism.[35] In Utrecht, he said, he had acknowledged that the basic outline of the book was his, but he was not asked for more, and since then had always wished that he could express himself about the details. But the worst thing was that Schoock declared that Voetius had several times required from him a false deposition in

---

[32] VIII, 2 p. 216.

[33] IV 178, line 7: Nullum vero maius crimen esse potest quam atheismi, quod ille mihi obiecit. Nulla manifestior calumnia, quam cuius probatio nulla est, nisi ex qua contrarium eius quod affirmatur possit inferri; ut ille non alio argumento me atheum probat, quam quod scripserim contra atheos, et, multorum iudicio, non male.

[34] According to the new style on April 20; IV 196–199.

[35] IV 198: Nolle ullo modo praetendere Cartesium esse alterum Cainum et Atheistam directum vel indirectum et qui cum Vanino paria faciat, aut dignum convitiis illis omnibus acrioribus, quae in scripto continentur sed e contrario eum habere pro viro erudito, bono et honesto.

which he should confess himself to be the sole author of the book and thus to absolve Voetius; this he did not do, rather replacing Voetius' draft with an ambiguous formulation. He produced the pertinent documents. Maresius published the documents and a number of letters, which made the shameful state of affairs clear enough,[36] although the younger Voet, Paul, did all he could to obscure it by means of new publications.[37] |

With the Groningen decision, Descartes turned again to the council of Utrecht, which, however, did not consent to rescind its judgment. Instead of revising the judgment, they issued, on June 12, 1645, a decree forbidding anyone henceforth to write for or against Descartes.[38] Once more the latter took up his pen and directed an *epistola* to the council, in which he set forth the whole affair anew.[39] Nothing further was changed thereby, the pamphlet war also went on, and Voetius even instituted a lawsuit against Schoock, as if the latter had wronged him; the suit did not, to be sure, reach a settlement.[40] Paul Voet continued to defend his father in several writings.[41] Nevertheless, the atmosphere in Utrecht gradually changed. Soon Cartesian professors were called there; theologians like Franz Burmann and Ludwig von Wolzogen (concerning whom more will be said below), took Voetius' place.[42]

2. *Voetius' Theological Method*

Now that the disputes in the first period of the encounter with Cartesianism have been depicted and thus the necessary historical framework sketched, we turn to the motives and arguments with which those on the orthodox side combatted the new philosophy. For this aspect Voetius is the best authority.

Voetius gives the rationale and the justification for his attitude in the aforementioned *Disputations concerning Atheism.*[43] These were printed in 1648 as part of his collected disputations. They have obviously been revised here,[44] so that we may, so to speak, regard them in this form as his final word. We shall follow his argument very closely, in order better to be able to judge the philosophical and theological motives of the disputatious

---

[36] Bonae fidei sacrum etc.: VIII, 2 p. 248, note.

[37] VIII, 2 p. 230, line 14.

[38] The text in VIII, 2 p. 226.

[39] June 16, 1645, published on February 21, 1648. French text: VIII, 2 p. 202–275; latin text: VIII, 2 p. 283–317.

[40] VIII, 2 p. 227.

[41] VIII, 2 p. 230.

[42] PETER VAN MASTRICHT (*Gangraena*, I, 2) relates an example how, in 1668, BURMANN and MANSVELT interceded in favor of a pro-Cartesian student.

[43] See above p. 22 note 11.

[44] For the basis of this assertion see below p. 36 note 80.

professors. The reader is begged in advance for pardon for the resulting length.

Voetius mentions no names in the disputations, but delineates his opponents so clearly that they cannot fail to be recognized. His most frequently | cited authority is the aforementioned Mersenne,[45] whose commentary on Genesis and "*Questions rares et curieuses theologiques*" are utilized with the greatest respect. Voetius begins,[46] as is customary, with a definition, which is then amplified by means of distinctions. He thus distinguishes between "real"[47] and merely "participating" atheism ("when someone becomes partaker of someone else's sin and furthers atheism"). The first of these is either „direct" or "indirect" ("when a point of view, through a conclusion necessarily derived from it, is apt to destroy the knowledge of God") (p. 118). This can occur "practically," in that one rejects or neglects religion (sometimes even while outwardly acknowledging it), or in that one denies God by one's life and conduct[48] – as in the case of the "neutrals" or Machiavellians, the slaves of the belly or of avarice. It happens "theoretically" when a point of view negates God and abolishes the Godhead by virtue of the consequence implicit in it (p. 119); and this, in turn, is "primary" when the consequence is immediate[49] or concerns necessary presuppositions (e. g., when someone denies the divinity or certainty of Scripture, but also when someone denies the *lumen naturale*,[50] or when the consequence includes the denial of God); it is "secondary" when the consequence is indeed evident but not immediate (as is the case with the Socinians and Arminians).

Through this scholastic classification Voetius makes it clear from the outset that he is concerned not only about real, theoretical and consequen-

---

[45] See above p. 22.

[46] *Disputationes Selectae*, I. p. 117.

[47] *Ibid.*, p. 118: cum quis omnem cognitionem, sensum et fidem numinis in corde suo quantum in se est extinguere conatur . . . summum ac perfectissimum Atheismi gradum.

[48] *Ibid.*, p. 119: Ad hanc classem referri possunt, qui neutrales et indifferentes sunt ad cuiuscumque religionis susceptionem et professionem, quique religione utuntur ut nummo, modo aiunt, modo negant, simulant, dissimulant.

[49] *Ibid.*, p. 119: ut exempli gratia, si quis neget omnem Dei providentiam, is proxima et immediata consequentia negat Deum.

[50] *Ibid.*, p. 119: Cum generalitas est negati antecedentis, quia scil. principium generale est religionis, ut si quis neget divinitatem Scripturae cum ethnicis aliisque extraneis, aut in dubium trahat cum pontificiis; aut si neget lumen naturale eiusque certitudinem, quae tamen post Scripturas est omnis cognitionis rerum tum divinarum tum humanarum principium. p. 120: Cum generalitas est negatorum consequentium seu conclusionum quo fit ut Deus negetur. Sic exempli gratia, si quis aut omnia aut pleraque Dei attributa neget, is consequenter Deum negat. Or: Cum per consequentiam non tantum certam et proximam, sed etiam lumine naturali evidentem negatur Deitas, exempli gratia cum quis negat Dei praescientiam.

tial atheism, but at least as much about "indirect" atheism, which can be either theoretical or practical – and which, when theoretical, | can be either primary or secondary. From the outset his attention is directed to atheism "in disguise," which can conceal itself under the cloak of religion or of dogma; he takes the exposure of this type as his special task as theologian and pastor.

Voetius next deals with the *causes* of atheism (pp. 125ff.). Concerning the *causa principalis* – man and the devil who urges him on – nothing will be said. The *causae impellentes*, however, are partly outer and partly inner; the inner partly general, partly more particular; and the more particular, in turn, are grounded partly in the intellect, partly in the will, in the emotions, or in actions. The *causae impellentes* are in the intellect when atheism arises from skepticism[51] and is scornful of all studies, or when the intellect wishes to know too much, then despairs of itself and is scornful of the *docta ignorantia*. A third class of such intellectuals is not willing to go beyond the senses or nature, or to be satisfied with knowledge of the "ὅτι"; in that class belong the "New Sadducees," who do not believe in the apparitions and operations of spirits[52] or who, in supernatural things (including the doctrine of the independent existence of souls), demand mathematical proofs.[53] Before they venture upon divine things, these people should take cognizance of the fact that the life of the individual and of the state rests upon very simple insights accepted on faith. From the *will*, however, come causes such as impatience, intellectual arrogance, flippant and presumptuous scorn of all wise men, of all previously discovered truth, all earlier intellectual achievement and its exponents – and therefore the intention of a completely new beginning[54] at the cost of everything | traditional. From

---

[51] *Ibid.*, p. 126: In intellectu, quando quis aut cum Scepticis et Pyrrhionis sive antiquis sive hodiernis omne scibile, omnem scientiae certitudinem explodit, ridet, in dubium trahit, aut quodlibetica quidlibet pro re nata amplectendo aut repudiando omnem naturalem veritatis conscientiam, omnem eius amorem, omne naturale sciendi desiderium hominibus inditum (iuxta Philosophum Metaphys. I, 1) quantum in se excutit.

[52] *Ibid.*, p. 126: Ad hanc classem refer novos Sadducaeos, qui operationes et apparitiones spirituum aut ad causas naturales aversis vestigiis et obtorto collo trahunt aut tamquam fabulas rident.

[53] *Ibid.*, p. 127: Tertii generis sunt, qui ἀπιστίαν aut δυσπιστίαν in eo ostendunt, quod in rebus supernaturalibus, quae Deum eiusque opera, adhaec bonos aut malos, animas separatas concernunt, non admittant nisi demonstrationes mathematicas et quidem τοῦ διότι seu potissimas pari certitudinis et evidentiae passu semper procedentes.

[54] Continuation of what is cited in the text above: Qui contemptus etiam ad propria quae olim bene didicerunt, se extendit, adeo ut agant, saltem agere se profiteantur, ut omnia obliviscantur et dediscant, quaecumque unquam ex aliorum scriptis aut institutione didicere, ut scil. miraculosum ipsorum ingenium instar rasae tabulae solummodo inventis et observationibus propriis inscribendis idoneum reddatur.

actions comes, e. g., the perverse method of building only on one's own experience and of acquiring the whole of knowledge anew (p. 128 f.). Finally, with respect to *outer* causes, he first mentions apologetic writings against atheism, which, to be sure, wish to ward off atheism, but in doing so in fact open the door to it – such writings, e. g., as the *"Amphitheatre"* of Vanini. [55] Further are named those who have taken natural phenomena for supernatural, but then have discovered the laws of this pseudo-supernatural and are now of the opinion that everything supernatural is to be explained in terms of certain laws. [56] Under "concomitant causes" he lists both "impious teachers," who from impure motives attract people to themselves, and the promises made by the new philosophers, "for they seem on the surface to promise something which is not incommensurate with the true and the good" (p. 131) – *viz.*, the ostensible freedom of philosophy to abolish or to place in doubt all principles or axioms of natural reason which have hitherto been valid; they promise freedom of speech *(prophetandi)* in divine and theological matters and the perfection and renewal of all sciences, "and this indeed by means of an abbreviated procedure, without toilsome and hard work, without the expense of books, teachers, writings, collections"; and, finally, they promise new knowledge, which is held out in prospect. However, all these things – like the scorpion – carry their poison in the tail; the *libertas philosophandi* leads necessarily to skeptical ἐποχή, and enthusiasm for the new teaching leads to skepticism or to "semi-skepticism," [57] in any case to blind submission to the teachers of these sciences. An appearance of being right is accorded to these teachers by the adroitness with which they point out the fallacies in the traditional academic procedure, and with which they polish up the ostensibly new knowledge terminologically. Not the least of their promises is the promise to refute the heresies and atheism – "that is their most refined and most dangerous | subterfuge." (p. 134) With such lures the fish can be landed. [58]

---

[55] *Ibid.*, p. 129: Indocti et male consueti libri, qui rerum sacrarum explicationem et definitionem prae se ferunt; 2) novae impugnationes atheorum minus solidae, quae dum ab una parte atheismo et libertinismo occurrere videntur, ab altera eidem portam aperiant. Tales sunt Vanini in Amphitheatro, sed quem consulto hoc id egisse catastrophe ipsius ostendit et passim notat Mersennus.

[56] *Ibid.*, p. 129: sic illi uni atque alteri experimento de virtutibus magneticis seu idiosyncrasiis et de viribus imaginationis perpetuo inhaerentes, illius legibus etiam maxime supernaturalia subiiciunt et ex iis aut ex occulta aliqua magiae naturalis sive astralis omnes illos effectus deducunt.

[57] *Ibid.*, p. 132: imo ipsas tenebras, utique vacuas, puras et perpurgatas tum aures tum mentes requirunt, atque adeo ad deletionem, oblivionem et praesentaneam erasionem atque abiectionem omnis scientiae et fidei, si quam antehac quis concepit aut admisit, hoc est scepticismi aut semiscepticismi, quin libertinismi professionem.

[58] *Ibid.*, p. 133: ut . . . ex elemento suo, hoc est principiis et axiomatis theologiae tum supernaturalis tum naturalis extrahi se patiantur . . .

In the second part of the disputations (pp. 140ff.), Voetius discusses dogmatic, practical and historical questions.

Among the dogmatic questions, which occupy the greatest amount of space, the most important is the answer to the question, "whether there is an innate, natural knowledge of God." Voetius' answer is, naturally, affirmative.[59] His authorities include Chrysostom, Aristotle, Seneca and Cicero. In what follows, this point is amplified, for the sake of the "juniors," in the form of a short outline of natural theology,[60] regarding which, however, it is noted that this knowledge still is not the saving knowledge which is really necessary.[61]

On the basis of these premises Voetius, to be sure, has some difficulty in showing that there can still be atheists. Previously, against a Socinian or Arminian opponent, he had already defended the proposition which he now repeats: "*Speculative nulli sunt athei, qui certo persuasi sunt non esse Deum.*" He also openly admits that calling the doctrine of innate ideas into question is the sharpest weapon of atheism.[62] In fact, from his viewpoint, there can be no habitual atheism, but only actual atheism, and the latter can never be sure of its case. Actual atheism is then judged as "negative," "privative," or "contrary." Considered in its "negative" aspect, it simply means that someone does not carry out the act of knowing God, as is the case, e.g., with children or with people who are occupied with other things. With respect to its "privative" form it signifies that, because of neglect or malice, someone does not carry out this act for a shorter or longer time, does not exercise the mind and memory with respect to it, and does not bring the seed to germination, or in any case does not develop possible individual acts into a habit. "Contrary," however, means | that someone (outwardly) disputes the proposition "God is" or (inwardly) persists in his reflection on it, or even comes to a negative conclusion in his deliberations. The Cartesians obviously belong in this category, in that

---

[59] Nostri communiter ... statuunt κοινὰς ἐννοίας seu notiones innatas latens scilicet rationis et religionis semen naturale, quod se habeat ad modum habitus principiorum, qui in adultis in actum educitur et unde actus theologiae elicitur absque demonstratione, percepta modo terminorum apprehensione; haud (text: aut!) aliter ac primorum principiorum veritas suo lumine radiat et in mentem nostram se infundit, simul ac enuntiationis termini percipiuntur, adeo ut nullius hominis adulti mens ab actuali istius veritatis coruscatione et sensu ad explicationem et perceptionem terminorum omnium possit esse libera (*ibid.*, p. 140).

[60] *Ibid.*, p. 141: consistit autem haec facultas etc.

[61] *Ibid.*, p. 142: aliud est cognitio salutaris et efficax, qua scil. immutamur, ut quae novimus opere ipso exprimere conemur; aliud non salutaris et inefficax et frigida, qua nihilo reddimur meliores, de qua I Joh. 2:4.

[62] *Ibid.*, p. 144: Mersennus ... ostendit primum et palmarium atheorum argumentum duci ex negatis notionibus menti humanae naturaliter et ἀχωρίστως impressis.

they persist in a state of doubt, and while they do not become negative in their deliberations, neither do they wish to reach a conclusion.[63]

The distinction between practical and speculative atheism is legitimate, yet both hang together so closely that the distinction does not imply separation. Just as every practice presupposes a certain kind of knowledge and all knowledge has its practical consequences, so is there no speculative atheism which does not also corrupt morals. Theory and practice condition each other, just as intellect and will always condition each other. On that point, Voetius invokes the testimony of scholasticism. With these observations[64] Voetius assumes the right, without further proofs, to deduce moral corruption from clearly established atheism; the charge of atheism includes immediately the charge of libertinism.

Nevertheless, Voetius still dwells on speculative atheism. As problem XI he poses the question whether Scripture alone is the real and sufficient proof, against the various kinds of atheists, of the knowledge of God.[65] An affirmative answer to this question is the thesis of the Arminians and Socinians; it is to be rejected, for it contradicts the whole theological tradition, renders the proofs of the existence of God impossible, and altogether fails in practice when one has to deal with people who reject the authority of Scripture, especially against pagans and Jews.[66] Against the Cartesians he defends the method of proving the existence of God hitherto common to the whole of Christianity, to all schools and all men of wisdom among theologians and philosophers.[67] | The wish to overthrow this method means not only to benefit the atheists, but is a sin, moreover, against sound reason, which is the gift of God, and against the Holy Spirit, who himself applied and used this method.[68] Here, therefore, is the point where he can convict

---

[63] *Ibid.*, p. 151: ad contrariam Dei ἀγνωσίαν refer conatum eorum, qui volentes scientes omnium rerum, conclusionum, principiorum, cognitionem et assensum abnegant et abiiciunt atque adeo universale mentis suae vacuum affectant, ut hac ratione ad veram scientiam perveniant.

[64] Concerning problema III, *ibid.*, p. 166.

[65] *Ibid.*, p. 169: An praestantissima, expeditissima, sufficientissima et unica ratio sit probandi Deitatem contra atheos et apud homines, quicumque tandem sint . . . ex revelationibus factis in vetere et novo Testamento?

[66] *Ibid.*, p. 170: Quomodo opponent illis, qui totam auctoritatem Scripturae negant aut in dubium trahunt, quod faciunt athei, inprimis si qui inter gentiles aut Turci educati sunt. Hic manus dandae erunt, et arma abiicienda.

[67] *Ibid.*, p. 172: Hanc universalem omnium saeculorum sapientiam otiose rideri et explodi nolimus, tritamque ac tutam hanc viam removeri, ut novam nondum inventam nondum exploratam, sed in mera potentia ac chao seu mavis imaginatione et vanitate promissorum et magnorum hiatuum adhuc haerentem ei substituant.

[68] *Ibid.*, p. 172: insuper in rectam rationem, lumen naturale et dona Dei injurii sunt, imo et in Spiritum Sanctum, qui hanc methodum ipse docuit et adhibuit. Is. 40, Psalm. 19, Act. 17, Rom. 1, ac . . . spero eos qui guttam pietatis habent, a temeraria et periculosa opinione recessuros, ne blasphemiis implicentur, quasi scil. Spiritus

the new school of deviating from Scripture. The point is still further elaborated. An essential feature of the traditional method is the inferring of the cause from the effect, or of the creator from the creation, a method utilized in Scripture in Rom. 1:19f.; Acts 14:15,17; Ps. 8:2,4; 19:1ff.; Job 38 and 39; Isa. 40:21,22,26; Jer. 10:10f. These passages, and the entire theological tradition, are now being contradicted by wholly unqualified people.[69] Moreover, the Bible also draws on sense experience (Isa. 40:21,26; Acts 17:27; Ps. 19:1ff.; Ps. 8:4; Rom. 1:19f.). The new pseudo-philosophy betrays its skeptical or semi-skeptical character by not allowing for the validity of experience in this matter. It thereby accuses the Holy Spirit of deception.[70]

After these statements it is clear how the question is to be answered, whether the new philosophy is to be accused of skepticism, libertinism, and atheism, even though its authors confess knowledge of God and a certain religiosity:[71] Just as Scripture designates as Epicureans and atheists even those who do not openly deny the existence of God; as it calls the greedy idolaters, although their dogmatic position is correct; as it speaks of sorcery even where no express covenant with the devil exists; as Paul charges the Galatians, in the matter of the doctrine of justification, with consequences that they would never have drawn themselves; as theologians at all times have labeled as atheism errors pertaining to God and his attributes, indeed even with respect to the word of God, the promises, and divine worship, | and as one charges the Pope with atheism – so are the consequences of *their* views to be charged to the new philosophers. When these men go so far as to assert that nobody has hitherto convincingly demonstrated natural theology and in its place institute their own theories, they must be led *ad absurdum* by a demonstration of the atheistic and skeptical consequences of their views, in order that their opinion not spread any further and seduce the imprudent.[72]

Sanctus in Sacra Scriptura rationem ac methodum convincendi Epicuraeos aut atheos incertam et minus evidentem ac tutam nobis tradidisset et ipse usurpasset, adeo ut ipsius conceptus nunc demum a philosophastro aliquo iuvari, perfici aut corrigi debeant.

[69] *Ibid.*, p. 172f.: Quibus hodie reclamatur ab uno atque altero inepto philosophastro aut ab otiosis quibusdam novaturientibus Atheniensibus (Act. 17) aut ab hominibus vix semi-literatis praesertim in metaphysica et theologia naturali tam hospitibus, ut ne terminos quidem didicerint aut fando de iis audiverint.

[70] *Ibid.*, p. 174: et consequenter tacite accusant Spiritum Sanctum, quod in Scriptura homines ad sensuum testimonium in his aliisque quaestionibus revocando a veritate abduxerit et deceperit. Cf. Jn. 20:27; Lc. 24:39f.

[71] Problema XV, *ibid.*, p. 174.

[72] *Ibid.*, p. 176: Jure merito infelices illi disputatores his absurdis et consequentiis pulsantur, qui praeiudiciis novi scepticismi Loiolithici contra autoritatem Scripturae imbuti, universalem dubitationem de omnibus principiis et veritatibus (inter quas et illae, quod sit Deus, quod Deus colendus, quod sit discrimen inter honestum et

In other respects, also, the new method offers a great deal that is offensive to orthodox understanding. The way of doubt in itself is sinful, because even when it is meant to be only experimental it intends to put man in a state of unbelief. The summons to doubt is a manifest summons to disobedience against the first commandment, and therefore a further, direct contradiction of the Holy Spirit.[73] Man thereby runs the danger of not finding his way back to knowledge, the more so as the way to it is admittedly difficult in the first place. The assertion that seekers of truth must pass through the state of doubt for the sake of truth is to be rejected, because one is not supposed to do evil in order to attain to the good.[74] The onset of a new hermeneutic is likewise rejected; those "who are suspicious of the authority of Holy Scripture because they find in it many things which do not suit their carnal mind, and who so little esteem the Mosaic and Scriptural physics, | which after all is dictated by the Holy Spirit, that they prefer their own theories of the world and of the nature of things," render themselves suspect. "They dispute the divinity of Scripture, accuse *implicite* the Holy Spirit of stupidity, and thereby further atheism."[75]

Finally, Voetius turns to the practical questions and asks, first of all, whether such speculative atheists are to be tolerated within the state, provided they harm no one and live according to the laws. With respect to the direct atheists the question is to be answered in the negative, but

---

turpe etc.) vanitati humani ingenii persuasum eunt, ut instar rasae tabulae cognitionem omnino novam de novo sibi quaerant.

[73] *Ibid.*, p. 176: Atqui homo adultus non potest absque peccato vel ad momentum esse in statu ἀγνωσίας Dei et cultus divini, hoc est in statu atheismi; non potest veritatem detinere in iniustitia, non potest dubitationibus suis aut affectata purae negationis ignorantia communes notiones de Deo et rebus divinis inducere aut obfuscare. Vera Dei cognitio primo decalogi praecepto nobis praescribitur, ut docent communiter omnes interpretes. Et quis ille vermis qui obloquatur Spiritui Sancto?

[74] *Ibid.*, p. 179: Atqui talis affectatio ignorantiae et sequestratio omnis cognitionis et oblivio veritatis, quam diximus, est malum, peccatum scil. contra primum decalogi praeceptum et contra Jn. 17:3, Phil. 1:9f., Prov. 4:5, 23f. Videntur hi homines similes illi fatuo philosopho, qui amore sapientiae oculos sibi eruebat, ut tanto liberius philosophari posset. Sensus enim externos abnegant et in impietatis abysso versari eos proclamant, qui ad cognitionem Dei sensuum auxilio utuntur. Insuper lumen internum principiorum naturalium ad tempus extinguere conantur, ut scil. lumen affectatae et admirandae suae cognitionis accendant. In utroque tacite accusare mihi videntur Spiritum Sanctum Rom. 1:19f., Is. 40, Act. 17:27, Rom. 2:14f., II Thess. 1:8; Jac. 2:19.

[75] *Ibid.*, p. 177: qui Scripturae autoritatem suspectam habent propter nonnulla, quae ibi occurrunt carnali ipsorum sensui minime congruentia, ... qui physicam Mosaicam et scripturariam a Spiritu Sancto dictatam tam parvi faciunt, ut suos conceptus de universo et rerum natura illi longe praeferre videantur ... quique consequenter deitatem Scripturae labefactant et Spiritum Sanctum ineptiae et pseudographematis in probatione Deitatis tacite insimulant et sic manus atheorum atque infidelium confirmant.

also with respect to the indirect ones when they advocate their error – for evil talk corrupts good morals, and that must be avoided. Atheists must be prosecuted by the authorities[76] and – in case they add blasphemies to their teaching – are also to be punished, the manner and severity of the punishment being left up to the laws and the jurists. Still, Voetius takes the pains of citing the relevant precedents of canon law in detail. Respectable people should have no traffic with atheists.[77] – One can understand Descartes' agitation over the defamatory charge and over the Utrecht judgment which was occasioned by it!

After Voetius has spoken up in favor of the punishment of atheists, he shows that, conversely, it is *not* a punishable action to charge atheists juridically with the consequences of their way of thinking. Otherwise one would have to punish the Reformed combatants against Arminianism, or even the King (James I) of England, who combatted Vorstius in the same manner. What would have become of Calvin, Melanchthon and the other Reformed Fathers if Papists and Jesuits could have brought action against them because the former charged the latter with atheism! Even if the defender of the truth should have erred himself, one must give him credit for his zeal for truth. This indeed is also shown in the practice of the political tribunals, which did not prosecute the defenders of the Reformed faith against Catholics, | Remonstrants, etc.[78] Voetius wanders far afield in penal consideration, in order to show that the accusation which he here raises could not really be decided in a court of law. In Problem XII he poses (with a view to the events related at the beginning) the question whether it behooves a Reformed university to condemn a professor for being a zealous advocate on behalf of orthodoxy and to take up the case of a papistical Jesuit or of a libertine who has made his complaint in petty epistles, and to decide the case to the effect that the accusation of skepticism and atheism has not been satisfactorily established. The question is to be answered in the negative, because the professor would have defended the case for which he was commissioned and, even if he should have erred in points of detail,

---

[76] Problema II, p. 179.

[77] Problema V, *ibid.*, p. 183: Absterrere eos [viros cetera honoratos] debebat timor et amor Dei et periculum seductionis propriae aut aliorum, scandalum piorum, impiorum neutralium, infirmorum etc.

[78] Problema VII, *ibid.*, p. 183: Artificium illud de politicandis controversiis aut argumentis et consequentiis pure theologicis ac theologico-philosophicis, iisque hac ratione ad tribunalia politica trahendis, ut veritatis defensoribus tanto compendiosius os obstruatur, novum non est in Gallia, Germania etc., ubi supremae potestates a religione nostra alienae sunt . . . Sed insolens et novum esse, siquidem invalesceret in regnis et rebus publicis reformatis, ut Judaei, Enthusiastae et Libertini . . . et similes arrepta occasione ex absurdis consequentibus, quibus orthodoxi eos urgent, actionem injuriarum instituerent et in iudicio triumpharent.

would have deserved thanks.[79] If such a judgment had to be handed down at all, it should have involved all schools, not just four or five professors.[80] Moreover, one should not doubt that the battle against atheism is also the business of the theologians, for it concerns natural theology, and *they* really know something about that.[81] It is into their care that the young theologians, who are studying philosophy | and who must be protected from a false philosophy, have been entrusted. To be sure, the opponents affirm that they do not wish to get involved in theology; but if the theologians permit themselves to be taken in by this affirmation, it would amount to surrendering the whole surrounding territory to the enemy and to being satisfied with the promise that the city itself would not be seized.[82]

---

[79] Problema XII, *ibid.*, p. 185: Quia professor ille communis ac receptae philosophiae ac theologiae naturalis (quae toti Christianismo imo et sanioribus et sapientioribus gentilibus, Judaeis, et Muhammedistis communis est) pro modulo suo ex principiis luminis naturalis et theologiae supernaturalis defendere studuit. Quod si in nexu consequentiae aut consequentiarum alicubi aberrasset, pro omissis venia, pro inventis gratia debebatur, non vero πληγαὶ ἀντὶ σώστρων. Videant, an hoc non sit tristitia afficere corda iustorum et confirmare manus impiorum.

[80] Here it seems to me to be clear that Voetius criticizes the Groningen decision. This is the reason why I asserted above that the disputation has been revised and must be regarded as Voetius' final word. Cf. the continuation, *ibid.*, p. 186: Denique cogitandum fuerat iudicibus illis, siquidem ipsorum sensu non satis solidae aut evidentes visae fuissent consequentiae, professorem illum communis veritatis et philosophiae vindicem errasse tamen errore erudito et cum multis aliis ipsi communi. Ita ut in ipso solo exemplum palinodiae et ludibrii in gratiam omnium novaturientium et fanaticorum non debuisset statui.

[81] Problema XV, *ibid.*, pp. 186 f.: Quibus conveniat invigilare adversus atheismos? Resp.: Omnibus, qui veritatem et pietatem amant. Sed peculiari ratione magistratibus ut potestate sua eos coerceant, et philosophis ac multo magis pastoribus et doctoribus, theologis, ut eos deprehendant et refutent. Frustra ergo eos ab his tanquam a canis physicis aut speculationibus mathematicis aliisque philosophicis arcere student nonulli, et res suas curare jubent. Nemo enim sanus negare potest, quin commentationes theologiae naturalis, pneumatologiae, et metaphysicae ad eruditionem et curam theologicam pertineant, non minus, immo multo magis quam ad mathematicos, medicos, iureconsultos, philologos, politicos, pragmaticos. Solent enim vulgo theologi non tantum in rebus theologicis sed etiam specialiter in logicis, metaphysicis et theologia scholastica haud paulo melius versati esse quam multi eorum, quos iam nominavimus.

[82] *Ibid.*, p. 187: Si in cursu philosophico ingenia illa pervertantur et pravis seminibus conserantur, frustra plerumque in cursu theologico ad restitutionem eorum laborant theologi ... Et quamvis paradoxi illi philosophi ... Scripturam et theologiam supernaturalem primo impetu non petant, immo maxime protestentur, se illam nolle tangere, indirecte tamen et per consequentias certitudinem eius in animis multorum extinguunt aut labefactant. Neque enim dextre explicari ac defendi potest theologia supernaturalis sine principiis, axiomatis, consequentiis et regulis consequentiarum, quae ex lumine naturali in artibus ac scientiis, praesertim logica et metaphysica resplendent ... Accedit quod per schema illud politicum seu philosophicum excussa omni cognoscendi tum certitudine tum modo ac methodo

I shall not go further into the historical problems which Voetius discusses here. There is, e. g., the polemic against the Socinians, who are accused of preparing the way for atheism because they abet neutralism and assert that each person can be saved within his own religion.[83] Drawing on Mersenne, the case of the atheist Vanini is discussed in detail.[84]

Our knowledge of atheism obligates us to be thankful that "we" are different,[85] but then requires caution and opposition. Among the means for this Voetius mentions, e. g., sound use of reason, right instruction, book-banning and a corresponding personnel policy,[86] especially in the universities,[87] caution in the use of the classical textbooks from antiquity; in that regard he recommends instead the reading of Thomas Aquinas, Raymond of Sabunde, and, among recent ones, Mersenne.

Finally, he summarizes the traditional proofs for the existence of God, wards off the Cartesian criticism thereof anew, and declares that | the damage which the destruction of natural theology causes cannot be made good again.[88]

---

hactenus probata, via munitur ad artem dubitandi aut nihil credendi et arma eripiuntur, sine quibus auctoritas Scripturae et mysteria contra fanaticos aut infideles defendi nequeunt.

[83] *Ibid.*, p. 194.

[84] *Ibid.*, p. 202.

[85] *Ibid.*, p. 208: ad gratiarum actionem, quod per Dei gratiam (per quam sumus quod sumus) non simus tales.

[86] *Ibid.*, p. 209: Ne locus, saltem ne honor sit impiis et ἀθέοις in re publica, contra ad dignitates promoveantur vere pii et religiosi. In primis hoc agendum, ne in aulis tanti fiant . . .

[87] *Ibid.*, p. 209: Ut inprimis in scholis et academiis praeficiantur viri pii et religiosi, quod speciatim observandum in professionibus facultatum et artium extra theologiam.

[88] *Ibid.*, p. 214: Tutissimam autem, expeditissimam et evidentissimam esse hanc methodum persuadent Christianis doctrina et exemplum Spiritus Sancti Rom. 1, Psal. 119, Act. 17, Is. 40 etc. Quem inscitiae aut pseudographaematis velle arguere, Atheismus est, latitans sub pallio Christiani: Quod si quis monitus pergat ineptire et seipsum ac veritatem involvere meris petitionibus principii, aut obscuris aut incertis consequentiis, quales 'cogito ergo sum,' et: 'cuius idea est in me, illud ipsum' etc. inducto prius scepticismo, omnique notitia naturali insita et acquisita erasa aut per dubitationem sequestrata, nec non negatis et ereptis omnibus principiis ac demonstrationibus ante hac toti Christianismo usitatis et quidem convenienter Scripturis, utique superbis illis causae proditoribus aut corruptoribus suggerendum est illud Tertulliani, scilicet 'Valentinianos et Marcionitas exspectabat liberanda veritas.' Iisdem etiam eorumque fautoribus dicere possent omnes omnium scientiarum, praesertim theologiae studiosi et magistri: 'Redde legiones.' Facilis enim descensus averni, sed revocare gradum etc. Ubi notitia omnis etiam de Deo et cultu Dei, de honesto et turpi, de nemine laedendo, suum cuique tribuendo, semel abjecta fuerit et principia luminis naturalis ac regulae consequentiarum cum tota logica et metaphysica profligata, unde quis sibi aut aliis ad placitum theologiam naturalem et supranaturalem restituit, unde arma suppetent? quibus utramque contra infideles, fanaticos, Scepticos, haereticos, libertinos defendat?

What are the consequences of these disputations with respect to the problem at hand? Voetius was obviously clear about the fact that Descartes could not be accused of being an atheist on the basis of his words; he accuses him not of direct, but of indirect, "contrary" atheism and bases his assertion on the method and consequences of Descartes' views. The method of radical doubt is *eo ipso* sin and disobedience against the first commandment; it implies skepticism or at any rate "semi-skepticism." The rejection of the cosmological proof for the existence of God means, in a material respect, a clear contradiction of Scripture, thus a denial of its divinity, and therefore "indirect" atheism. Voetius is fully conscious of the problematic character of his proof-method; nevertheless he has a good conscience, and appeals to Scripture itself and to the theological practice which, since the Apostle Paul, works by inferring consequences, which, to be sure, the opponent himself does not draw, but which are implicit. When his method is acknowledged he has no reason to be ashamed of his assertions. His work is in its own way irreproachable, a beautiful example of the analytical method of this orthodoxy. Voetius knows himself to be free from offensive intentions, he is not concerned with persons but with the subject matter and its consequences.

Nevertheless one would hardly want to say that the Utrecht professor has conducted his case well. The charge of skepticism against | Cartesianism is unjustified not only on formal grounds; it fails to recognize the optimism regarding knowledge which is integral to this philosophy. It confuses methodical with skeptical doubt, and has no feeling for the fact that this doubt has broken in upon the age with a kind of elementary force, so that the customary procedures could no longer be effective against it. For the retrospective observer, the strangest thing of all is Voetius' passionate defense of the cosmological proof for the existence of God and of natural theology, on the strength of which, for him, faith stands and falls. Here his heart pulses. But at the same time that is his weakness: Voetius defends not just faith, but the whole traditional system of theology – they are manifestly one and the same thing for him. He measures the new by the standard of the old, whereas the new was only able to come into existence because the old standards had proved to be insufficient; and he does not understand that here a question has also been posed to him which he cannot evade. In order to be convincing he would have had to argue from the very center of his faith – but did his faith really have such a center?

3. Descartes and the University of Leiden

A course similar in its outcome to the one in Utrecht was taken by the dispute between orthodox theologians and Cartesians in Leiden. In Leiden, too, Descartes had friends at the university. The philosopher Adriaan

Heereboord was the foremost representative of his cause. His opponents were the theologians Trigland, the head of the faculty, and Revius, who knew Descartes from Deventer and had repeatedly tried to convert him to Protestantism. In a disputation on April 7, 1647, Trigland raised the charge of Pelagianism, Revius of blasphemy,[89] while Voetius added fuel to the flames from Utrecht. Descartes defended himself through letters to the trustees and to the "consuls" of Leiden, and again mobilized his powerful friends. The preliminary outcome was a decree of May 20, 1647, which forbade the Leiden professors to mention Descartes in lectures and disputations. Descartes himself was commanded to keep silence about the points named in the charge.[90] This decree meant little, for they continued to discuss the case without naming names. Already | on December 23, 1647, there was another tumultuous disputation, at which Johannes de Raey stepped forward as a Cartesian; he also continued to lecture on the new metaphysics. Soon Heereboord and Revius reopened the dispute. On the one side, the influence of the Cartesian method was constantly growing; on the other side, the Church exerted its pressure.[91] Decisive for some time was a new decree, which was issued on October 6, 1656, at the instigation of the retired councilman, Jan de Witt: The word of God is more to be trusted than the judgment of men, and therefore, out of love for peace and order, one must stop defending theses from the philosophy of Mr. Descartes, which have given offense to many people.[92] The formulation itself shows the political intent of the decree; in the more metropolitan Leiden one was much more susceptible to political considerations than in the narrow confines of Utrecht.[93] The professors were sworn to this decree

---

[89] DESCARTES, IV 631 ff.

[90] PH. C. MOLHUYSEN, Bronnen tot de geschiedenis der Leidsche Unversiteit (1574–1811), 7 vols., The Hague, 1913 ff.; A. EEKHOF, De theologische Faculteit te Leiden in de XVIIe eeuw, Utrecht, 1921; J. A. CRAMER, Abraham Heidanus en zijn Cartesianisme, Utrecht, 1889, Hoofdstuk II.

[91] FR. SPANHEIM, Opera, II, col. 960.

[92] MOLHUYSEN, Bronnen, III, append. 716 and 717; SPANHEIM, col. 960.

[93] MARESIUS, De abusus etc., § 23, relates that in 1664 HEIDANUS himself suppressed a disputation 'De dubitatione.' WITTICH, Theologia pacifica, § 36, mentions general political reasons for the rejection: causam supprimendi fuisse praesidio, non quod pro falso habuerit axiomata, sed pro cruda quadam locutione, quem aliqui concoquere non potuerint. SPANHEIM, col. 959, does not mention HEIDANUS' name but relates that the Amsterdam synod thanked the professors, quod hi tanta fide invigilassent, ut in eandem deinceps curam incumberent, ne in theses publice propositas influerent huiusmodi, quae iustissimam offensionis ansam et scandali materiam ecclesiis suppeditarent. PETER VAN MASTRICHT, Gangraena, II, 2, names a further case of December 3, 1665, and quotes the offensive propositions. SPANHEIM says expressly that this time COCCEIUS was also among the opponents. – MASTRICHT makes further reference to particularly offensive disputations of January 31, 1671, and June 7, 1674, in which the thesis was proposed that the doubt has to be applied

– and (with the exception of Heereboord) performed the oath, since (as Heidanus wrote to Jan de Witt) the theses were, after all, not stated precisely with respect to their content.[94] In the following year the Synod of Delft forbade the admission of candidates for the office of preacher who did not expressly disavow the new philosophy.[95] A doctoral disputation, *De veritate religionis christianae*, was cancelled in 1659 because of all too offensive theses.[96] | The debate even encroached upon the Leiden theological faculty, where Heidanus represented the case for Cartesianism, while Hoornbeek, in a public disputation, turned against him; Cocceius held back, maintaining that he still did not understand the (new) philosophy.[97]

After the downfall of the Witt brothers, there followed on January 16, 1676 a new decree, now forbidding, on pain of dismissal, discussion of twenty philosophical and theological theses as harmful innovations. No lecturing was to be done either publicly or privately on Descartes' metaphysics. We sense behind these developments the larger political context of the time of the second predatory war of Louis XIV. William III of Orange, the Dutch Stadtholder, was more attached to the "prince-minded" orthodoxy than to the "democratic" Cocceians (who at the same time sympathized with the Cartesian philosophy). A victim of the above-mentioned decree was the aged Heidanus. He refuted the twenty theses as unfounded accusations and was therefore removed from his chair. His book

---

even to the question of the existence of God and to the principles of practical behavior (*Gangraena*, I, 2 and I, 8). Cf. MOLHUYSEN, Bronnen, III, p. 313 (proceedings concerning the case of JOHANNES SUARTENHENGST, professor of philosophy, on November 9, 1675).

[94] The text of the decree is found in LEYDEKKER, *Fax veritatis*, p. 17, quoting from HORN, Historia ecclesiastica. Cf. MOLHUYSEN, Bronnen, III, pp. 317 ff., esp. p. 320.

[95] SPANHEIM, II, col. 960: ... Synodus Delphensis, anno succedente LVII. iniunxit classibus et consistoriis, ne candidatos ullos admitterent, nisi qui fidem ultro darent, neque permixturos se sacrae doctrinae noxia e philosophia principia,' nec 'propagaturos ea philosophemata quae, ex Cartesio prompta essent offensioni multorum.'

[96] SPANHEIM, II, col. 960: Nam et 'praeparationem euangelicam' appellabat (philosophiam Cartesianam), cuius praecepta viam praemonstrarent, qua posset mens vere 'Deum sequi', consequi 'perfectam virtutem,' ac gaudere de 'plenaria sui perfectione;' et praeter quaedam sententiae ambiguae insperserat etiam nonnulla theologis injuria et contumeliosa, v. gr. traducendo ascerta de coelorum omnium terminis, deque omnibus in terra 'propter hominem' factis, ut 'omnis impietatis et atheismi fundamentum.'

[97] SPANHEIM, II, cols. 960 f.: ... opposuit Cl. Hoornbeekius ... publicam disputationem de capitibus decem, puta de dubitatione, mundo infinito etc. quiritatus, theologiam sic a philosophia 'impugnari vel destrui,' eamque probandam philosophiam solam, 'quae theologiae se accommodans ei nullam vim adferret aut damnum.' Nec aliter Vener. Cocceius, ut modo visum, quanquam ob arctam deinceps cum altero collegarum necessitudinem parceret Cartesii nomini; deque eius philosophia universa, quam sibi 'nondum licuisset perdiscere,' iudicium declinaret.

Consideratiën over eenige saken onlenghs voorgevallen in der Universiteit, Leiden, 1676, on which Wittich collaborated, went through three editions in the course of one year, and in 1678 also appeared in Latin in Hamburg. On the other hand, Fr. Spanheim the younger defended the proceedings against Heidanus in the famous *Epistola de novissimis circa res sacras in Belgio dissidiis* (October 31, 1676).

One may hardly ask about the theological fruit of these battles. They do not show the persuasive power of arguments, but rather the alliance of orthodoxy with the existing order. For that reason they were scarcely suited in the long run to arrest the new philosophy's progress toward victory. The decrees against it did not remain in force for long, the much less so as even | theologians attached themselves to the new ideas and the discussion had to be carried on at another level.

As is well known, Descartes himself left the Netherlands in 1649 in order to accept an invitation of Queen Christina to go to Sweden. There he died on Feb. 11, 1650.[98]

II. The Problem of Hermeneutics

In the second period of the discussion the question of hermeneutics steps into the foreground. It is raised by the physician Ludwig Meyer and by the theologians Ludwig Wolzogen and Christoph Wittich.

1. Ludwig Meyer, the "Paradoxical Fencing-master"

In the year 1666 a booklet appeared anonymously in Eleutheropolis, i. e., in Amsterdam, bearing the title: *Philosophia Sacrae Scripturae Interpres. Exercitatio paradoxa, in qua veram philosophiam infallibilem Sacras Litteras interpretandi norman esse apodictice demonstratur et discrepantes ab hac sententia expenduntur ac refutantur.* The author was an Amsterdam physician, Ludwig Meyer, who had studied in Leiden and now belonged to the wider circle of Spinoza's; he was, however, no Spinozist in the real sense, but rather a Spinozian Cartesian,[99] and had made a name for himself as a physicist and a philologist. The book, moreover, was republished by Semler in Halle in 1776. With its first appearance it stirred up a great deal of dust; it has the merit of having posed the hermeneutical question in a way that it could not be ignored.

The preface begins with a challenge to the theologians. The condition of modern theology, it says, corresponds to the former condition of philosophy; just as dogmatists and skeptics once quarreled in philosophy, so

---

[98] CH. E. ADAM, Vie et Oeuvres de Descartes. Etude historique, Paris, 1910.

[99] Descartes et le cartésianisme hollandais (see above, p. 21 note 6), p. 254.

today in theology the orthodox stand fast on their conviction but are not of one mind among themselves, so that Christendom has been split into various parties, each of which insists on its special dogmas, – dogmas which, however, do not rest on Holy Scripture or, if they do claim to be grounded in it, cannot be proved as being in accordance with Scripture. All parties appeal to Scripture without their quarrel ever being resolved. Others admit that much can be derived from Scripture only as probability | and therefore expound their case with certain reservations. [100] Help comes, however, from the new Cartesian method; with its support, Meyer wishes to make the attempt in theology, too, to demolish everything uncertain, in order to get at the principle of the whole. [101] In theology the first principle is Holy Scripture. But then the question arises about its interpretation. It is necessary to find a method by which the true meaning of Holy Scripture can be discovered and demonstrated as being contained in it, and through which at the same time the opposite explanations can be proved to be false – both of these things in a certain and infallible manner. [102] He has hitherto not found such a thing among the theologians; for that reason he wishes to set forth the result of his own efforts.

Meyer's point of departure is the heart of the traditional doctrine of Scripture: Scripture contains the truth and only the truth. Moreover, it distinguishes itself from all other books in that here no difference may be made between the truth of the statement and the truth of the matter (IV, 4). The task, therefore, is simply to ascertain the meaning of the biblical statements, just as with a royal decree whose genuineness is established, it is a matter of lifting the real meaning of the prince from the wording. But this simple task proves to be insoluble to the author because language, including the language of the Bible, is always ambiguous. The proof of this ambiguity fills the first chapters of Meyer's book. From his initial point he further infers that every exegesis according to which the Bible says something false must itself necessarily be false. This yields, as it were, a negative criterion for correct exegesis. But the reverse is also asserted: every truth which one derives from the Bible also hits upon the

---

[100] *Exercit.*, prologue: cum autem contra alii, si non omnia sua, quam plurima tamen religionem Christianam concernentia tantum verisimiliter a Scripturis petita atque deducta esse ingenue fateantur, adeoque illa tanquam incerta et dubia, meliori aliorum saniorique iudicio subiiciant ac sub correctione, ut aiunt, loquentes quasi ab illis emendanda proponant.

[101] Diu multumque reputavi mecum sedulo, an quemadmodum illi in philosophia. Sic et mihi in theologia liceret conduceretque in dubium revocare quicquid in dubium revocari posset, idque continuo tanquam falsum reiicere, donec tandem ad aliquid in theologia firmum et stabile, quo tuto pedem figere possem, pervenirem.

[102] Qua verus S. litterarum sensus erui ac erutum esse demonstrari et aliorum falsa interpretamenta delegi ac istiusmodi esse ostendi queat, atque haec omnia quidem certo atque infallibiliter.

true meaning of the scriptural statement. [103] That is shown in the following way: | 1. God has foreseen all the possible interpretations of Scripture from the beginning; 2. God's truthfulness does not permit him to give the reader something other than the truth; from this it follows that all possible interpretations of a passage have been willed and incorporated into it by God, and consequently they are true – to the extent that they contain only truth. [104] Scripture is, in its meaning, inexhaustibly varied, as the rabbinic scholars already asserted and as Augustine and the Fathers taught (IV, 9). There is, therefore, only *one* criterion of correct exegesis, namely, that exegesis must contain truth. Therefore, he counters both the Catholic and the Protestant conception with his own thesis: the office of interpreter belongs to the true philosophy, which is the sure and undeceptive norm as much for the exegesis of Holy Scripture as for the testing of the exegesis. [105] To be sure, by philosophy we are not to understand the opinions of the "divine Plato" or of the "great Aristotle," but rather the method of Descartes; [106] the knowledge which is gained thereby is, according to the testimony of Scripture and of the philosophers, given by God. [107] How undeserved is the scorn for the philosophers which is customary among theologians, may be shown by mathematics, physics and the methodology of Descartes (V, 4). Only ignorant persons can despise them. Nature and grace, reason and revelation contain basically the same truth. [108] To the extent that philosophy interprets Scripture, God himself is his own interpreter. [109] Thus the

---

[103] *Exercit.*, IV, 6: omnem veritatem esse verum sensum. – IV, 8: omnes alicuius loci veritates, quae lectori occurrere possunt, etiam esse veros sensus.

[104] *Exercit.*, IV, 8: sequitur omnes illas (veritates) eo in loco ab ipso intentas significatasque fuisse, adeoque esse veros sensus.

[105] scilicet hoc munus (interpretis) verae competere philosophiae hancque esse norman certam ac minime fallacem tam sacros libros explicandi quam illorum explicationes explorandi (V, 17; cf. VI, 1).

[106] *Exercit.*, V, 2: Philosophiae nomenclatura intelligimus . . . illarum veram ac indubitato certam notitiam, quam ratio, ab omni praeiudiciorum in volucro libera naturalique intellectus lumine et acumine suffulta ac studio, sedulitate, exercitatione, experimentis, rerumque usu exculta atque adiuta ex immotis ac per se cognitis principiis per legitimas consequentias apodicticasque demonstrationes clare et distincte perceptas eruit ac certissima veritatis luce collocat.

[107] *Exercit.*, V, 3: Hanc autem Deo Opt. Max. luminum patri, sapientiae fonti suam debere originem nulli non notum.

[108] *Exercit.*, V, 7: Ex antedictis porro etiam facile colligi potest, quam futilis sit illorum sententia, qui naturam gratiae, scientiam revelationi, veritatem ordinarie veritati extraordinarie patefactae non tantum quoad certitudinem suppositam, sed etiam oppositam esse volunt; cum utraque uno eodemque loco atque ordine habenda sit. Non enim Veritas sibi ipsi, quamquam diverso modo parta atque acquisita, aut contraria esse aut antecellere potest.

[109] *Exercit.*, VI, 1: Quapropter, cum . . . philosophiae autor sit (Deus), ipsi etiam adscribenda erit omnis interpretatio, quae illa dirigente atque approbante in medium adducitur. Ac proinde illi quoque verae interpretationi nomen denegari nulla poterit ratione.

theologians, too, have in practice interpreted Scripture on the basis of their | philosophy, the Reformed theologians especially with respect to the doctrine of the Lord's Supper.[110] Even in the Scriptures true philosophy is nowhere rejected (VII); it can never contradict true theology (VIII). The Catholic thesis that only the Church can expound Scripture is refuted in detail. Not less false is the Protestant method of explaining Scripture by Scripture; this method obliterates the peculiarities of the individual writers;[111] one cannot say that one passage must have the same meaning as another in which the same expressions occur.[112] The expedient of using the unequivocal and clear passages is of no help, because these would have to be clear by themselves; if this were the case, one would simply make the *communis loquendi usus* the interpreter of Scripture, out of which, however, all unclarity arises; besides, those passages are not clear, as is shown by a closer look. Frequently that which seems clear to one reader is by no means clear to another (XI); *every* passage can be explained in different ways.[113] The *hapaxlegomena*, lastly, can by no means be elucidated by comparison with other passages (XI, 7). The customary hermeneutical rules have only obscured the understanding. Enlightenment by the Holy Spirit, finally, can in no way whatever be a hermeneutical principle; either it means enlightenment by means of the text – in which case the problems indicated remain – or it means sectarian fanaticism. At the end of the book Meyer tries to set himself apart from the Remonstrants and the Socinians. In a epilogue he recommends the use of his method for the Church: the certainty of exegesis which hitherto has been missing will now be obtained, the controversies | will cease; one will no longer need to inquire after the *one* literal meaning, the exegete will be freed from the ballast of the exegetical

---

[110] At harum trium discrepantium explicationum [i. e., the Catholic, the Lutheran, and the Reformed] quaenam est vera? quaenam falsa? quaenam sensui respondet, quam in anima habuit Christus, dum haec verba proferebat? Edocuit haec philosophia. Reformati enim illius ope suam stabilierunt, ac Pontificiorum et Lutheranorum sententiam absurdam esse ostenderunt, dum ex physicis demonstrarunt, panem, salvis remanentibus illius accidentibus, in illud caput non posse transsubstantiari, nec unum idemque corpus posse pluribus locis simul inesse, nec duo corpora in uno eodemque loco, et alias absurditates, quae horum opinionem necessario consequuntur.

[111] *Exercit.*, XI, 2: Sane cuilibet S. Scripturarum loco sua constat auctoritas, sua inest veritas atque proprius sensus, qui nec ab alio dependet nec per alium determinari debet; nec unquam unius apostoli scriptis aliquod interpretationis ius in alterius datum legimus.

[112] *Exercit.*, XI, 2: qua quaeso ratione certi esse possumus, unius loci mentem plane eandem esse quae alterius? Quamvis enim eadem aut similia in utroque occurrant iocabula, potest tamen sensus esse diversus vocabulaque in uno loco proprie, in alio vmproprie aut allegorice aut alio quovis modo sumi.

[113] *Exercit.*, XI, 6: Cum igitur nihil non in S. Litteris reperiatur ambiguum, nec quilibet sensus sit verus, sed ille duntaxat, qui menti scriptoris congruerit, nec hic per se pateat, nullus locus erit per se clarus.

tradition and of textual criticism; the reader will become independent of the errors of textual transmission and of translations. – As one can see, this means that all theological difficulties of the time can be solved with the new method, but only for a price: the surrender of theology itself.

2. Ludwig von Wolzogen and the Pietistic Critique

The theological faculty at Leiden reported a very unfavorable judgment of Meyer's writing to the estates of Holland; Cocceius and Heidanus were the authors. Among the theses forbidden in Leiden in 1676 was the proposition: "Philosophy is the interpreter of the word of God." Heidanus and his collaborators found it easy to disavow this proposition, since they had never maintained it. The "paradoxical fencing-master" (according to the subtitle of Meyer's anonymous tract: *exercitatio* = fencing-practice) henceforth figures in all writings of the time as the rationalistic bugbear. The most important and effective refutation is that of the Utrecht Professor Ludwig von Wolzogen: *De scripturarum interprete adversus exercitatorem paradoxum*, Utrecht, 1668.[114] The author was considered a Cartesian and had long been a thorn in the flesh of the punctilious reform party because he sabotaged their efforts to tighten church discipline by admitting people into the Walloon congregation who had been censured by the Dutch congregation – and also because he made no secret of his pleasure in card playing and moving about in fashionable circles.[115]

In comparison with Meyer, Wolzogen is much the better theologian and also the better writer, although his booklet suffers from the fact that it follows the train of thought of his opponent and often tries to be more ingenious than serves the cause of clarity. For him, too, it is a firmly established fact that Scripture contains the truth and only the truth and that it is to be believed unconditionally once its meaning is clearly determined. Moreover, "he shows himself to be a Cartesian. For him the *clare distincteque per|cipi* is the measure of all knowledge of truth."[116] He does not go in for the Cartesian conception of the universe *(Weltbild)*, and prefers to leave it out of the discussion. In posing the problem he follows his opponent: faith depends on the right interpretation of Scripture.[117] But

---

[114] Reprint in: LUDOVICI WOLZOGEN, *Orthodoxa Fides sive adversus Johannem de Labadie Censura Censurae Medioburgensis in libellum De interprete Scripturarum*, Utrecht, 1668. – In what follows I shall cite the *Censura Censurae* (abbr.: *Censura Cens.*), which in many respects brings WOLZOGEN's opinion to clearer expression than the main writing does.

[115] Cf. W. GOETERS, Die Vorbereitung des Pietismus in der reformierten Kirche der Niederlande bis zur Labadistischen Krise 1670, Leipzig, 1911.

[116] GOETERS, p. 218.

[117] WOLZOGEN, *De Scripturarum Interprete*, p. 129: Quid credat fides non habet,

his hermeneutical thesis is the orthodox one: *Scriptura Scripturae interpres*. For him this means not only that a passage is always to be explained
by means of another, but that Scripture is to be expounded according to its
own usage.[118] He contests the assertion that this usage must necessarily be
obscure and ambiguous, for when God speaks with men, his speech must
be understandable.[119] He is in agreement with the "fencing-master" in
his understanding of language: Words are first of all arbitrary signs which
are intelligible only to the initiated. But Wolzogen is of quite another
opinion with respect to its intelligibility: speech *becomes* intelligible to the
initiated because the *usus loquendi* is accessible to philological investigation,
which is indispensable for determining that. Where Scripture is not
understood, it is not Scripture's fault, but the reader's.[120] Every rational
reader of Scripture necessarily becomes its interpreter;[121] for that, he
needs nothing besides sound reason and familiarity with language usage,
so that basically even a heathen can understand Scripture.[122] Many a thing
remains obscure, to be sure, but the essential thing is accessible to investiga-
tion. In the first place Scripture is, for the interpreter, a | human book,[123]
and is not to be treated differently from a writing of Livy or of Polybius.
Like the writings of these historians it is, insofar as it is an act of communication,[124] a historical account – different, to be sure, from other historical
accounts in that it merits unconditional trust because of its author. Wolzogen

---

nisi docuerit interpres. *Censura Cens.*, p. 137: Ut fides credere possit, habere debet
quod credat; id omne in Scriptura continetur. Ut autem sciam quid in Scriptura con-
tineatur, est ea explicanda; hoc facit interpres. Censor putat solam lectionem auditionemque verbi sufficere ut credamus. Hic opponit lectionem auditionemque interpretationi, quasi sine interpretatione possit audiri legive verbum Dei. Quod falsissi-
mum. – Cf. *Censura Cens.*, p. 151.

[118] *Int.*, p. 205: Et ii qui Scripturam faciunt interpretem Scripturae, si se intelli-
gant, non possunt aliud intelligere quam usum loquendi Scripturae, qui tamen usus
habet etiam anteriorem usum universae linguae. – Cf. *Censura Cens.*, pp. 220ff.,
where he appeals to WALAEUS and HEINRICH ALTING.

[119] *Int.*, p. 11; *Censura Cens.*, p. 3: intelligi posse debere statuo, quia sunt ad
intelligendum datae.

[120] *Int.*, p. 13; *Censura Cens.*, p. 57.

[121] *Int.*, p. 49; *Censura Cens.*, p. 79: sive Deus sit sive angelus, isque an ater an
albus sit, nil refert, sive homo, is mihi interpres dicendus, si cum intelligentia legit.
Quisquis enim iudicio comprehensa verba cum sensu connectit interpres est; qui
modo ratione sit praeditus, ut facere nexum illum possit, qui sola ratione formatur,
iam meretur suam appellationem.

[122] *Censura Cens.*, p. 47: Sine isto tamen lumine Spiritus Sancti ipsi Athei et
Ethnici et Grammatici non omnes quidem sensus Scripturarum attingent, quod ne
facient quidem adiuti Spiritu fideles; sed omnes tamen eos, qui sunt clari, theoretice
percipient, etsi nulla cum oboedientia fidei. Sic Ethnici inter Christianos saepe iudices
fuerunt et disceptatores controversiarum. Sed ista non est salutaris intelligentia.

[123] *Int.*, p. 27; *Censura Cens.*, p. 45.

[124] *Censura Cens.*, p. 53.

still has unbroken confidence in his philological method;[125] the "fencing-master" can also be refuted by referring to the historical character of Scripture, since reason has nothing special to say about it, at least finds nothing to criticize;[126] the fencing-master's method necessarily fails in the face of the historical. Wolzogen, on the other hand, does indeed know something of the historical character of understanding: one does not understand everything in every .age; primitive Christianity understood many things better than we understand them today; other things, e. g., the prophecies, are understood better by the later age, which witnesses their fulfillment.

With respect to the reasonableness of the content of Scripture, also, Wolzogen differs from his opponent, who no longer made a distinction between reason and revelation. Wolzogen is more careful: Scripture contains something which constantly remains inaccessible to reason – e. g., the doctrines of the Trinity, the Incarnation, and the like;[127] other things can subsequently be shown by reason to be rational – as, e. g., the doctrine of satisfaction and justification, or the form of worship;[128] it contains, thirdly, much for which reason is just as competent as revelation – the existence of God, the doctrine of the nature and immortality of the soul. With regard to all these themes it is generally true that Scripture indeed contains something supra-rational, but can contain nothing contra-rational. If, however, a contradiction does arise, it is only apparent and is to be resolved by means of right, i. e., rational, exegesis; at no time can something contrary to reason be the meaning of Scripture.[129] Moreover, many a dogmatic point is not | stated directly, but can only be obtained from Scripture by way of logical inference; this inference is the task of reason[130]

---

[125] *Int.*, p. 86: Ita adhibitis omnibus legibus interpretandi, quas fert natura textus, si iuxta eas sensum deprehendam Scripturarum, aut verus ille est, aut non sunt a perfecte bono Deo profectae Scripturae.

[126] *Censura Cens.*, pp. 171 f.

[127] *Int.*, p. 32: Hic sola fides agit; nil a ratione iuvatur.

[128] *Int.*, p. 68: Posteriora, etsi habeant in revelatione fontem, quicquid tamen inde profluit itidem debent acceptum ferri rationi.

[129] *Int.*, p. 67; *Censura Cens.*, p. 93: affirmate licet pronuntiare, Scripturarum hanc mentem non esse posse. – *Int.*, p. 20; *Censura Cens.*, p. 18; (cf. *Int.*, p. 21): Si quid de cursu siderum, de terrae constitutione, de rebus naturalibus universe videatur affirmare Scriptura, quod invictae rationi, quod omnium hominum contestatae iudiciis experientiae contrarium esse deprehendatur, ego vel pietatis esse credo, sic explicare loquentem Deum in Scripturis, ut non sibi sit in natura loquenti contrarius. – *Censura Cens.*, p. 24: Rationem naturalem recte adhibitam recte iudicare posse statuo de rebus naturalibus. Vim Spiritus autem facere affirmo, ut et in coelestibus videre clarum possit. – *Censura Cens.*, p. 26: Si sit certa experientia et rerum evidenti inspectione firmata, nego quicquam docere Scripturam, quod ei sit contrarium . . .; quae cognoscuntur experientia, ea dico non confutari a Scriptura, quia nec ipsa veritas ab ea confutatur.

[130] *Int.*, p. 22; *Censura Cens.*, p. 28.

– just as a decision concerning ambiguous assertions is to be obtained only with the help of reason. However, Wolzogen does not mean that he would correct Scripture by means of reason; rather, he is convinced that if a contradiction between rational knowledge and Scripture appears, one has not yet correctly understood Scripture.[131] Labadie refers to creation, the Trinity, and the Resurrection as contra-rational truths; Wolzogen answers that he would not believe these articles of faith if they really contained a contradiction. For already in school one learns that something self-contradictory cannot be. "I confess that I cannot understand these mysteries; but I do understand that they can contain no contradiction, for that is as foreign to the word of God as falsehood itself."[132]

Naturally Wolzogen must meet the objection that reason as such is corrupt, and therefore is no longer capable of interpreting in the way described by him, but needs the help of the Holy Spirit. He answers that he was speaking of the *recta ratio*, which is still present even in corrupt man. A corrupted reason is no longer reason;[133] man, who uses reason, can err, but not reason as such. In the sphere of the natural no special | illumination is necessary,[134] but such illumination *is* necessary for knowledge of the supernatural. This illumination takes place, however, in the process of understanding and consists of the fact that natural means lead to the goal, i. e., objectively: that Scripture becomes intelligible to me, subjectively: that I apply the correct means. To this extent Wolzogen can also speak of the need for the help of the Holy Spirit and he most emphatically did so in opposition to Labadie![135] Only through the help of the Holy

---

[131] *Censura Cens.*, p. 96.

[132] *Censura Cens.*, pp. 18 f : Id quidem adolescens olim didici a magistris, multa supra rationem esse, at contra eam nihil posse. Ista mysteria me minime assequi fateor; id tamen assequor, nihil habere contradictionis, quae a Dei verbo tam est aliena quam falsitas ipsa.

[133] *Censura Cens.*, p. 200: Nam corrupta ratio, qua parte corrupta est, iam non est magis ratio quam luminosum dici astrum possit, qua parte deficit et extinguitur. Et licet homines, qui utuntur ratione, saepe decipiant iuxta ac decipiantur, ipsa tamen ratio recta numquam decepta, numquam fuit deceptrix. – p. 34: Corrupta ratio et involuta tenebris nequidem ratio dici debet. – p. 35: Nec enim de corrupta ratione agimus, sed de ea, quae sit expurgata ope philosophiae in rebus naturalibus, in coelestibus vi quadam singulari Spiritus Sancti. – p. 59: Quae fallit aut fallitur ratio, minime ratio dicenda. Ego certam illam et immotam intelligo, positam in demonstrationis evidentia; non quae spectatur in Aristotele aut Cartesio aut ullo mortali, qui possunt omnes falli, quando non recte utuntur ratione, sed quae est a Deo profecta.

[134] *Censura Cens.*, p. 166: Illud gratiae auxilium non est necessarium in multis rebus explicandis, quae non pertinent ad occulta mysteria religionis; solum verborum accuratum examen hic sufficit, nec est necessarium, ubi non agitur de salutari et efficaci persuasione, quia et impii et daemones, qui destituuntur utique Spiritus Sancti auxilio, intelligere tamen theoretice Scripturam possunt.

[135] *Censura Cens.*, pp. 148 f.: Etsi enim duci ratio per certas regulas possit, ut ne erret, sicque regulas interpretandi queat observare in explicatione Scripturarum,

Spirit can the inertia of the human intellect be overcome, so that the latter may apply the method correctly; only through this help does constant faith arise from the knowledge obtained. Like the "fencing-master"[136] Wolzogen opposes the idea of a direct illumination through the spirit, "as if, by means of the Holy Spirit, a special organ for knowledge, a 'light,' is given to man."[137] The Reformers have bound illumination wholly to the arguments which God has set down in Scripture.[138] The Holy Spirit is not an exegetical principle or tool; it does not furnish new arguments,[139] but induces me and helps me – and | for that it is necessary – to do what is reasonable in the right way.[140] Here he sees himself in opposition to the "fencing-master"; for the latter no longer needs the Holy Spirit at all.[141]

---

tamen ut salutariter et ad finem usque persuadeamur, solus potest efficere Spiritus Dei. Salutariter dico, quia potest aliqua levis et tenui luce micans cognitio menti affulgere, quam licet theoreticam nominare, qua etiam impii possunt affici in lectione Scripturarum; sed salutaris cognitio praecedenti ignem adhibet potentissimum sanctae applicationis, qua non credo tantum haec dicere Deum, sed quia Deus dicit, ea verissima esse mihique fore salutaria. Debet quoque perseverans esse ista cognitio, quod a solo Dei Spiritu possumus exspectare. – *Int.*, pp. 64 f; cf. *Censura Cens.*, pp. 87 f.: Potest enim sensum quoque Scripturarum interdum assequi qui Spiritu non regitur, quia sufficit lumen naturale, ut ad ea attendat, ex quibus pendet intelligentia. Sed quia non ita attendit, non scrutatur, non movetur hoc Spiritu non excitatus aut edoctus ductusve, hinc fit, ut non eos faciat progressus, nec semper assequi veritatem interpretationis possit. Hanc ergo vim hic tribuimus Spiritui, ut excitet inertem animum, ut ad verum scopum ducat utque per illas semitas ducat, quibus tandem perveniat ad salutarem interpretationis veritatem faciatque omnia illa quae requiruntur ad hanc veluti actionem animae. Nam alterum quod in nobis desideratur, videtur ad passionem aliquam nostram . . . referri posse, suntque omnia impedimenta, quae intercedere possunt, quominus res uti sunt pervidere queamus. Quae nec possem hic recensere omnia, quia sunt innumerabilia, nec si possem opus tamen foret, quod satis intelligatur Spiritum, quando ea removet impedimenta, tantum id facere, ut discussis nebulis umbrisque dissipatis, ea possim clare animadvertere quae sunt in Scriptura, quibus penetrare in earum sensum detur.

[136] *Int.*, p. 126.

[137] GOETERS, Pietismus, p. 220.

[138] GOETERS, Pietismus, p. 220.

[139] *Censura Cens.*, p. 89: Nam nulla suppeditat nobis nova argumenta Spiritus Sanctus. – p. 145: Spiritus docet quis sit Scripturarum sensus, non immediate, sed per Scripturam, quae omnia habet argumenta.

[140] *Censura Cens.*, pp. 109 f.: Imo Spiritum Sanctum nullo modo inter leges interpretandi colloco; id est cum absurdum sententia tum dictu quoque absonum. Non potest enim legis vicem obtinere aut inducere naturam Spiritus Sanctus. Sed id facit potenti vi sua divinus ille Spiritus, ut legibus istis recte utamur. Inter leges quas fert natura textus, minime comparet Spiritus Sanctus; illum tamen intelligi volui, cum dixi, adhibendas leges, quia adhiberi rite sine Spiritu non possunt. – Cf. *Int.*, p. 250; *Censura Cens.*, p. 263.

[141] Id lector omnis observabit facillime Exercitatorem repudiare Spiritum, quem non distinguit a ratione; me sine Spiritu rationem nil salutariter interpretari posse ubique affirmare.

Nevertheless, in the case of Wolzogen, one has the impression of a thoroughgoing rationalist. But with his presuppositions, can it be otherwise? His concept of faith is simply the orthodox one. "For him Scripture is a complex of supra-rational truths transmitted by God himself. To accept it on God's authority means, according to him, to expound Scripture in faith and by means of Scripture." [142] On the other hand, however, he so emphatically asserts that Scritpure is consonant with reason and, in case of doubt, is to be expounded rationally, that in actuality, despite all reservations, reason must become the yardstick of exegesis. To be sure, he is here in harmony with Reformed orthodoxy – to which he in fact appeals most emphatically.

Wolzogen's short writing was conceived primarily as an answer to the "fencing-master." However, it stirred the orthodox-pietistic party most deeply; about twenty opponents gradually arose from its ranks against Wolzogen. [143] The most important among them is Jean de Labadie. As pastor of Middelburg he had brought Wolzogen's writing before his consistory and the latter entrusted its delegates to the Vlissingen Walloon-Synod with the commission to raise charges; the writing, so it was said, contains erroneous and scandalous Socinian, Arminian, Pelagian, Semi-Pelagian, and Popish propositions; it is profane and blasphemous against Holy Scripture. [144] Already at the opening of the synod, when Wolzogen was to give the invocation, Labadie declared that he could not pray with him; how Labadie subsequently operated in assemblies and from the chancel is described by Wolzogen in the preface to the *Fides Orthodoxa*; [145] it need not be elaborated here. At this synod, early in the year 1668, | there occurred "the first characteristic clash of the pietistic conception of the scriptural principle with rationalism." [146]

But behind Wolzogen there stood the university, the city council, and the estates of Utrecht, which demanded of the next synod an examination of the charges. This is how the proceedings at the Synod of Naerden (Sept. 5–15, 1668) came about. There, after all kinds of evasions, Labadie produced a written *censura* of Wolzogen in which, following his opponent point by point, he annotates every expression which appears to him to be questionable, and passes around the aforementioned heresy-labels very lavishly. He bases the charge of Pelagianism on the allegation that Wolzogen

---

[142] GOETERS, Pietismus, p. 221.

[143] The most important writings are mentioned by GOETERS, Pietismus, p. 227.

[144] Cf. the preface to the *Orthodoxa Fides*; *Censura Cens.*, p. 327.

[145] Preface to *Orthodoxa Fides* 3, 4 b: Est quidam quasi ritus maledicendi consuetudoque recepta; non iam opiniones examinantur, sed studia partium spectantur; quae si quis contraria sectari credatur, solemni quasi carmine devovetur diceres ex formula pronunciari anathema.

[146] GOETERS, Pietismus, p. 215.

regards the diligence of man as more important than the activity of the Holy Spirit.[147] Wolzogen, he asserts, makes man the judge of Holy Scripture. That there is a kernel of truth in this has already been stated; but when Labadie bases the charge on the assertion that faith is being made dependent on the work of the interpreter,[148] he thereby simply shows that he himself has abandoned the Reformation doctrine of Scripture. On the other hand, he reverts for his part to the "Reformation" doctrine that only the Holy Spirit can explain Scripture; with persistent monotony he repeats that Wolzogen has nothing to say about the Holy Spirit and its efficacy. "Does not the Holy Spirit cause a new light to rise up in man when it converts hearts, when it makes unbelievers into believers, when it daily opens hearts and illumines the mind, as was the case when Christ was with his disciples so that they understood the Scriptures? How can the Spirit move hearts if it does not also illumine the mind?"[149] Here indeed the decisive difference is specified. At the close of his book Wolzogen had drawn a drastic picture of the "enthusiast," in which Labadie obviously recognized himself and, correspondingly, took offense at his opponent.[150] While his | objections against Wolzogen are clear, his own position is far from clear; how it differs from the position of the enthusiast attacked so harshly by Wolzogen remains obscure.[151]

The Synod of Naerden became a catastrophe for Labadie. After careful examination the assembly decided that Wolzogen's book was to be regarded as orthodox "et par conséquent que le Sieur de Labadie et son consistoire a eu grand tort de l'accuser d'une façon si atroce."[152] They demanded of Labadie that he acknowledge his wrong and henceforth abstain from similar actions. Labadie made evasive excuses and when, in addition, he was

---

[147] *Censura Cens.*, p. 289: Passim videre est, eum persuasionem potius ad mentem ipsam eiusque industriam quam ad Spiritum Sanctum eiusque potentissimum motum et vim referre.

[148] *Censura Cens.*, p. 151; LABADIE comments: Ergo ab homine interprete et ab humanis et humanitus latis interpretandi legibus pendebit fide assensusque supernaturalis. Apage Pelagiane! To which WOLZOGEN replies (p. 154): Aut non pendent a Scriptura res credendae, aut debent ab interpretatione pendere, quia Scripturae sensus cognitio pendet ab interpretatione. Cf. p. 162.

[149] *Censura Cens.*, pp. 277 f.

[150] *Int.*, p. 257; *Censura Cens.*, pp. 295 ff. – In *Censura Cens.*, p. 299, WOLZOGEN says that the whole *Censura* could be disposed of with the one sentence: si dicatur de Spiritu Sancto accipere Labadie, quae de Spiritu enthusiastico affirmavi. Cf. p. 290: Hic illum locum ingreditur Censura notare, quo maxime motum existimem, ut adversum me calamum stringeret. Passim enim et in concionibus et in scriptis quoque publicis vult videri Spiritu afflatus, quem non quidem propheticum audet nominare, sed quasi propheticum vocat et medium collocat inter communem Spiritum fidelium et propheticum. Eum singulari libello explicuit, qui merum continet enthusiasmum.

[151] I am unable to share in the positive evaluation of LABADIE's work by GOETERS.

[152] "Jugement du Synode de Naerde," printed at the end of the *Censura Censurae.*

himself accused on account of his "Héraut du grand Roy Jésus," he departed.
The synod excluded him from the Lord's Supper and divested him of his
ecclesiastical offices. This was the beginning of the Labadist separation –
which was brought about, not exclusively, but certainly also by the difference in the question of hermeneutics. Wolzogen, on the other hand, had
been acknowledged to be orthodox – and thereby orthodoxy itself had
conceded its own rationalistic roots. Goeters[153] rightly refers to the embarrassment into which Voetius fell because of Wolzogen's writing. The
orthodox had to decide between the rationalism of Wolzogen and the
"enthusiasm" of Labadie, and not a few followed the latter, so that his
likes could indeed now appear as the real pillars of orthodoxy.[154]

3. Christoph Wittich and His Hermeneutical Advance

The hermeneutical discussion was brought to a preliminary conclusion
by Christoph Wittich's book: Consensus veritatis in Scriptura divina et
infallibili revelatae cum veritate philosophica a Renato Des Cartes detecta,
Leiden, 1682 (422 pp. in quarto). This work is important for us because
there come into view not only the questions of method, but also those of
the new conception of the universe, which now for the first time becomes
a theological problem. |

The preface relates the occasion of the book, and in this context gives us
some interesting literary information about the rise and scope of the
controversy: during Wittich's teaching activity in Herborn, Cyriacus
Lentulus[155] began to write against him and the Cartesian philosopher
Clauberg, calling them atheists and innovators.[156] It was rumored that
they denied the resurrection. What was especially offensive, however,
was the doctrine that the origin of night and day is to be explained by
means of the rotation of the earth, and that the earth moves around the
sun, because this stands in open contradiction to the Bible. Jacobus Revius
of Leiden, whom we have mentioned above, had already attacked this
"doctrine" in several writings.[157] Thereupon Clauberg wrote his Defensio
Cartesiana[158] against both attackers, and Wittich dealt with the question of

---

[153] GOETERS, Pietismus, pp. 226f.

[154] WOLZOGEN reprinted LABADIE's Censura and his refutation of it in the Orthodoxa
Fides. The foreword is dated V Cal. Decembr. 1668 (= Nov. 27).

[155] eloquentiae et historiarum professor (ad quem nihil attinebat philosophia, sed
putabat suis luminibus a nobis affici).

[156] CYRIACUS LENTULUS (Lentz), Nova Renati Des Cartes Sapientia faciliori quam
antehac methodo detecta, Herborn, 1651.

[157] JACOBUS REVIUS, Methodi Cartesianae consideratio theologica, Leiden, 1648;
and: Statera philosophiae Cartesianae, Leiden, 1650. – About REVIUS, see RE XVI,
1905, pp. 710–713.

[158] JOHANNES CLAUBERGIUS, Defensio Cartesiana adversus Jacobum Revium . . . et
Cyriacum Lentulum, Pars prior exoterica, Amsterdam, 1652.

the movement of the earth in two disputations (1659). [159] The latter showed, "after the manner of Copernicus," that there is no contradiction of Scripture involved. New attacks resulted, first in the form of some Utrecht disputations, which repeated the old objections, namely that Wittich destroys the authority of Scripture and doubts the reliability of the Holy Spirit in things philosophical. Wittich sought to counter them initially by means of a Duisburg disputation *"Consideratio theologica de stylo Scripturae."* (Apparently his three disputations were then published together in book form.) Other theologians joined the Utrecht opposition: Jacobus du Bois, [160] Peter van Mastricht, [161] and Johannes Herbinius, [162] all of whom joined in charging that Wittich was attacking the authority and truth of Scripture. As for Herbinius, Wittich reports that he later (1664) came to concur with him and gave up his opposition. The Church took the case up in *Classes* and at synods; Lentulus wrote a new pamphlet which, apart from the style, Wittich designated as *scriptum ineptissimum.* [163] To these attacks | Wittich now proposes to reply with a fresh reworking of the disputations mentioned. [164]

After this historical survey, Wittich unfolds the plan of his book in the preface. He begins with the basic distinction between philosophical and revealed knowledge. The former is not given by the Holy Spirit, but corresponds to the *lumen naturale* and serves the natural striving for truth; Descartes has shown that one can thereby arrive at sure results. Philosophical knowledge cannot be obtained from Holy Scripture (this argument is to be set forth in detail in Chs. 2–8). Just as certain for Wittich is Descartes'

---

[159] The date can be inferred from the remark in the preface: anni enim viginti tres inter hanc et primam editionem intercesserunt. The reference obviously is to the publication in book-form.

[160] JACOBUS DU BOIS, Dialogus theologico-astronomicus, Leiden, 1653; and: Veritas et auctoritas sacra in naturalibus et astronomicis asserta et vindicata, Utrecht, 1655.

[161] PETER VAN MASTRICHT, Vindiciae auctoritatis et veritatis Scripturae in rebus philosophicis.

[162] JOHANNES HERBINIUS, Famosae de Solis vel Telluris motu controversiae examen theologico-philosophicum, Utrecht, 1655.

[163] Nova Renati des Cartes Sapientia – in quo acerbius et iniquius in Cartesium a Revio iacta iterantur et inculcantur novisque calumniis detortae sententiae Cartesii proscinduntur.

[164] *Consensus*, Praef., p. 5: Est ea dissertationum secunda editio, dispositione commodiori et alio titulo. – Concerning the first edition he says that it had hitherto been sold in publicis librorum auctionibus iniquo pretio – which may explain the fact that today it apparently can no longer be found. – As for Cartesian counter-writings against those mentioned, WITTICH quotes the following (Praef., p. 11): L. VELTHUSEN, Naeder Bewijs dat noch de Leere van der Sonne stillstandt en des aerdtrycks beweging etc. strijdigh zijn met Godes woordt tegens J. du Bois; IRENAEUS PHILALETHIUS, De verstrickte Astronomus Jacobus du Bois.

supernaturalism; like Descartes, he would, in any case, if he knew that God had revealed something contradictory to reason, rather give credence to divine authority than to reason. The Cartesian doubt means simply the careful testing of all traditional opinions, and whoever seeks certain truth will have to admit that this not only is permitted but is necessary. [165] Is one really not permitted to hold firmly to faith in God and at the same time to examine whether His existence may be proved on the basis of the *lumen naturale*?! [166]

As to the hermeneutical problem, Wittich observes that Scripture speaks in the customary expressions of the language of its time. To be sure, along with them Scripture has also taken over the *praeiudicia* of this language. Expressions thus encumbered (e. g., when they speak of the rising and setting of the sun) are on that account, however, not simply false; they contain, on the contrary, a truth which, independently of the prejudices contained in the words, is directed toward man. [167] The question then is not | whether Scripture is to be believed or whether it teaches something false, but whether one can distinguish between the language and the substance. [168] Language is in general an expression of the world-view of the speaker. [169] Scripture just makes use of the language at hand, even though this language does not correspond exactly to the things spoken about; the truth intended in the instruction may be explained independently of the language in which it is clothed. In taking this position Wittich knows himself to be in agreement with Scripture and with the Reformed confessions; [170] furthermore, he appeals to a letter of Descartes [171] and to a cloud

---

[165] *Consensus*, Praef., p. 8: quod non tantum licitum, sed etiam necessarium esse ei, qui certam et indubitatam quaerit scientiam, quis non videat?

[166] *Ibid.*, p. 8: Quidni etiam, dum fide firmiter teneas Dei existentiam, liceat inquirere, num eadem ex lumine naturae possit cognosci et demonstrari?

[167] *Ibid.*, p. 6: Scripturam uti formulis receptis etsi praeiudiciis innitantur; or: Scripturam uti talibus loquendi modis, qui veritatem aliquam, sed generalem tantum atque relatam ad homines et praeiudiciis quoad verba involutam significant. – His earlier formulation had been: Scripturam saepe de rebus naturalibus loqui secundum opinionem vulgi, non secundum accuratam veritatem.

[168] *Ibid.*, p. 7: Non quaeritur, an Scripturae sit credendum? An Scriptura falsum loquatur? An Scriptura multis falsitatibus scateat? . . . Sed quaestio est: An non Scriptura utatur sermone e trivio desumpto et phrasibus, quae ex praeiudiciis habent ortum, non tamen illa ipsa praeiudicia docendo, sed veritatem generalem talibus verbis quasi involutam? ubi ego affirmantium sententiam sequor.

[169] *Ibid.*, p. 7: Quis enim negabit quin sermo quavis in lingua multis praeiudiciis sit involutus?

[170] *Ibid.*, p. 6: Nos utique, praeterquam quod verbi divini auctoritati libenter omnes nostros sensus et opiniones subiicimus, nihil quicquam innovamus in Confessionibus receptis, nihil reprehendimus, sed eas tanquam communis Reformatorum fidei tesseras recipimus atque subscribendo probavimus et ex animo etiamnum probamus.

[171] *Epist.* 100; *Theologia pacifica defensa*, p. 27.

of Reformed witnesses from Calvin to Cappellus.[172] For the Faith, the
controversy has no real interest.[173] Asked what then his interest in the
matter is, Wittich refers to the universal obligation of truthfulness; the
devil attempts in every possible way to obstruct truth, and he could not
do it any better than by offering it to the world cloaked in lies and absurdities.[174] At the very least one must demand the freedom to discuss these
questions, and at the very least the opponents should admit that this free
discussion does not concern things which affect the Faith.[175] As a rule for
exegesis, he declares that, in giving attention to the intent and circumstances of the text, we are to ask what the Holy Spirit wants to teach us
in a given passage.[176] Scripture itself, naturally, does not distinguish between
the assertion and its truth, | but the question is whether, where it speaks
pre-scientifically and from a particular world-view, *we* cannot distinguish
between the intended truth and the form in which this truth is expressed,
and thus can transform scriptural assertions concerning "philosophical"
things into philosophical assertions without doing harm to their content.
The *"praeiudicium"* in which the biblical writers were caught thus remains
"in medio"; it does not concern faith, but only knowledge, which is of no
consequence to faith. Finally, Wittich formulates his directions for the
exegete as follows: "When exegetes have found the universal truth which
satisfies the text . . ., they are to see whether a prejudice is perhaps implicit
in these expressions, which does not have its origin in the Holy Spirit, but
rather in common usage, and whether, therefore, the language is 'vulgar,'
or is precise and brings pure truth to expression."[177] Incidentally, that one
may depart from the biblical wording he frequently shows by referring to
the treatment of the eucharistic words of institution in Reformed theology;

---

[172] *Consensus*, § 31.

[173] *Consensus*, Praef., p. 6: Non fidem spectant, non theologiam revelatam controversiae, quas excitare placuit sophistis.

[174] *Ibid.*, p. 8: quam si larvis mendaciorum et absurditatum dedecoratum mundo
exhiberet. Cum enim omnis veritas mentem perfectione ornet eique iucunda et
grata accidat vera multarum rerum et causarum naturalium cognitio, non potest
non menti veritatis cupidae esse molestum, quod propter istas calumniarum et
mendaciorum nebulas sibi aditum ad eam videat esse factum difficilem, aliis etiam,
eas non sentientibus et propterea nec discutere conantibus impervium.

[175] *Ibid.*, p. 10: . . . fruantur (adversarii) suo iudicio, sed et permittant nos frui
nostro habeantque has quaestiones eo loco, citra quas salvo religionis reformatae
vinculo liceat modeste dissentire, prout tales multas ipsa etiam in theologia dari
omnes theologi agnoscunt.

[176] *Ibid.*, p. 8.

[177] *Consensus*, p. 209: ut postquam (interpretes) per generalis veritatis significa-
tionem scopo Spiritus Sancti satisfactum esse viderint, videant, num in iis formulis
forte praeiudicium aliquod sit implicatum, quod non a Spiritu Sancto, sed a vulgo,
dum tali formula utitur, significatur, atque sic sint vulgares num accuratae et nudam
veritatem exprimant.

it is the Lutherans who defend the wording, whereas the Reformed theologians point out the inner contradiction and therefore subscribe to a "metonymous" interpretation. Even Wittich's opponent, Du Bois, can only say that one must not depart from the wording without a compelling reason, so that the whole argument can really only revolve around the question whether the reasons given in the particular instance are valid or not.[178] The rationalism in the doctrine of the Lord's Supper obviously facilitates the connection with modern rationalism.

A large portion of Wittich's book is devoted to the presentation and defense of the Cartesian conception of the universe (Chs. 9–19). He deals with the extension of the universe and defends its endlessness, with the center of the universe, with the movement of the planets, with the annual revolution of the earth around the sun, and the like. What matters to him here is to prove that this conception of the universe is based on reason, so that, on its account, he is justified in departing from the biblical wording. Next, the hermeneutical thesis is set down and defended (Chs. 21–30), the consensus with the theological "authorities" is established (Ch. 31), and, finally, the thesis of the author is defended against twenty objections (Chs. 32–40). For each thesis Wittich reproduces | the defense of the counter-thesis and quotes his opponents in great detail. For proof of his own asser-tions he simply collects examples which show that Scripture often enough is to be understood figuratively, since it proceeds in popular manner from sense perception,[179] in that, e.g., it presupposes the heart to be the seat of the soul and its faculties, and the like. These examples are, to be sure, not related to the question in dispute regarding the earth's revolution, but they show that Scripture avails itself of customary speech and thereby, at the same time, that making the same presupposition in other cases as well is not against Scripture.[180] In the closing chapters (44–50) Wittich demon-strates his method from the biblical passages which are usually quoted against

---

[178] E. g., *Consensus*, Praef., p. 7; *Theologia pacifica defensa*, XII 4, 290.

[179] *Consensus*, cap. XXI, § 461: Primum argumentum . . . desumimus ex Jes. 8:1, ubi mandatur Esaiae, ut scriberet stylo humano, hoc est tali scriptura, quam quilibet posset legere, vel secundum modum, qui erat in usu, vel iuxta stylum communem et consuetudinem, interpretibus Belgis. Ergo non debebat aliter loqui quam verbis, quae a quovis intelligi possent. Ergo porro dum incideret in mentionem rerum naturalium, debuit adhibere formulas communi usu tritas, non accuratas. Atqui tales formulae usu tritae saepe innituntur praeiudiciis.

[180] *Consensus*, cap. XXXI, § 679: Si enim non sit blasphemum, Scripturam loqui secundum opinionem non accuratam semper veritatem, hoc est, ut interpretor, si utitur formulis receptis veritatem praeiudiciis involutam referentibus: si certum sit in genere, tales locutiones in Scriptura saepe reperiri, uti testantur tot theologi, quaestio tantum erit, an etiam in locis pro Solis motu adductis sint agnoscenda? propter quod solum, si generalis sententia consensu tot theologorum est confirmata, tot fluctus non fuissent movendi ab adversariis.

him. Thus, for example, he examines the intent and context of Josh. 10:12f., and establishes that it is very well possible that in the case of the miracle of the sun standing still, Joshua did not understand the physical phenomenon. "Even though he was full of the Holy Spirit, the latter was not given to him for that purpose."[181] Whatever the case may have been, he simply wished – without doubt at the prompting of the Holy Spirit, who had kindled the belief in miracles in his heart – that the day of battle would be longer for him.[182] He expressed this prayer in the customary manner, just as every man of that time would have expressed it – and, even if he had been informed about the revolution of the earth, he would not have needed to express it differently; yet God gave him that for which he had prayed. "He wished that the sun would stand still for him in order that he could attain his objective, i.e., he wished that the sun would remain above his horizon longer. Now, if the apparent course of the sun was checked, this could just as well have happened by the earth standing still as by the sun standing still," – for this explanation Wittich refers | to Kepler.[183] It is not his intention to question the factuality of the miracle. For Joshua a miracle *has* happened. In closing he says: "For the breath of the Holy Spirit is not to be extended further than to that for which it was given."[184] As to the second passage, Isa. 38:8, the wording gives no reason to suppose a real movement of the sun; it is only said that the shadow retreated.[185] In Ps. 19:2–7 there are many popular expressions which are to be explained by means of the usual *praeiudicium* arising from sense-perception. The intent of the passage is the manifestation of the glory of God in the works of creation; and no harm is done to that intent if one explains the movement of the stars according to Descartes.[186] The "general truth" which is intended in the expressions used is the change of position of the stars in

---

[181] *Consensus*, cap. XLIV, § 811: quamvis Spiritu Sancto fuerit plenus, non enim ad hoc ipsi Spiritus Sanctus erat datus.

[182] *Ibid.*, § 812.

[183] *Ibid.*, § 813.

[184] *Ibid.*, § 814: Non enim afflatus Spiritus Sancti ulterius extendendus quam ad id, ad quod datus fuit.

[185] *Consensus*, cap. XLV, § 854: Solem mutasse situm suum decem gradibus respectu solarii Achazi, quod aeque fieri potuit per terrae quam per corporis solaris retrogradum motum.

[186] *Consensus*, cap. XLVI, § 875: imo quaenam philosophia gloriam Dei magis in coelis agnoscit? illane, quae gloriam Dei ex ipsorum pulchritudine, motus directione secundum leges naturae, eorum immensa magnitudine, nullis terminis . . . circumscripta etc. immensam agnoscit, quod Cartesiana facit, an vero Aristotelica, ut vulgo traditur, quae vix aliquid distincte de iis intelligit? . . . Narrari autem gloria Dei in Psalmo dicitur non praecise et determinate per causam istius vicissitudinis, quam vellent adversarii, sed simpliciter tantum a Psalte per variationem situs et vicissitudinem dierum agnosci dicitur posse . . . § 891: At ego nego, quod a motu

the firmament, but not the cause of this change. The remarks on Ps. 93:1; 104:5 and 19; Mt. 5:45 and Eccl. 1:4,5 add nothing essentially new. The method is clear enough: Wittich seeks to fix the intent of the text in relation to man and shows that no harm is done to this intent when one accepts the modern conception of the universe. He can conclude his book, therefore, with the claim that the views of Descartes do not contradict the Bible; from a rational point of view, the sole task could consist in verifying its truth on the basis of the *lumen naturale*.[187]

In 1655 Wittich came to Nymwegen and had to stand trial in 1660 before the Synod of Gelder, which, however, confirmed his orthodoxy in August 1661. In 1671 he went to Leiden, where he taught as the colleague of | Abraham Heidanus and, in spite of his known attitude toward Heidanus' deposition, was not molested. There, during a new discussion – which will occupy us below – he died, on May 19, 1687. There can be no doubt that with the introduction of the concept of the *intent* of the text into the debate he made a decisive advance over Wolzogen. He was the first to succeed in distinguishing between theory of the universe and theology, and thereby to show a way out of the dilemma into which theology had fallen.[188]

III. The Dispute about the Conception of the Universe
(Wittich and Maresius)

With this development, however, the battle was not yet at an end and not yet decided. We must still try to picture the "Cartesian" theology proper and to follow its further struggle with orthodoxy, in order to make clear the motives of the latter and to understand the reasons for its failure.

First of all, the remarkable fact is to be observed that the Cartesians at the same time were all Cocceians. Their contemporaries already felt this bond between rationalism and biblicism to be unnatural.[189] It has been

---

Solis in Psalmo desumitur argumentum ad Dei gloriam manifestandam . . . nego enim de Sole motum a Psalte affirmari, sed tantum variationem situs, quae cum vulgo recepta formula per cursum exprimatur dico etiam Spiritum Sanctum eam voluisse adhibere. Cf. § 892.

[187] *Consensus*, cap. L, § 938: Cum ex dictis pateat, sententiis Cartesii nullum esse cum sacris litteris dissidium, nihil aliud restare, quam ut eae num verae num falsae sint, per lumen rationis examinentur, quod ex parte etiam in hoc tractatu est factum.

[188] For biographical details cf. CUNO in: Allgemeine Deutsche Biographie; for material information cf. the summary in SPANHEIM, II, cols. 967 f. – Neither the RE nor the RGG has devoted an article to WITTICH.

[189] Cf. SPANHEIM, *Epistola de novissimis circa res sacras in Belgio dissidiis* (in: Opera, II, cols. 942 ff.). – *Ibid.*, col. 973: Factum tamen est, ut utriusque filii, quo illos, uti quidem videtur, 'defendat numerus iunctaeque umbone phanlanges,' nosque ἀνάριθμοι simus, et pro eo quo utrique feruntur in methodum priorem,

regarded as purely external and accidental; others tried to understand it in the light of the defensive situation which was common to both groups over against the inflexible caretakers of the orthodox heritage. In reality this alliance probably had theological grounds. Descartes had claimed the knowledge of the universe for philosophy, but by that very claim had removed revelation from the sphere of reason and had bound knowledge of revelation | all the more strictly to Scripture. It was therefore natural that the Cartesians now also adopted the new "scriptural" theology of Cocceius and sought to adhere, within the inner theological domain, as much as possible to the terminology of the Bible. The development which can be observed among the late medieval Nominalists is here repeated: the more profane philosophy becomes, the more biblicistic theology becomes.

The ideal type of such a Cartesian Cocceian is *Abraham Heidanus*, whom we have already met as Wittich's colleague. Heidanus proceeds from the separation of philosophy from theology, as Descartes proclaimed it, but is also convinced that between philosophy and theology no contradiction is possible, since both, in different ways, are grounded in God. Thus, he also justifies the methodical doubt: it is indeed very possible to believe a truth on the basis of Scripture, whose authority assuredly stands firm, and, at the same time, to question it on the basis of reason, in order to arrive at a surer knowledge of it; for many things which we believe on the basis of Scripture can also be investigated by reason and accordingly are subject to *its* method .The Cartesian doubt is thus only one stage on the way to truth; "*dubito ut intelligam.*" However, the "mysteries" stand above reason, and "revealed theology" exists independently of all philosophy. Therefore, their truths remain entirely outside the range of philosophy, while "natural theology" offers simply a synopsis of the Cartesian system.

It remains an open question, of course, whether this juxtaposition may be accomplished as neatly as the plan provides for. Will not the real certitude rest finally with the clear and distinct perceptions of natural theology? This question will be posed at the moment when the authority of revelation is challenged from the standpoint of history.

As mentioned above, Heidanus was dismissed in his old age. As yet unmolested at the time of his dismissal (see above), *Christoph Wittich* later had to fight out the real battle. In Nymwegen he had based his lectures

---

in personas, in causam veterem affectu, ut iam alia sileam, factum (inquam) est ut iunxerint dextras in mutua foedera, ut sint deinceps mutuae defensiones, praeconia mutua, arma communia, et vix a Cartesii sacris quisquam ad theologica, quin hoc ipso ad Cocceianae sapientiae adyta gradum moveat, quantus etiam sit inter illa hiatus. Nisi tamen vicerit sententia horum sapientium unius, ad quaesitum, quid Cocceio rei cum Cartesio, non inscite reponentis, 'veritates se mutuo et agnoscere et amplecti,' sic quoque cultores veritatis, quod de Fratribus Roseae Crucis legisse memini.

on the *Systema theologicum* of Samuel Maresius, but had dictated annotations to his students which corrected Maresius in accordance with a Cartesian interpretation. When a copy of these annotations (moreover, one full of mistakes) fell into Maresius' hands (whom Wittich regarded as his teacher and of whom he spoke with highest regard initially), he published as a refutation his *Dissertatio theologica de abusu philo-|sophiae Cartesianae surrepente et vitando in rebus theologicis et fidei*, Groningen, 1670. Wittich retorted with his *Theologia pacifica, in qua varia problemata theologica inter reformatos theologos agitari solita ventilantur, simul usus philosophiae Cartesianae in diversis theologiae partibus demonstratur et ad dissertationem celeberrimi viri Samuelis Maresii . . . modeste respondetur* (1671). Soon thereafter Wittich was called to Leiden; his book, which follows the remarks of Maresius very closely and for that reason was not exactly lucid, appeared in a third edition in 1683, supplemented by an appendix against Maresius' *Indiculus controversiarum*, which had appeared in the meantime. Maresius replied once again by adding "*annotationes*" to the ninth edition of his textbook (1673); Wittich replied to this with the *Theologia pacifica defensa*, published posthumously in Amsterdam in 1689. It is a volume of 1104 quarto pages in which the author with tiresome verbosity in 21 chapters and 681 paragraphs, again following the plan of the *Theologia pacifica*, sets forth and refutes the objections of Maresius in fullest detail.

Wittich repeatedly asserts his orthodoxy and is clearly conscious that theology is bound to Scripture and confessions.[190] For him the Cartesian distinction between philosophy and theology is fundamental;[191] the Cartesians do not wish to establish a new theology, but, quite to the contrary, reproach the scholastics for having mixed philosophy and theology. The separation of the two disciplines means that no theological conclusions can be established on philosophical principles, but also, conversely, that no philosophical knowledge can be established on the basis of theological knowledge, i. e., on Scripture.[192] As examples of the confusion of the

---

[190] *Theol. def.*, Preface: Sequor ego Scripturam sacram tanquam unicam regulam et normam fidei et vitae, firmiter adhaereo formulis consensus inter Reformatos receptis, Catechismo Heidelbergensi, Confessioni Belgicae, Synodi Dordracenae canonibus aliisque confessionibus Reformatorum. Si quis per consequentiam elicere conetur ex mea sententia dogmata heterodoxa et haeretica, caveat tamen oportet, ne istas conclusiones . . . mihi tribuat tanquam mea dogmata. Scio libertatem quidvis sentiendi in religione esse restrictam et limitatam canone verbi divini, a quo si recedat, in meram et nulla ratione tolerandam licentiam abituram . . . (developed in cap. IV).

[191] *Theol. def.*, I, 1: Philosophiam non esse miscendam cum theologia docui in Theologia pacifica, ostendique primariam inter theologiam et philosophiam distinctionem in diversitate principiorum esse fundatam, quod theologiae principium sit divinum verbum et revelatio, philosophiae vero lumen rationis.

[192] *Theol. def.*, II, 27: non esse vice versa theologiam miscendam cum philosophia,

two he names such venerable | people as Valesius, Danaeus, Casmannus, [193] Alsted – and naturally has Maresius in mind, too; if the latter had not crowded so much philosophy into his theology, the discussion would have proceeded differently *(Theol. pac.* 370, *Theol. def.* I, 23*)*. As authority for his own thesis Wittich cites Luther among others *(Theol. pac.* 3*)*. He insists that one makes use of biblical terminology for theology, "especially with regard to things which depend on revelation alone" (p. 10); theology could thus also obtain a new lustre. The thesis is demonstrated in detail with examples from physics; people who, like Du Bois, write a "Mosaic" or "Christian" physics overstep the boundaries established for theology. However, Maresius' charge that the Cartesians cannot believe in the resurrection is unjust, because it would never occur to them to doubt something so clearly attested in Scripture. [194]

Naturally it does not rest with this simple drawing of boundaries. To begin with, difficulties are created by those propositions which can be proved philosophically as well as theologically. [195] The scope of these propositions is a moot question; Wittich does not count the doctrine of the Trinity among them, but Maresius definitely does, and Wittich admits that many of the orthodox agree with him. [196] His general rule is that one must assent without reservation to truths which are revealed in Scripture, even when reason cannot attain them; [197] but the demand that philosophy has to subordinate itself to theology as its handmaiden is senseless, since true philosophy and true theology cannot contradict each other; both are gifts of God. [198] "The | philosopher" sets up an impossible case when he assumes

---

sive conclusiones mere philosophicas non debere probari ex Scriptura, sed ex solo lumine rationis legitima methodo et certis demonstrationibus esse deducendas . . .

[193] About OTTO CASMANN, who taught at Burgsteinfurt since 1589, see D. MAHNKE, in: Stader Archiv, 1914 (Heft 4), pp. 142–190.

[194] *Theol. def.*, XII, 4, 287: Noverat enim, etsi ex philosophia non possit haberi certa spes resurrectionis (nec enim putem ex philosophia scholastica sua eam voluisse ostendere), haberi tamen ex Scriptura certissimam et indubitatam eamque Cartesianos, quos dicit, theologos credere et ubique profiteri.

[195] *Theol. def.*, I, 1: Ita enim Deum esse omnipotentem probari potest ex lumine rationis postestque idem demonstrari ex Scriptura; idem iudica de Dei aeternitate aliisque eius attributis.

[196] *Theol. def.*, I, 2: Ego vero libenter quidem fateor, non deesse theologos quosdam ex nostris, qui hac in parte scholasticos sequuntur, alios tamen certum est esse qui malint mecum . . . simpliciter credere τὸ ὅτι ex Scripturis, quia est revelatum, at in τὸ διότι nolint inquirere, etsi per magnam admodum hyperbolen ad mille provocet.

[197] *Theol, pac.*, 37; *Theol. def.*, I, 23.

[198] *Theol. pac.*, 15; *Theol. def.*, IV, 54: Potius igitur (Maresius) distinxisset inter lumen rectae rationis et eius abusum, quod abusus sit rectae rationis, quando pugna videtur intercedere inter rationem et Scripturam, non ipsum lumen rectae rationis, quod cum sit a Deo patre luminum revera, non potest cum revelatione pugnare.

that revelation could contradict the *lumen naturale*.[199] Nevertheless, the
two disciplines mesh and render mutual help: theology obtains clear and
distinct concepts from philosophy and is referred by it to the wonders of
God in nature *(Theol. pac.* 16*)*. Philosophy, in return, learns from theology
that man is made in God's image and is burdened with original sin; both
points are relevant to its task.[200] But it does not end with merely formal
help. To the extent that both treat of the same material, philosophy also
gives certitude about theological matters.[201] Maresius[202] asserts, to be sure,
that theological certitude is stronger; Wittich disputes this, since certitude
knows no degrees; the assertion that reason could err even apart from false
use, is a blasphemy in his view.[203] Reason and revelation – presupposing
that they rest on clear and definite perception – have an equal degree of
certitude. But is it not a fact that reason nevertheless gains the ascendancy
at this point because it *proves* what theology can assert only on the strength
of authority? The tendency in that direction seems to me to be unmistak-
able when Wittich says: *De Dei | natura agit et philosophus et theologus,
et hunc iuvat ille in formandis distinctis conceptibus de Dei natura et attributis. Imprimis probat philosophia Dei existentiam ex lumine naturae,*

---

[199] *Theol. pac.*, cap. XI, esp. § 134; *Theol. def.*, I, 23. – Maresius' objection
is (*Theol. def.*, XI, 5, 198): Licet enim omnis vera, solida et recta ratiocinatio sit
a Patre luminum directive, ipsa tamen ratio nostra, ex qua elicitur, est in se corrupta,
tenebris obsita et errori obnoxia, quod in revelationem divinam cadere nequit.
Wittich replies (*ibid.*): Ratio quidem corrupta dici potest, sed ratio recta quomodo
corrupta dicatur, intelligi non potest. Si enim recta sit, corrupta utique non est.
Fateor quidem mentem nostram corruptam per peccatum originale, ut in Spiri-
tualibus nihil boni cogitare possit, et plane sit mortua in peccatis; potest tamen verum
aliquod cognoscere, potest bonum aliquod morale externum edere, fatentibus id
omnibus reformatis et nostro Cl. antagonista.

[200] *Theol. def.*, I, 25.

[201] *Theol. pac.*, 134: Ratiocinia humana recta eandem generant certitudinem
sive fundentur in ratione sive in Scriptura.

[202] *Theol. def.*, XI, 5, 199.

[203] *Theol. def.*, XI, 5, 199: Ceterum 'falsum aut errorem subesse posse iis, quae
luce rationis humanae percipimus' vellem non dixisse virum clarissimum, cum sit
summe injurium in Deum. Cum enim Deus sit auctor lucis rationis, si iis, quae luce
rationis humanae percipimus, possit subesse falsum, utique Deus per id quod nobis
dedit nos dicendus erit decepisse, quod cum veracitate eius pugnat . . . Mirum autem
merito mihi videtur, esse homines qui serio negent aequalem esse certitudinem ex
evidenti demonstratione exortam ei, quae clara verbi divini revelatione nititur. Et
forte tales non intelligunt certitudinis formalem rationem illudque quod probabile
tantum est cum certo confundunt . . . Pertinet illa certitudo, quae menti convenit,
ad reliquias imaginis divinae, quas homo retinuit post lapsum; etsi enim per lapsum
ita sit depravatus, ut in multis cespitet, non tamen est aestimandum, per illum ita
imaginem divinam esse deletam, ut nulla ne quidem rudera vel reliquiae eius re-
manserint. Iudicare itaque potest et quidem recte iudicare potest de quibusdam;
quando recte iudicat, certum est eius iudicium, neque enim rectum iudicium a
iudicio certo ullo modo potest dinstingui.

quam supponere opportet theologum, dum auctoritatem Sacrae Scripturae demonstrat (Theol. pac. 191*).*

Theologically, Wittich, too, shows himself to be a Cocceian and repeats not only the Cocceianic division of salvation-history *(Heilsgeschichte)*, but also the distinction between the Old and New Testaments by means of the terms πάρεσις and ἄφεσις. With respect to the doctrine of justification he advocates Cartesian voluntarism and cites Amesius;[204] he calls *notitia* an act which precedes redemptive faith *(Heilsglauben)*,[205] whose *actus essentialis* is the *assensus*, and thus makes love (for Christ) into the (second, in order of succession) *actus essentialis* of faith *(Theol. def.* XI, 4, 206*).*[206]

---

[204] *Theol. def.*, XI, 3, Superscription: Intellectui nullum imperium competit in voluntatem. Sedes fidei salvificae est voluntas, intellectus vero sive perceptio rerum credendarum est necessarium antecedens ad fidem. – MARESIUS asserted that the seat of redemptive faith is exclusively (later he says: "primarily") the intellect. WITTICH replies: Ego vero ·subiectum fidei salvificae dico solam esse voluntatem, intellectum vero rerum credendarum considero tanquam necessarium antecedens ad fidem. Qua in sententia habeo ὁμόψηφον Amesium in Medulla Theol. (*Theol. def.*, XI, 3, 166; cf. XI, 3, 171). Besides Amesius he also mentions VOETIUS and COCCEIUS as authorities. MARESIUS sees here again hidden Pelagianism: Non vult (Wittich) fidei sedem esse intellectum, quia intellectus irresistibiliter illuminatur, sed eam assignat voluntati, quia ipsa a se sola determinatur, ut etiam fidem suam potius suo adscribat libero arbitrio, quo se fabrum suae fortunae constituat, quam Dei illuminationi et gratiae. (*Theol. def.*, XI, 3, 169).

[205] *Theol. def.*, XI, 4, 205 and 213: Notitia enim illa revelationis mihi non est primus actus fidei, sed est actus fidem antecedens.

[206] He defends himself against MARESIUS who wants to maintain the orthodox concept of faith, i. e., to base the *unio* with Christ on the intellectual act alone. *Theol. def.*, XI, 4, 207: Si voluntas immediate determinatur ab intellectu, prout loqui solet Vir Cl. sive, prout ego malo dicere, si voluntas certo et infallibiliter sequitur claram perceptionem intellectus, quomodo fieri potest, ut Christo clare cognito tanquam unico nostro bono non feratur immediate in eum voluntas, non eum sibi uniat, quod est amare? Illa ipsa unio cum Christo tanquam capite nostro est actus amoris; sic enim formamus voluntate nostra totum aliquod ex Christo et nobis, cuius Christus primaria est pars, quatenus spectatur ut caput, nos vero pars longe inferior et minoris momenti ... Non igitur caritas *tendit* ad ulteriorem coniunctionem cum Christo, sed ipsa iungit nos Christo. In § 208 he emphasizes that the distinction between *fides* and *caritas* can only be a theoretical one; caritatis actum illum in fide comprehendi satis (Apostolus) ostendit, quando fidei tribuit, quod nos cum Christo uniat, ... credere in Deum est credendo amare, in eum ire et membris eius incorporari. Fides est cognitio, per quam non quaerendo volitamus, sed inhaerendo Deum diligimus. – To define his position over against that of Catholicism he says (*Theol. pac.*, 138): ... si per formam intelligatur generaliter quicquid rei essentiale est eamque distinguit ab alia, caritas illa non quidem integra fidei forma dici debet, sed tamen pars formae. Si vero forma stricte accipiatur, ut debet, pro intimo rei attributo, ex quo reliqua oriuntur, dicimus caritatem quidem illam esse fidei salvificae proprietatem, sed non ipsam formam fidei sive essentiam, quam constituimus in acquiescentia cordis in Deo et Auctore et fonte salutis (*Theol. def.*, XI, 5, 216). MARESIUS finds this distinction monstrous; satis habebant (orthodoxi)

'Wittich can, to be sure, correctly set forth the forensic | doctrine of justification, designating, in the endeavor to differentiate the individual acts, the imputations as *fundamentum justificationis*, the *vindicatio a merito condemnationis* as its *forma*;[207]/when at the same time he mentions the supernatural motivations and experiences which are awakened by means of faith, this probably is in the line of the Reformed tradition.[208] If Maresius here again suspects Pelagianism, Wittich retorts that it is, after all, not a matter of a *causa meritoria* of justification, but only of signs from which it is to be understood *a posteriori* that we are in God's grace, so that one can, on that basis, once more express the judgment that we have been justified. He refers to the coexistence of Paul and James in Scripture and also cites Martin Bucer as an authority *(Theol. def.* XVI, 379;380;387*)*. A substantial difference from Maresius obviously does not exist at this point (cf. 381).

The special material points of Descartes also have a place. Wittich defends not only the principle of doubt as a proper methodical principle for students, but the *clara et distincta perceptio* is the criterion of truth in theology also. To the question of Maresius concerning the criterion of the *perceptio* Wittich replies, with reference to his master, that there is no need for such a criterion, since clarity and distinctness, like light, bear witness to themselves. He turns against the theological view of nature in favor of the causal, because we do not really know God's intentions with respect to the existing things; this obviously serves to replace the anthropocentric conception of the universe with an "objective" one.[209] Here, | Maresius

---

defendere caritatem esse a fide, ut effectum a sua causa, filiam a sua matre, fructum a sua radice *(Theol. def.*, XI, 5, 217).

[207] To be sure, MARESIUS also objects to the mode of expression when WITTICH suggests one could in a certain respect also say that by faith we justify ourselves. WITTICH's reasoning is as follows *(Theol. def.*, XVI, 373): Si igitur fides nostra, actus nostra, possit dici nos iustificare, non video quid obstet, quominus possimus dici hoc sensu nosmet ipsos iustificare . . . Haec est vera ὁμολογία, quando id, quod Deus, etiam cor nostrum dicit Dei vicem.

[208] *Theol. pac.*, 245: Hunc actum alii actus iustificationis in conscientia sequuntur, quatenus reflectentes super actus fidei et bonorum operum, quos actus novimus nos propriis viribus edere non potuisse, eos habemus pro certis signis et testimoniis redemptionis nostrae per Christum, atque sic nos iterum pronuntiamus iustos et immunes a merito condemnationis. Quia tamen hi actus in conscientia vim et efficaciam accipiunt ab actu primo, quo Christus in coelis nostram causam agit et Pater nos absolvit, hinc Scriptura solet passive loqui de nostra iustificatione eamque Christo et Patri tamquam causae efficienti attribuere.

[209] This is the basis of the warning, *Theol. pac.*, 106: cavendum nobis esse, ne nimis superbe de nobis ipsis sentiamus, quod fieret, si dicamus, omnia propter nos solos ita esse facta, ut nullus alius sit eorum usus. *Theol. def.*, IX, superscription: Deus nobis quidem revelavit generales fines suorum operum, non particulares. Quamvis sano sensu possit dici, omnia propter hominem esse facta, non ita tamen loquitur Scriptura. To be sure, in Confessio Belgica, art. 21, it says that all things

reproaches him, by citing Col. 2 : 18, for sham humility and sees the authority of the *Confessio Belgica* abandoned. Wittich adopts Descartes' concept of God and proof of God's existence without scruple, and comes close to the assertion about the best of all worlds.[210] Of course, he passionately defends the modern conception of the universe and repeats that it does no harm to faith. He readily disposes of Maresius'[211] repeated references to the biblical sun-miracles, as already refuted by something he had said earlier (see above pp. 54ff.). For Maresius, on the other hand, the characteristic remark is that "it is certain that this world of ours is everywhere equally far removed from the upper heaven," by which he wishes to prove that the earth is the center of the universe. Here Wittich finds it easy to mock by saying that he wished his opponent had proved this assertion,[212] and easy to claim that Maresius still lacks even the rudiments of astronomy and optics,[213] while he himself argues just as confidently from the infinity of the universe.[214]

For Wittich, the whole dispute so presents itself that it revolves around philosophical, not theological matters. As for theological questions, which he treats in the second part of his books, there remain the exegesis of a few passages over which he differs with Maresius, and some *problemata* about which one can have more than one opinion without endangering faith. Among these he mentions,[215] e. g., | the question *de ordine in decretis (scil. de praedestinatione)*. Maresius was an infralapsarian. Wittich explains that the finiteness of our condition permits no sure judgment, but he confesses that "in the winter of the year 70" he finally came, through the influence

---

may be to the service of man, but it does not say: omnia absolute facta esse propter hominem neque ea ullum habere alium usum. MARESIUS replies (*Theol. def.*, IX, 121): ita pari ratione accusaveris fideles cum Pontificiis, quod iusto superbius de se sentiant, dum se profitentur Dei filios et certos suae salutis . . . illi sunt humiliter impii, qui metuunt nimium de Dei amore et bonitate erga se praesumere. *Theol. def.*, IX, 124: Qui negant saltem secundario omnia esse destinata ad homines, non possunt bona fide sine restrictione et reservatione mentali Jesuitica profiteri, se ambabus manibus amplecti hanc Confessionis doctrinam, quam aperte reiciunt, ut suo Cartesio, homini quoad vixit religionis sic satis securo, velificentur.

[210] *Theol. def.*, XVI, 344: Deum semper facere id quod est optimum ostendi Theol. pac. § 233, quod tamen ita censui explicandum, ut quamvis res singulae sint perfectae in suo genere et respectu perfectionis essentialis atque prout considerantur tamquam partes universi, possint tamen absolute et in se spectatae fieri meliores atque perfici magis accidentaliter. Hoc ostenderam exemplo hominum, qui potuerunt fieri impeccabiles sicut angeli boni impeccabiles sunt redditi, sed ad varietatem creaturarum ostenderam debuisse esse et creaturas peccabiles, cuiusmodi sunt homines, et creaturas impeccabiles, quales sunt angeli.

[211] *Theol. def.*, II, 38.

[212] *Theol. def.*, II, 28 and 35: eius certitudinis vellem, ut fundamentum aliquod solidum adduxisset . . . At Ptolemaicorum sententia haec iam diu est explosa.

[213] *Theol. def.*, II, 29.

[214] *Theol. def.*, II, 30.

[215] *Theol. pac.*, 255; *Theol. def.*, 392.

of Twiss and after overcoming some scruples, to adopt supralapsarianism
– which certainly does correspond better to his thought *(Theol. def.* XVII,
393f.). It is revealing that he numbers even this question among the
problematica, whereas Maresius, with an appeal to the Synod of Dort,
asserts that infralapsarianism is the only doctrine confessionally sound.
Under the heading of *Problematica* Wittich likewise advocates (Ch. XVIII)
the teachings of Cocceius, whom he follows with regard to the sabbath-
question, the distinction between the Old Testament and the New Testament
according to πάρεσις and ἄφεσις, and the doctrine of the covenant (see
above, pp. 63f.), among other things. [216] Since the Cartesians were generally
accused of a tendency toward the dissolution of church government and
church discipline, the doctrine of church government is treated broadly; [217]
but in the eyes of Wittich it does not concern a question of faith, insofar as
it is controversial.

What is astonishing on the whole is that the objections brought forth
with such passion by Maresius have so little relevance theologically. He is
concerned, of course, with serious things. He sees the authority of the Bible
and Confession endangered; with this, and by the dissolution of church
government, he sees the whole Church endangered. The Wittichian
hermeneutic is blasphemous because it asserts that the Bible contains
popular errors; [218] Maresius regards his opponents as devil's advocates and
as innovators who rank with Marcion and the Papists. Nevertheless, when
it comes to substance, the differences frequently disappear. Maresius himself
finally admits that he does not want to accuse his opponent of heresy, but
wishes only to make him attentive to dangers. He does not know how to
express his right insights suitably because his dogmatics are not sufficient
for that purpose. Maresius, for example, raises the charge of | Pelagianism
(Theol. def. V, 49) – but Wittich's intention is only to work out the special
character of the volitional [219] act and not to make God the author of sin; he

---

[216] Cf. *Theol. def.*, XVIII, 433: Progredior ad nobilem quaestionem de differentia
Veteris et Novi Testamenti, quam nemo clarius et felicius observavit in plurimis
Scripturae locis quam Cl. Cocceius ὁ μακαρίτης, quamvis quoad rem ipsam ei
praeiverint veteres theologi ad unum omnes. – Concerning ἄφεσις and πάρεσις, cf.
Theol. def., XVIII, 434 and 442.

[217] *Theol. pac.*, 295: et sane notum est de regimine externo ecclesiae non eadem
sentire Reformatos . . . ac proin minori animorum agitatione est tractanda.

[218] *Theol. def.*, II, 40: . . . blasphemant Scripturam ac si loquatur de rebus non
uti sunt, sed uti apparent et suis expressionibus errores vulgi et sensuum implicet.
Pari facilitate dixerit Marcionita Scripturas profiteri de Christo . . . ex apparentia
sensuum, non ex rei veritate, et Pontificius, Paulum asserere de pane eucharistico,
quod frangatur et edatur propter apparentiam sensuum . . . Haec sane istorum
stultitia esset irridenda, nisi haberet coniunctam impietatem et enervandae imo
evertendae autoritati et veracitati verbi divini unice destinaretur.

[219] *Theol. def.*, XI, 3, 152: De corruptione quae per peccatum est introducta, nulla
inter me et Cl. Virum fuit unquam dissensio, quamvis id studiose voluerit, ut iure

does not deny original sin at all, and repeatedly avows the decrees of Dort. Maresius accuses the Cartesians of relying, like the Weigelians, on the Inner Light; Wittich replies that Maresius should prove that, and refers to his oft-stressed principle: *non debere mysteria fidei ex lumine rationis probari*.[220] With respect to the doctrine of predestination, Wittich outdoes Maresius in consistency; it is difficult to convict a supralapsarian of Pelagianism. On the other hand, Maresius outdoes his opponent in manifest rationalism with respect to the doctrine of God. Wittich at least leaves the possibility open[221] that God, in his *potentia absoluta*, is not bound to the proposition of contradiction, even if this should be only a theoretical possibility.[222] For Maresius, however, even this irrational residue is not tolerable – without any embarrassment he appeals in this case to medieval scholasticism. For the rest, his objections, particularly with respect to the doctrine of God, are only of a terminological sort.[223] The objections which he considers essential in fact concern the domain of philosophy; he defends Aristotelianism and its conception of the universe. For example, he defends the proposition *Quod non est in sensu, non est in intellectu* even with respect to the doctrine of God,[224] or he defends the *Ubi definitivum* of souls (which are separated from the body) and of angels, and maintains that Christianity thereby stands or falls.[225] The Copernican conception of the universe can thus appear to him only as an *opinio lunatica*. No wonder Wittich subjects Maresius to the reproach that he himself confuses theology with philosophy, i.e., with a specific | conception of the universe – and therefore limits the battlefield to the domain of philosophy.

It becomes clear at this point that Cartesianism in the first instance operated as a critical philosophy. To be sure, the Cartesian theologians, for

---

me Pelagianismi accusare posset. *Ibid.*, 157: dum autem statuo, voluntatem semet ipsam determinare, id non dico opposite ad operationem divinam, sed potius subordinate . . . Attentionem requiro eodem modo, quo ad videndum requiritur apertio oculorum. Cf. XI, 4, 178 f.

[220] *Theol. def.*, III, 45.

[221] *Theol. pac.*, 201 ff.; *Theol. def.*, XIV, 324.

[222] *Theol. def.*, XIV, 325: (Maresius) Novatoribus sic dictis affingit id, quod non dicunt: 'Deum posse ea, quae implicant contradictionem.' Illi revera hoc non affirmant, quamvis etiam non audent negare, veriti, ne limites ponent Dei infinitae potentiae, si id negarent, sed iudicium suum ea de phrasi suspendunt, relinquentes aliis hanc audaciam determinandi suis phrasibus potentiam Dei infinitam.

[223] Cf. *Theol. pac.*, 193; 202.

[224] *Theol. pac.*, 131 f.; *Theol. def.*, XI, 4, 189.

[225] *Theol. def.*, XII, 4, 287 (according to WITTICH's quotation): In coelo ergo est anima vel in inferno respectu status felicis vel infelicis. At vero hoc est illudere Christianis, dum evertis sacrilege fundamenta Christianismi. Statum tribuis animae separatae felicem vel infelicem, sed quem nullibi obtinet, cum ipsa nusquam sit. Si sit in coelo felix vel in inferno infelix, debet in alterutro esse tanquam in loco felicitati vel infelicitati suae assignato, aut tibi nihil sunt coelum et infernum.

their part, also took over the elements of their new philosophy which concerned the conception of the universe, and these elements certainly had
subsequent dogmatic consequences; but in the beginning the critique of
the previous connection between the conception of the universe and
theology was the decisive thing, while the orthodox Maresius was obviously
not capable of distinguishing between the two.

IV. Two Orthodox Opponents of Theological Cartesianism

Among the opponents of Cartesianism Peter van Mastricht and Melchior
Leydekker stand out. [226] I will elaborate on them because all themes of the
debate are here combined, and finally, because here the theological
weaknesses of the two partners once more become visible.

1. Peter van Mastricht

Peter van Mastricht published his chief work – "*Novitatum Cartesianarum
Gangraena, nobiliores plerasque corporis theologici | partes arrodens et
excedens, seu Theologia Cartesiana detecta*" – in 1677 in Amsterdam. [227]
In the first part he treats the *novitates generaliores*, i. e., the fundamentals
of the new philosophy (Chs. 3–4) and the problems of scriptural exegesis

---

[226] I lack the material on LEONARDUS RIJSSEN. The work of PETRUS ALLINGA,
Funus D. Leonardis Rijssenii, is cited and dicussed in detail in MASTRICHT, *Gangraena*,
Praef., VIII. In the same Praefatio, chs. XXIff., extracts are cited of CEPHA
PISTOPHILUS' *Diatribe* against GISBERT VOETIUS. MASTRICHT asserts that he identifies
faith with love. MARESIUS reproaches him for acknowledging in faith "ne γϱὺ
quidem" which is not love. According to this information he appears to be a repre-
sentative of voluntarism. – SPANHEIM, II, cols. 962f., lists a large number of anti-
Cartesians from England. The citations which he gives show the same picture throughout. By way of example, I can only quote the following: Samuel Gott Armiger,
acutissimus philosophus, in praefatione historiae Geneseos (London, 1670), praemissa
Cartesii hypothesi (qua hic ex corpusculorum diverso motu, figuris diversis, deducit
omnia mundi adspectabilis phaenomena, ac solem, planetas, stellas constituit centra
omnium vorticum) revocans lectorem ad Mosaicas tabulas 'aut haec,' inquit, 'non
est Scriptura, aut ista non est philosophia.' Vocatque in eo loco 'Cartaceam' philosophiam, quae mundum aliter in charta describit, quam illum Deus in natura et in
verbo. Robertus Fergusson libro vernaculo cui titulus: 'Interesse rationis in religione'
(London, 1675) ista habet: 'Affirmare mihi liceat, esse facillimum probare,'
Cartesianam hypothesim 'tam esse adversam religioni quam fuit ulla hactenus
philosophia orbi cognita.' Mox: 'Mire haec videntur amica Atheis.' Insistitque vir
eruditus his potissimum hypothesibus tribus, ut inimicis religioni: primae de 'motu
materiae secundum leges mechanicas,' unde exsurgere possint omnia mundi
phaenomena; alteri de 'Dubitatione' seu suspensione assensus, ut quae ad scepticis-
mum ducat; tertiae 'de clara et distincta perceptione,' quae sit cuique 'mensura
veritatis.'

[227] The copy which the author donated to the Theological Academy of Duisburg
is extant in the university library in Bonn.

(Chs. 5–10). In the second part he goes through the entire dogmatics in thirty-seven chapters, in order to list the *novitates speciales* chapter by chapter. They concern natural theology first of all (to which the doctrine of God also belongs), then the doctrine of the Trinity (Chs. 17f.), the doctrine of creation (Ch. 19), to which are joined the questions of cosmology; further, the doctrine of the angels (Chs. 20–24), of man (Chs. 25–29), of God's providence, of original sin, of free will; but also christology (Ch. 34), and the doctrine of grace (Ch. 35); last of all he treats *de fide et lege divina* and *de novissimis*. His opinion manifestly is that the whole of dogmatics is being altered by the Cartesians. The latter are extensively quoted, in every instance their thesis is contrasted with the orthodox doctrine; at the conclusion of every chapter the "absurdities" to which the new teaching necessarily leads are enumerated. His method amounts to this: Cartesianism – which, despite the extensive quotations, is often enough misrepresented, e. g., when the "paradoxical fencing-master" is invoked as the chief witness – is simply measured by the standards of orthodoxy. This is not a forthright attack, with drums beating, on basic positions of the adversary, but a broad, very carefully worked out confrontation of the two standpoints, which is occasionally beset by a contrived logic. The enumeration of "absurdities" is by no means convicing, because for Mastricht traditional orthodoxy stands absolutely firm and he therefore neither understands nor takes seriously the position of his opponents.

For him the radical opposition of the two points of view is an incontestable fact. The Cartesians are the dangerous heirs of Arminianism *(Praef.*, Ch.3*)*. Mastricht does not question their personal integrity, but their innovations can only be explained as a special trick of the devil (Ch. 5); they are irreconcilable with the Christian faith and are therefore to be fought with the utmost seriousness. Mastricht invokes the decision of a Duisburg synod of 1656 (Ch. 13). The battle is all the more necessary inasmuch as the young people run after the Cartesians and consequently neglect the study of the old theology. In particular Mastricht sees all his efforts (the efforts of an ethicist!) on behalf of the practice of Christianity endangered. [228]

This sharp judgment is based on the consideration of the fundamentals of Cartesian philosophy. Mastricht begins his discussion with a chapter (Ch. 2) on Cartesian doubt and categorically sets the biblical demand for

---

[228] *Gangr.*, Praef., ch. 5: Videbam enim omnes conatus meos, quos in practica impendebam et praxin, vanos fieri; omnes artes quibus ad practica et praxin studiosos pellicere allaborabam, cassos esse, quamdiu his novitatibus inescati, solidiora quaevis fastidirent. Videbam insuper voce pariter ac scriptis studium theologiae practicae negligi, contemni, rideri, quibusvis artibus denigrari, labores Anglorum πρακτικωτάτους quibusvis dicteriis explodi ac iuventuti e manibus excuti. Videbam scripta theologica praelectiones, conciones, seposita praxi, novitatibus perstrepere, tantum, proculdubio, ut plus mentis et otii iuventuti suppeteret novitatibus venandis excolendisque etc.

faith against it. "In that God commands us to have faith, he forbids us to
doubt, because divine faith is irreconcilable with doubt, which destroys
assensus." On this point he cites Rom. 4:20f., Jn. 3:33 and I Jn. 5:10
(I, 2, 4 p. 21). Doubt about God's existence destroys every foundation of
faith and salvation; for he who wishes to come to God must believe that
He exists (Heb. 11:6). In support of his view he cites the scholastic saying:
Dubius in fide est haereticus. To be sure, what he wants is not simply blind
acquiescence (hearing *"de trivio"*); every Christian is obliged to examine
the reasons for the articles of faith from Scripture and elsewhere. But faith
does not wait until it has found the reasons. He who does not believe and
does not make an effort concerning the reasons of faith commits a double
sin; he who believes without reasons sins only once in that he omits the
examination of Scripture. Mastricht obviously wishes to exclude faith
merely on authority – but does he not concede more than a little finger's
worth to his opponents when he flatly designates this faith as sin? Concerning particular points there is certainly much correct insight; [229] but since
faith is fundamentally understood in terms of belief in something as true
– that will be made clearer immediately – and since the résumé of the
"Gangraena" proceeds essentially on the basis of practical considerations,
the argumentation is not really convincing, and, in any case, does not
stand up against an existential doubt.

Mastricht's concern becomes especially clear in the section on the validity
of Scripture with regard to physical phenomena and with regard to the
hermeneutical question. He is concerned with the authority, certitude and
unambiguous exegesis of Scripture. He finds that if the | Cartesians were
right, the Catholics would be better off then the Protestants. [230] He observes
that the Cartesians would make faith into knowledge [231] and that the
"exercitator" no longer actually needs Scripture because he would build
entirely upon reason.

But in order to avoid that, God's authority is now used to cover the
whole content of Scripture, i.e., it also guarantees the correctness of
assertions pertaining to nature and physics. Mastricht fears the emergence

---

[229] *Gangr.*, I, 2, 4: ut tenearis credere, sola praerequiritur clara et sufficiens
revelatio, nequaquam autem clara et distincta perceptio. Hic Rhodus, hic salta.
I, 2, 5: Dubitationem saltem volunt, quae pars sit corruptionis nativae, qua alienati
sumus a vita Dei per ignorantiam. Eph. 4: 18. – I, 2, 8: Proinde dubitatio fidem
tollit, quippe, iuxta Scripturas, cum ea ἀσύστατος.

[230] *Gangr.*, I, 6, 9 (p. 80): Numquid enim praestat, fidem in ecclesiam resolvere,
pronunciaturam secundum dictata conciliorum, patrum, traditionum ecclesiastica-
rum, quam in philosophos, secundum philosophiam Cartesianam pronunciaturos?

[231] *Gangr.*, I, 9, 10 (p. 103): Quid enim est credere, nisi verbis Dei assentiri
propter solam ἀξιοπιστίαν dicentis Dei? Quodsi igitur verbis Dei assensum commo-
des propter ea, quod congruant cum ratione seu philosophia, numquid fidem in
scientiam converties?

of a pagan philosophy which will be in a state of perpetual strife with Christianity. To be sure, the Cartesians assert that theology and philosophy are only one truth and must therefore agree; but they cannot annul the contradiction between the assertions of Scripture and the assertions of philosophy – the latter understood here as a new natural science. When, e. g., philosophy asserts that the earth revolves around the sun, the protest becomes a matter of conscience (I, 3, 13). The origin or the *proton pseudos* of the new doctrine of scriptural exegesis lies in the *systema mundi*. [232] One must, in questions of physics, simply follow Scripture; thus it appears to be lack of faith when one engages in criticism. [233] Mastricht calls it an insult to the Holy Spirit to say that one receives from Scripture no sure instruction concerning natural things, since Scripture does not always speak *secundum veritatem* concerning them, and its notions could therefore be corrected by knowledge derived from the observation of nature. Accordingly, the attempts to propound a biblical physics are also defended by Mastricht, who appeals to the classical models from Danaeus to Alsted – which is not to say that such a biblical physics could be complete (which, indeed, | Cartesian physics is not either), but nevertheless is sufficient, so that no doubt is permissible. [234] Precisely with regard to physical phenomena philosophy has to take its direction from theology.

The new hermeneutic is rejected just as unequivocally. Neither with respect to physical phenomena, nor with respect to natural theology, nor with respect to theological propositions which are equally accessible to reason, is it permissible to proceed from the assumption that the Bible

---

[232] *Gangr.*, I, 5, 1: Origo seu πρῶτον ψεῦδος novitii statuti a systemate mundi omnino repetenda est. Credit enim philosophia Cartesiana, quiescente sole terram duplici motu rotari circa eum; contra Scripturam audit constanter sibi obloquentem; huic igitur quo satisfieret excogitari coepit Scripturam in istis locis non agere secundum accuratam veritatem, sed secundum erroneam opinionem vulgi.

[233] *Gangr.*, I, 6, 4 (p. 78): . . . hoc ipsa dictat ratio, ut nimirum ratio cedat Deo, primae veritati, subordinata quaevis dictata naturae dictatis creatoris, qui procul omni dubio, accuratissime earum callet naturem. I, 6, 5 (p. 78): . . . cum prima veritas quibusvis secundis, intellectu nostro certior, manet omnino, has ad illam, nec vicissim conferendas et examinandas esse. I, 5, 7 (p. 69): De rebus naturalibus certam cognitionem e Scripturis non posse obtineri, eo quod non semper loquantur 'secundum veritatem' . . . Atque adeo conceptus illos parum accuratos . . . ex lumine rationis posse corrigi.

[234] *Gangr.*, I, 7, 4 (p. 85): The controversy is about the question ,an loca Scripturae de rebus naturalibus per universum sacri codicis corpus dispersa, congesta, digesta, confirmata, explicata, tum per Scripturam tum per philosophiam nec sint nec dici mereantur philosophia quaedam sacra, physica Mosaica, Christiana. An vero hoc sit theologiam cum philosophia male permiscere et confundere? Hic Zanchius, Danaeus, Casmanus, Alstedius, aliique prius affirmant, posterius negant; Cl. D. Wittichius cum suis contrarium arbitratus et arbitrari debet, ut legitime cum iis pugnet. I, 7, 6 (p. 88): Spectant igitur omnia ista de naturalibus dicta ad doctrinam II Tim. 3:16.

speaks inaccurately and therefore falsely. The hermeneutical thesis of the
Cartesians means for Mastricht that one makes of God a false witness.[235]
He cites, e.g., I Cor. 15:14f. and asserts that just as God is made a liar there
by the denial of the resurrection, so God is also made a liar by the new
conception of the universe because, according to the latter, God would have
willfully made false assertions.[236] Furthermore, Mastricht seeks to demonstrate to his opponents that they do not keep within their own boundary-
lines since they do not respect revealed truths, but rather subject them
likewise to philosophy,[237] and he devotes his whole eighth chapter to
proving that, according to Wittich, Scripture must submit to philosophy
even in practical and moral questions – for which, however, he can adduce
only one chapter title from Wittich's book.

I need not elaborate further on Mastricht's detailed exposition of the
Cartesian dogmatics. He simply lists the deviations from custom and
tradition. He defends, e.g., the independence of natural theology against
the endeavor to assign it | to philosophy. Like Maresius, he resists the
proposition that God could do something contradictory; one of the reasons
for this is that the Reformed position regarding the doctrine of the Lord's
Supper would then be abandoned in favor of that of the Lutherans.[238] He
likewise turns against the efforts of many a Cartesian to deduce the Trinity
rationally instead of letting it stand as a mystery. In Chapter 21 he opposes
the "philosophical" view "that on the moon there are probably mountains,
forests, human beings, or that the moon does not actually emit light," and,
concerning the position of the earth in the cosmos, "that the earth could be
reckoned among the planets and the sun among the fixed stars"; and naturally he opposes the doctrine of the movement of the celestial bodies ("that
the sun stands still, but the earth revolves in a double movement around
the sun" is the title of the chapter). With respect to the doctrine of original
sin, the attempt to explain it by hereditary transmission makes him frown.
The most important point of all may well be that (in the chapters *de gratia
conversionis*) he finds in Velthusen, and concealed also in Wittich, the irresist-

---

[235] *Gangr.*, I, 5, 10 (p. 71): Deum (absit blasphemia dicto) falsum esse in verbo
suo testem. Qui enim ea loquitur ac testatur, quae in se non sunt vera, sed speciem
tantum et apparentiam quandam veritatis habent, per quam a vulgo habeantur pro
veris, ille profecto testimonium dicit, cui cum re non convenit quodque proinde
falsum est.

[236] *Ibid.:* Sic pari ratione, si v.g. Sol non movetur et terra non quiescit, tum . . .
Deus falsus testis reperietur, quoniam in Scriptura testatus est, Solem moveri, qui
non movetur, et terram quiescere, quae non quiescit.

[237] He admits, to be sure, that this is not done 'apertis verbis,' but he asserts that it
is done 'in praxi' (*Gangr.*, I, 9, 2, p. 96). However, his examples – the Melchizedek
passage; Jn. 5:31; II Pet. 2:1 – are not convincing, because he himself can deal
with them only in the manner of WITTICH.

[238] *Gangr.*, cap. XI, pp. 257f.

ibility of grace disputed, and in the doctrine of faith,[239] he combats the fundamental voluntarism of the Cartesians and the identification of faith and love. At this point, Wittich has made the *notitia fidei* a presupposition, instead of a part of faith, and has defined this faith as a hungering and thirsting after righteousness, indeed has designated *caritas* as *integra fidei forma;* and Gronewegen simply identified faith with love:[240] all virtue – and therefore also faith – may be called love. To the definition of *fides* as a hungering and thirsting Mastricht objects:[241] if this were so, then precisely the faithful who "possess God and the Mediator *actu* and have already had faith for a long time" would be excluded from faith. Whereas the Cartesians speak of faith as the *opus instrumentale* of justification, because in justification an active part is ascribed to faith, Mastricht wishes to designate faith as only a *causa sine qua non*, in order not to let it become the *causa nativa et congenita*, and not to endanger the sole efficacy of grace. But he is far from making this aspect the decisive one and from seeing in it the heart of his resistance; it appears, almost at the very end, as simply one aspect among many others. |

2. Melchior Leydekker

Melchior Leydekker, the true disciple and heir of Voetius in Utrecht, engaged Cartesianism in discussion in a book which appeared in Leiden in 1677. Its shortened title is: *"Fax veritatis."* [242]

In the preface he compiles the accusations which the parties level against each other. The Cartesians reproach the orthodox to the effect that their theology is not scriptural, that they have re-introduced Catholic scholasticism into the Church; that they hinder every advance in knowledge

---

[239] *Gangr.*, cap. XXVI, p. 545; cf. cap. XXVII, De hominis intellectu et voluntate.

[240] *Ibid.*, p. 546: quando Deus consideratur ut testis verax, a nobis exigens assensum versus sua testimonia et fiduciam in sua veracitate et infallibilitate, tum caritas appellatur fides!

[241] *Gangr.*, cap. XXXVI, 5, p. 548.

[242] *Fax veritatis* seu exercitationes ad nonnullas controversias, quae hodie in Belgio potissimum moventur, multa ex parte theologico-philosophicae. Praefixa est praefatio de statu Belgicae Ecclesiae et suffixa dissertatio de providentia Dei. – In his preface he mentions a book which appeared four years earlier and which I have not seen. It is entitled *Sulamyth*. – Of special interest is the book: *Vis veritatis* seu disquisitionum ad nonnullas controversias, quae hodie in Belgio potissimum moventur, de oeconomia foederum Dei libri quinque. Suffixa est autoris oratio inauguralis ut et Johannis Voet . . . epistola ad amicum de Petri Allingae praefatione erotematum decadibus praemissa, Utrecht, 1679. This book contains a detailed discussion and criticism of Federal Theology.

and their work does not have scientific character;[243] that they prefer the study of dogmatics[244] to the detriment of the general scientific education of theologians; that they exaggerate the importance of controversies and are not prepared to examine the new theology without prejudice, indeed, they work heedlessly toward a schism in the Church. The orthodox, conversely, defend themselves against the continued innovations[245] and | against the disesteem for the confessional writings.[246] In the alliance between Cocceians and Cartesians they see a *confoederatio* which has no basis in substance. Leydekker sketches its history: There was a time when a famous Cartesian philosopher confessed that he did not understand the obscure mysteries, and when Cocceius himself feared Cartesian philosophy like the plague, as can be proved from his "Last Words of Moses" (1650), § 74; but after being called to Leiden, he began traffic with its defenders, for which reference is made to Cocceius' letters and his *Summa theologiae* (VII, 26 to 28).[247] The orthodox complain that the errors become progressively greater;

---

[243] Praef.: quod theologiam doceamus nullis rationibus suffultam, fratrum opiniones oppugnemus, nosque solo saeculari bracchio tueamur.

[244] LEYDEKKER replies: Surely the theologians have first of all to learn the principles of pure doctrine; novimus non nullos novae theologiae discipulos academiam reliquisse inexercitatis animis quod religionis articulos, quamvis novorum mysteriorum expertissimi haberentur, quibus melius fuisset suos locos communes (quod locos cum nugis dicunt) bene addidicisse, quam iis contemptis solummodo novis τερατο-λογήμασιν incubuisse. Atque hi scilicet illi sunt, qui de eruditionis apud nostros neglectu conqueruntur, qui se filios lucis existimant, reliquis volitantibus sicuti umbris. Nos nostris suadere non desinemus, ut norint imprimis locos communes . . . quo exercitatas mentes habeant ad malum et bonum verumque et falsum discernendum et refutandos quosvis errores novos, qui antiquo vero adversantur.

[245] *Fax ver.*, Praef.: agnoscimus satis uti fidei ita et cognitionis imperfectionem, neque obsistimus doctis doctissimorum virorum laboribus, manus vero damus illis, qui laborant ut ulteriore lumine ecclesia collustretur. At de receptae in ecclesiis doctrinae et explicationis articulorum fidei desertione, de inventis novis veritatibus et σχήματος totius religionis immutatione dolemus neque istiusmodi profectum laudamus, qui vetera destruat, ut nova aedificet, ne continua fidei incertitudo dominetur, et theologia mutetur in menses et annos ad arbitrium quorumcumque, qui αὐθάδεις sua commendant, cetera aliorum alto supercilio despiciunt . . . At versatilis nimis illa religio est, cui continua mutatio inducitur, non illam fides tolerat, quae de veritate certa nihil dubitat, non ex mutabilium hominum opinionibus dependet.

[246] *Ibid.:* quod fratres istiusmodi dogmata doceant, quae cum libris symbolicis non congruunt, non vana multorum reprehensio fuit.

[247] *Ibid.*: Atque hinc errorum in ecclesia colluvies, hinc novatoribus robur et vires, factis potentioribus, malo ecclesiae fato, dum ante annum 1672 soli ad cathedram promoverentur superiorum favore et academica commendatione, qui a vetere theologia alieni, novae nomen et fidem dederant. Atque haec, de qua loquimur, confoederatio hoc tempore arctius adstringitur, ubi veritas extollit caput nec patitur amplius se negligi et supprimi, excitatis theologis et philosophis, quin et academiarum curatoribus et magnatibus, quorum corda zelus pro domo Dei accendit. Hinc libelli ex communi collegio et concilio scripti, anonymi, quibus quaevis defenduntur, excusantur, emolliuntur (nam sic tempora ferunt) dogmata, quae cum veritate ut

Cocceius himself has become more radical, and the disciples go beyond their master; the innovators have become the authors of discord in the Netherlands. To be lamented is their *licentiosa prophetandi libertas, ubi se fratres ad S. Scripturarum interpretationem accingunt*, i. e., the typological and *heilsgeschichtliche* exegesis of the Cocceians, to whom Leydekker attributes the rule: *Verba valent quod valere possunt*.[248] Finally, he complains about the insubordination of the innovators with respect to church order.

The book then treats in ten *loci*[249] the questions which have been especially fomented by Cartesianism. Every *locus* begins with a synopsis of the *proton pseudos* of the Cartesian thesis. Next, the individual *"controversiae"* of the *locus* are discussed by means of arguments in the form of theses; every chapter includes a section, *"fontes solutionum,"* in which Leydekker offers his solution to the problems. |

Leydekker's book is written with great care and a tremendous knowledge of the literature. In substance, however, it offers scarcely anything new. To be sure, there are, with respect to particular points, good formulations and theologically sound perceptions. The first chapter, *De sacra theologia*, is concerned with the question whether the Cartesian doubt is admissible as a theological method; naturally the question is answered in the negative.[250] For example, Leydekker argues that to doubt the knowledge we have gained from the testimony of conscience or from innate principles is simply ludicrous, especially when, on the whole, the "methodists" arrive only at truths long familiar; many will not be able to find their way out of methodical doubt again.[251] Radical doubt seems to him to be altogether impossible (I, 5 p. 3). For our first ancestors in paradise, doubt was the beginning of the satanic temptation – one sees that this is rather the way

---

tenebrae cum luce conveniunt. Imo quamvis quis liber alicuius nomen gerat in fronte, diversi tamen scriptoris opus est, unoquoque aliquid addente de suo, quod ipsi typographi non negant, experti loquimur.

[248] *Ibid.:* Huic si obsistas canoni nescis potentiam et vim Scripturae; nimirum ut Scripturarum divinitas credatur, debet id dicere, quod mens praeiudiciis imbuta eius verbis affingit.

[249] De sacra theologia, De sacra Scriptura, De Deo et attributis, De trinitate, De decretis et aeterna Dei providentia, De creatione, De creatione angelorum, hominum, brutorum, De providentia Dei actuali, De statu hominis ante lapsum.

[250] *Fax ver.*, I, 1 (p. 1): πρῶτον ψεῦδος: Statuunt id novatores nominatimque Cartesius, ut facilius hominum animos occupent et usque adhuc veritatibus defensis et probatis suas substituant novas opiniones et dogmata, non protinus recipienda ab iis, quorum animus receptis principiis seu hypothesibus imbutus est.

[251] *Fax ver.*, I, 1, 4 (p. 3): Imo perpendendum, an animus in voluntaria sui quasi excaecatione satis aptus sit sese liberando et dubitatione extricando aut recti iudicii capax, quo de argumentis bene iudicet et de veritate comperta sese certum reddat; est enim dubitatio haec animi morbus et aegritudo, corruptionis, imbecillitatis et naturalis post lapsum caecitatis evidentissimum testimonium.

and method of the devil than of God (I, 6 p. 3). Doubt contradicts the certitude of faith,[252] so that intentional doubt means (according to Rom. 1:19f.) to keep faith down in unrighteousness (I, 9 p. 3). Doubt about God and his existence goes against nature;[253] it means that one lays aside his conscience; it is sheer disobedience[254] and is dangerous, because one may die in a state of doubt.[255] This doubt comes from the devil and is to be fended off with the | shield of faith;[256] in the end it leads to atheism.[257] To transfer the method of doubt to theology means to make theological schools into academies of skeptics in which ἐποχή and want of faith are more essential than faith. Rather, the example of Timothy (II Tim. 1:5; 3:15f.) is to be commended to students. The Holy Spirit is not the spirit of doubt, but of unchanging faith.[258] Thus Leydekker energetically disputes the

---

[252] *Fax ver.*, I, 1, 8 (p. 3): Dubitatio adversatur per se certitudini fidei et passim a Deo in S. Scriptura condemnatur, uti fides commendatur. Unde perperam affectatur dubitatio, ut ad fidem, veram et certam sapientiam, recta et prona via et methodus. I, 1, 11 (p. 4): Spiritus Sanctus, qui est Spiritus veritatis et sapientiae non producit in nobis fidem et certitudinem per scepticam dubitationem, sed eam ut vitiosam expugnat. Contraria diaboli methodus est in filiis inoboedientiae, ut qui infidelitatem in ipsis operatur per omnimodam ad dubitationes impias tentationem.

[253] *Fax ver.*, I, 2, 4 (p. 7): Ne dubitemus de Deo alte impressus est conscientiae existentiae divinae sensus, quem ne quidem pessimi et perditissimi impii eiurare potuerunt. Calvini Inst. I, 3 etc.

[254] *Fax. ver.*, I, 2, 8 (p. 7): Dependentia moralis a nostro creatore, per quam exigitur quovis momento erga Deum amor, honor, timor, cultus etc. omnem de existentia illius omni tempore dubitationem excludit. Nullo enim non momento cultus Dei a nobis postulatur, uti de Deo et in Deum fides, sine qua impossibile est ipsi placere. Heb. 11:6.

[255] *Fax ver.*, I, 2. 10 (p. 7): Quidni extimescat hominis conscientia in tali statu audire vocem iudicis: Fatue, hac nocte animam postulabunt a te (Lc. 12:20). Nonne periculum est, ut homo dubitans in peccatis moriatur et sine spe salutis aeternae? aut forte Deus animae pie et honeste dubitantis miserebitur? Beati qui in domino moriuntur et fide etc. (Apc. 14:17; Heb. 11:13).

[256] *Fax ver.*, I, 2, 13 (p. 8): Dubitationes de Deo aut ad dubitationem tentationes sunt ignita spicula diaboli ad quae pii exhorrescunt, quibusque sese opponunt clypeo fidei, tantum abest, ut pius easdem dubitationes animo nutrire et fovere debeat. Ps. 73, 77, 88; Eph. 6.

[257] *Fax ver.*, I, 2, 14 (p. 8): Prona est haec dubitatio ad atheismum via, praecipue ubi teneris et dissolutis animis, ut sunt plurimorum, commendatur. Multi enim ex dubitatione exitum non quaerent, vel ob imbecillitatem intellectus et cordis profanitatem invenire non poterunt. Imo ad omnia argumenta studebunt exceptiones et responsiones comminisci, et rationes quaevis non satisfient iis, qui ad conscientiae testimonium non attendunt, et dum vellent profani non esse, facile sibi persuadebunt Deum non existere, quodvis excogitantes quo cuicunque demonstrationi aliquid respondeant et obiiciant, quin tantisper quis atheus est, quamdiu de Dei existentia dubitat.

[258] *Fax ver.*, I, 3, 8 (p. 12): Methodus studii theologici non est naturalis et philosophica, sed Christiana et theologica, quae fidem, pietatem et preces postulat ac supponit.

proposition of the Cartesians that reason is just as sure as God's revelation; [259] reason is from God, to be sure, but it is exercised by us and is thereby fallible and subject to deception; trust in it is sectarian fanaticism. [260] Leydekker is well aware of the new kind of piety which is nourished by a faith based on reason: as someone has said, the true religion of Descartes was Cartesianism. [261] That natural | and revealed truth do not contradict each other is, to be sure, basically true; Leydekker shares this opinion, but natural truth is not simply the truth of reason. [262] Moreover, one is to distinguish between the principles of knowledge and the conclusions drawn therefrom, which are not self-evident. [263] From this it follows finally that the long-standing handmaiden relationship of philosophy to theology is to be maintained (I, 5) and that philosophy and theology cannot simply be sciences of equal stature.

---

[259] *Fax ver.*, I, 4, 1 (p. 15): Ratio humana caeca est in rebus fidei post lapsum, infirma et obtenebrata vero in naturalibus, maxime iis, quae ad τὸ γνωστὸν τοῦ θεοῦ pertinent, quod nullus nisi Pelagianus negaverit. Quare rationem naturalem adeo superbe cum revelatione conferre videtur non satis orthodoxae hypothesi de naturae et rationis naturalis corruptione convenire.

[260] *Fax ver.*, I, 4, 3 (p. 16): Etenim est quidem a Deo directive et effective in genere entis, elicitur tamen et a nostra mente, ut causa proxima et formali, a qua habet, quod sit fallibilis et fallatur in multis. Nec omne verum cernit et perspicit, ut de errore nullum periculum esse possit. Quare usum rationis cum revelatione vel respectu certitudinis vel authoritatis, id est obligationis ad fidem aequiparare est semetipsum θεόπνευστον asserere in conceptibus, et infallibilitatem sibi arrogare, vel tantum non in conceptibus sese prophetis et apostolis coaequare, maxime cum eousque proceditur, 'quod ea, quae per rectam rationem cognoscimus interne, Deus censendus sit nobis revelare, utpote qui author sit istius usus rectae rationis.'

[261] *Fax ver.*, I, 4, 7 (p. 16): Hoc pacto regulae, conclusiones et axiomata philosophica pari pietatis affectu recipienda forent, quo theologica et Scripturaria, sunt enim utraque ex divina revelatione. On the other hand, he says in Solutiones II (p. 18): Lumen quidem naturae Dei est opus, non tamen eodem modo philosophia ex eo lumine deducta rationis humanae beneficio. Ratio cum fallitur et fallit non est a Deo, et quamvis actu non falleretur, fallibilis tamen est, neutiquam infallibili revelationi, nequidem fidei conferenda et coaequanda; semper enim suae fallibilitatis debet esse conscia, nec temere fidendum illi ut infallibili, quae saepe fallit et fallitur.

[262] *Fax ver.*, I, 4, Sol. IV (p. 18): Licet veritas naturalis et revelata sibi mutuo non repugnent, attamen ipsa veritas naturalis non est id, quod saepe dictat humana ratio. Potest veritas revelata adversari ratiocinationi et humanis conceptibus, licet congruat cum veritate in natura patefacta, quam ratio humana saepe non videt, non capit nec perspicit.

[263] *Fax ver.*, I, 4, Sol. VI (p. 18): Distinguenda sunt principia prima naturae per se nota a conclusionibus et conceptibus rationis: non hic agitur solum de principiis primis, sed conclusionibus, conceptibus sive rationis usu; falsum est conclusionum et conceptuum eandem esse certidudinem, quae est primorum principiorum, ergo et multo minus eadem est certitudo rationis humanae seu philosophicae quae est fidei seu revelationis in Scripturis.

With respect to the doctrine of Holy Scripture, the thesis of the Cartesians that Scripture accomodates itself in certain passages to the popular
opinion (and therefore also to the false prejudices) of its age is to be flatly
rejected. Leydekker sees their new conception of the universe as the *proton
pseudos* of all the efforts of his opponents.²⁶⁴ Their thesis would mean that
the testimony of Scripture is false – which cannot be.²⁶⁵ In that case God
would have deceived us and taught us an error and would be requiring
faith in something false²⁶⁶ – and all that without reason and to no |
purpose.²⁶⁷ The thesis of the erroneous opinions of Scripture destroys its
credibility as a whole, and with it faith in Christ himself. For in this way
one subjects Scripture, at least in regard to natural phenomena, to reason,
sets up a double standard for faith,²⁶⁸ and annuls the doctrine of original
sin.²⁶⁹ One will not stop here but continue on to the dogmas which rest
partially on reason and partially on revelation (the so-called *articuli mixti*),
indeed even to the revealed mysteries, for the explanation of which

---

²⁶⁴ *Fax ver.*, II, 1 (p. 24): πρῶτον ψεῦδος: Hypothesis de motu terrae et quiete
Solis mordicus defensa.

²⁶⁵ *Fax ver.*, II, 1, 1 (p. 24): Erronea opinio vulgi est falsa, Sacrae Scripturae
testimonium nequit esse falsum, cum ea sit divinitus inspirata, uti nec Dei, qui est
mentiri nescius.

²⁶⁶ *Fax ver.*, II, 1, 2 (p. 24): Deus sic de facto fefelisset nos et errorem docuisset.
II, 1, 6 (p. 25): indignum est enim fingere, id ideo Deum fecisse, ut in aliis mysteriis
foret credibilior S. Scriptura, quasi vero ἀξιοπιστίᾳ Sacrae Scripturae quid demeret
motus terrae et quietis Solis revelatio, posito quod illa moveretur, hic quiesceret.
Superantne mysteria fidei hoc naturae admirandum? Quin incredibile videtur si non
impossibile adversariis terram quiescere, Solem vero tam rapido motu ex nostra
hypothesi moveri, et suam scilicet veresimiliorem commendant, ergo vanam causam
praetexunt. At quidni verentur ipsi, ne absterreant a sua philosophia sua suppositione
de quiete Solis et terrae motu quoscunque, qui nostro praeiudicio et quidem communi
laborant, si Deus debuit eandem tacere communemque errorem, qui est et noster,
fovere, ne habeatur, minus fide dignus in rebus gravioribus, quaeque sola revelatione
innotescunt? Causa ergo sic continuo loquendi non fuit, imo contra quid obest, quare
Deus sic loqui perpetuo non potuerit convenire; obstat enim eius veracitas omnis
falsi nescia et speciem falsi non ferens, tum scopus Spiritus Sancti in verbo tradendo,
uti et Scripturae ipsius dignitas, sinceritas et puritas, cui omnis supra omnia fides
debuit adhiberi.

²⁶⁷ *Fax ver.*, II, 1, 8 (p. 25): Sic enim ex parte Scriptura non foret certa, αὐτό-
πιστος et propter seipsam credenda; quinimo si potuit Scriptura scribere non verum
in hoc vel illo argumento, quidni in aliis et pluribus? in historiis rebusque
doctrinae levioribus? etc. Labascit sane ex hac hypothesi eius infallibilitas θεοπνευσ-
τία ἐν πᾶσι et αὐτοπιστία, adeoque illius dignitas et authoritas et divinitas etc.
palam prostituitur, imo et fides nostra de ipso Christo eiusque vera humana natura.

²⁶⁸ *Fax ver.*, II, 2, 4 (p. 30): Volunt duplicem esse normam credendorum et interpretationis S. Scripturae, ipsam S. Scripturam et rationem humanam (quae hucusque
apud orthodoxos in theologicis numquam regulae aut normae vicem obtinuit) cum
Socinianis et Remonstrantibus.

²⁶⁹ *Fax ver.*, II, 2, 2 (p. 31): Ex obliquo negatur rationis humanae corruptio post
lapsum dum ad conceptus eius mens et sensus Spiritus Sancti exigi debere statuitur.

Scripture makes use of concepts and images which indeed are also known from nature (II, 2, 3 p. 31). To explain Scripture, faith is necessary; to it reason and philosophy must subject themselves.[270] Otherwise one makes theology dependent on philosophy, and thereby uncertain.[271] At this point Leydekker himself seems to advocate the *theologia regenitorum* and, for his part, to make not faith, but piety *(Gläubigkeit)* the presupposition of the exegesis of Scripture, in that he expressly defends the Pietists against the reproaches of the Cartesians.[272] – In the fourth controversy he defends the rôle of the synods and their right to give binding scriptural interpretation and to pass binding judgment against innovations;[273] in the fifth he defends the authority of the Dutch translation of the Bible | against the Cocceian interpretations. What then follows is directed especially against the peculiarities of the Cocceians.

Leydekker's commitment to a particular world-view comes clearly to light when, with respect to the doctrine of creation,[274] he declares it to be absolutely impossible that a theologian could take the Copernican-Cartesian system of the universe to be true, and staunchly appeals to the familiar biblical passages as the basis of this rejection. He finds among his opponents only an unrestrained enthusiasm for philosophical hypotheses and a boundless faith in the infallibility of philosophy. When the Cartesians say: "The light of reason does not contradict the light of revelation, for truth is not opposed to truth," he answers: the Copernican hypothesis is not so certain that one may permit himself to be dissuaded from the uniform doctrine of Scripture; philosophy rather than Scripture must give way, so that the honor of the word of God may remain intact.[275] The prophets were

---

[270] *Fax ver.*, II, 2, 6 (p. 35): Interpres S. Scripturae extra S. Scripturam est fides, cui ratio et philosophia subordinari debet ac subiici.

[271] *Fax ver.*, II, 2, 15 (p. 34): Ac prout varia erit philosophia, varia erit theologia et incerta S. S. interpretatio, quae omnis philosophiae basis ac fundamentum.

[272] *Fax ver.*, II, 3, Sol. VIII (p. 40): Falsum est eos enthusiasmum revocare in ecclesiam, qui mentis illuminationem internam per Spiritum Sanctum postulant ad S. Scripturae intelligentiam eiusque mentem percipiendam; sed se a Pelagianismo, Socinianismo, Papismo, et Remonstrantismo liberant iuxta Scripturas I Jn. 2:2 etc.

[273] *Fax ver.*, II, 4, 4 (p. 41): Publici interpretis contemptus vergit in profanam et libertinisticam libertatem, ecclesiae divisionem eiusque perturbationem, qua ecclesia sit in Babel convertenda, ubi confusa labia et corda, sine ullo consensu, imo et veritatis stuprum, adulterium et corruptionem per luxuriantia ingenia, a quibus ecclesia sibi cavere debet. II, 4, 9 (p. 42): Pluris est publica doctorum ecclesiae in Synodo legitima interpretatio quam privata; nec tantum aestimanda propter interpretum eruditionem et probitatem, verum etiam legitimam eorundem vocationem et divinam missionem. Synodica Sacrae Scripturae interpretatio vera fit nomine Dei adeoque illi debetur reverentia nisi divinae in ecclesia ordinationi refragemur.

[274] *Fax ver.*, VI, 7 (p. 291).

[275] *Fax ver.*, VI, 7, Sol. I (p. 293): 'Lumen lumini non est contrarium, uti nec veritas veritati.' Bene; at negamus hypothesin Copernico-Cartesianam veram esse,

not ordinary, run-of-the-mill people, but *viri magni, prophetae et maximi philosophi* –not to mention Christ himself. As testimony for the old view we have the words and narratives of Scripture, we have their confirmation by the divine miracles, and the uniform and reliable witness of Scripture regarding the motion of the sun.[276] That the passages concerning the motion of the sun and its miraculous standing-still | can truly make sense when one takes the new hypothesis as a basis, is to be denied; the meaning which the opponents attribute to them is not drawn from Scripture, but is pressed upon it *ex pertinaci praeiudicio*. There is no need for theology to reply to the objections of philosophy as long as it stands firmly on the foundation of revelation; but theologians who latch on to the new doctrine are no longer theologians, and would do well to consider the example of the Catholics, who have, after all, condemned Galileo.[277] Leydekker (VI, 8) just as firmly contradicts Wittich's view that animals and human beings could possibly be found on the moon. The *proton pseudos* in this instance is, for him, the proposition that, like the moon, the earth is a planet which moves around the sun as its center. That is contradicted by Acts 17:26, Psalm 115:16, and Gen. 1:26, as well as by the purpose which God has given to the stars,[278] by the redemptive work of Christ, and the threat of judgment on the *earth* (II Pt. 3 and Mt. 25). The appeal to God's unlimited omnipotence in favor of the opposite notion is illegiti-

---

atque usque adeo certam, ut Scriptura a nativo sensu, quem clare et ubique semper exhibet, debeat detorqueri in eum, quem philosophia dictat. Potius debet philosophia cadere quam Scriptura, convenit magis cum Scriptura philosophiam conciliari quam contra. Ut stet verbi divini honos, intemerata eius veritas atque αὐτοπιστία.

[276] *Fax ver.*, VI, 7, Sol. III (p. 294): 1. Expressa verba et historiae, 2. historias confirmantia divina miracula, 3. perpetuum et uniforme Sacrae Scripturae de motu Solis testimonium; numquam enim vel per speciem docet contrarium; 4. Sacrae Scripturae veritas, integritas, auctoritas, αὐτοπιστία etc. quae patiuntur maximum praeiudicium, si adversus communia, multiplicia, uniformia et evidentissima, ut Solis radiis descripta, testimonia philosophi conceptus et hypotheses opponantur.

[277] *Fax ver.*, VI, 7, Sol. V (p. 295): Theologi vero cum Cartesianorum partibus accedunt et hac in parte philosophiam certitudine supra theologiam extollunt, suo nomine indigni sunt ac subsidunt infra modestiam pontificiorum in hac ipsa controversia, quamvis alias Sacram Scripturam contemptim satis habeant. Cum enim Galilaeus de Galilaeo ad sacrum tribunal inquisitionis raperetur propter hypothesin astronomicam de quiete Solis et motu terrae defensam libro edito 'De systemate mundi' non aliunde eius sententia fuit reiecta Romae quam quod dicta Sacrae Scripturae illi adversarentur.

[278] *Fax ver.*, VI, 8, 6 (p. 297): Lunam cum Sole ceteraque sidera Deus condidit quarto creationis die, et quidem eo fine, ut lucem terrae praeberent distinguerentque nobis tempora, diem ac noctem, menses etc. atque ita eorundem distinctiva nostro orbi signa forent. Gen. 1:14f. Alius finis ex Scripturis non patescit. Planetica et lunatica opinio est alium usum fingere in praebendo multis hominum aliorum myriadibus hospitio ac receptaculo.

mate; for that establishes at best the possibility, but not the probability, of this thesis. With equal right one could imagine still other cosmic systems beyond the visible heaven and the heaven of the blessed.[279] Finally, there is the brief and concise statement: that the sun is the center of the universe and that the earth, like Saturn or Jupiter ... and the moon, is a planet, contradicts Scripture. This can be shown, first, by the assumption of Scripture that the earth stands fast and the sun moves ..., second, by the words of Scripture concerning the earth and its inhabitants ..., third, by the fact that Scripture constantly | distinguishes between the earth and the celestial bodies, and opposes them to each other.[280]

No one will fail to see that in the arguments of these anti-Cartesians a legitimate theological interest comes to expression. They have rightly seen that the scientific attitude which Descartes demands is different from the attitude of faith which the Bible demands. Leydekker was justified in his fear that reason would not be satisfied to investigate natural theology; it subsequently extended its competence to the revealed truths, by first trying to demonstrate their rationality and then by making this rationality the yardstick of their truth. But no one can fail to see also that the defenders put themselves in the wrong. Their concept of truth is obviously the same as that of the philosophy they are combatting. They made faith dependent on the prior acknowledgment of certain truths which had to be accepted on the authority of the Bible. They thus invite an examination of this authority in its formal aspect, with respect to which the rising historical science will in turn work havoc. The rejection of the concept of intent introduced by Wittich made it impossible to differentiate within revelation between statements concerning a world-view and theological statements. The orthodox were bound to confuse their outmoded world-view with their faith. This union of theology with world-view had finally and unavoidably discredited their case. If – as one can suppose without further ado – they really preached in accordance with their dogmatics, how weary must a nation of seafarers and merchants have become of their polemical preaching, while the "new philosophy" experienced one confirmation after another! No wonder the old-style orthodoxy simply gave

---

[279] *Fax ver.*, VI, 8, Sol. I (p. 299): Est Deus immensae potentiae, quidni facit ex infinita materia infinita et diversae formae alia systemata? In iis diversa corpora? Ibique hominum infinitae diversitatis et speciei habitacula? Vides, philosophe, quo te adigat Christianus, qui infinitam potentiam Dei urges, ut lunaticae opinioni concilies veresimilitudinem.

[280] *Fax ver.*, VI, 8, Sol. III: Solem esse centrum mundi ac terram esse cum Saturno, Jove ... luna planetam, Scripturae adversatur. Probatur 1. ex hypothesi Scripturaria de quiete terrae et motu Solis ... 2. ex phrasibus Sacrae Scripturae de terra et terrae incolis ... 3. ex perpetua in Scripturis terrae a coelo et coelestibus corporibus distinctione et mutua oppositione.

out. The Reformed tradition was carried on by the Cocceians and Pietists; the work of Wittich, to my knowledge, had no continuation.

The victory of Cartesianism was a milestone in Europe. The "goulden eeuw" was definitely at an end. But orthodoxy itself had helped its opponent into the saddle. In its concept of truth, and in the intellectualism which flowed from it, it was closer to the "new philosophy" | than it suspected. But inasmuch as it bound its case to a superannuated philosophy, it destroyed its own credibility – which it would have needed more than ever at this moment of intellectual history. The recollection of this era seems to me to be of more than merely antiquarian interest. [281]

---

[281] I would not dare repeat KARL BARTH's verdict (in his essay: "Samuel Werenfels und die Theologie seiner Zeit," Evangelische Theologie, 3, 1936, pp. 190f.) that TROELTSCH and his school had "considerably over-estimated the critical significance of the so-called new *Weltbild*." It obviously rests on observations made with respect to a later generation, which believed it had survived the crisis.

The Idea of God and Modern Man *

Rudolf Bultmann

Translated by Robert W. Funk

At the beginning of 1963 there appeared the book of the Anglican
bishop John A. T. Robinson, *Honest to God* (honest to and about God).**
In both England and Germany (as well as in America) it has provoked a
debate that was in part heated. Articles appeared in the Hamburg news-
paper, *Die Zeit*, with captions "Is God a metaphor?" "Is our image of
God dated?" "Is faith in God finished?" – questions that were evoked by
Robinson's book. Some theologians who expressed their opinions rightly
observed that the ideas advanced by Robinson are not new in contemporary theology. Now Robinson had not made this claim at all. He calls
repeatedly on Paul Tillich, Dietrich Bonhoeffer and others.*** But in the
process of assimilating their thoughts, he sees that they add up to the following sum, so to speak: *a revolution is necessary*. For, since the traditional
ecclesiastical image of God is not longer credible to contemporary man, *a
new image of God* is required; the old one is obsolete.

It is comprehensible that for many readers – especially for readers
among the laity to whom the book is directed – this thesis is frightening.
With the disposal of the old image of God, is not faith in God and thereby
also God himself finished? That this question forces itself upon men today
is not signalized by Robinson's book alone. As early as 1961 there appeared
the book, *The Death of God*,[1] by the American theologian, Gabriel Vahanian, which is a peculiar and theologically more independent parallel to
Robinson's book. The title of Vahanian's book takes up the famous pro-
nouncement of Nietzsche: "God is dead."

The note *"God is dead"* was struck almost a hundred years before
Nietzsche by Jean Paul in his *Siebenkäs*, which appeared in 1796–7, and

---

* "Der Gottesgedanke und der moderne Mensch," ZThK, 60, 1963, pp. 335–348.
** SCM Press (England), Westminster Press (U.S.A.), 1963.
*** Translator's note: Professor BULTMANN's modesty prevents him from men-
tioning that ROBINSON also calls frequently on him.
[1] G. VAHANIAN, The Death of God. The Culture of Our Post-Christian Era, New
York: George Braziller, 1961. By the same author, "Beyond the Death of God: The
Need of Cultural Revolution," Dialog I, 4, 1962, pp. 18–21.

there in a ghastly vision: "Discourse of the dead Christ from atop the cos | mos: there is no God."[2] This discourse is not a philosophical discussion of atheism. The import of the vision consists rather in showing that atheism is nihilism (in this respect also a precursor of Nietzsche): "The whole universe is burst asunder by the hand of atheism and fragmented into innumerable quick-silver particles of I's, which twinkle, roll about, wander, flee together and from each other without unity and stability. No one is so very much alone in the universe as the one who denies God... Alas, if every I is its own father and creator, why can it not also be its own angel of destruction?"

Nietzsche permits the "madman" to proclaim the message of the death of God in his work *Die fröhliche Wissenschaft* (1882). Martin Heidegger says in his essay "Nietzsches Wort 'Gott ist tot' "[3]: "Nietzsche's word names the destiny of two thousand years of Western history." This remarkable assertion rests on the conviction that Western history has been determined for two thousand years by Greek metaphysics, through which in the last analysis the secularization of the world, brought to completion in modern times, has been established. We may here suspend jugdment with respect to the correctness of this assertion. Explicit atheism, in any case, is a phenomenon of the modern period, and Gerhard Ebeling has rightly said that this atheism is a countermovement against Christianity.[4] It is also clear that the death of God for Nietzsche means the death of the Christian God. "But," Heidegger adds, "it is not less certain and is to be borne in mind in advance that the names of God and the Christian God are used by Nietzsche to designate the supersensory world generally. God is the name for the realm of ideas and ideals."[5]

The "madman" calls it out in a figure: "What did we do when we unchained this earth from its sun?", and he continues: "Where is it moving to now? Where are we moving to? Away from all suns? Do we not stumble all the time? Backwards, sidewards, forward, in every direction? Is there an above and a below any more? Are we not wandering as through

---

[2] G. BORNKAMM has reprinted the speech as an appendix to the second volume of his collected essays: Studien zu Antike und Urchristentum. Gesammelte Aufsätze II (Beiträge zur evangelischen Theologie, Band 28), Munich, 1959, pp. 245–250. – HEGEL had also said that God is dead, namely the God of church dogmatics. On this point cf. W. ANZ, "Tod und Unsterblichkeit" (in: Einsichten. Festschrift für G. KRÜGER, Frankfurt, 1962, pp. 11–35), p. 25. The "atheism" of HEGEL, however, is not nihilism in the sense of JEAN PAUL and NIETZSCHE.

[3] M. HEIDEGGER, Holzwege, Frankfurt, 1950, pp. 103–247. Cf. also K. LÖWITH, "Nietzsches antichristliche Bergpredigt," Heidelberger Jahrbücher, 6, 1962, pp. 39–50.

[4] G. EBELING, The Nature of Faith, London, 1961, p. 80f.; Word and Faith, London, 1963, pp. 135f., 343.

[5] HEIDEGGER, Holzwege, pp. 199.

|an endless nothingness?" The consequence of the death of God is therefore *nihilism*, as Jean Paul had pictured it.

We must guard against viewing atheism merely or even basically as a consequence of natural science and its world-view. To be sure, modern natural science has found the hypothesis "God" unnecessary, according to the well-known *dictum* of La Place, and the atheism of natural science has without doubt been widely influential, leading even to absurdity in Russia, where as the result of space-flight it is given out that there was no trace of God in the space above the earth. Nevertheless, even when there are natural scientists today who again hold the hypothesis "God" to be possible and appropriate, atheism is not thereby contradicted. For it has far deeper roots.

Atheism, as Jean Paul and Nietzsche understood it, is indeed nihilism, and this is not necessarily a consequence of the way in which natural science understands the world. In this respect the loss of the supernatural can be and was replaced in the eighteenth and nineteenth centuries by the belief in progress and its accompanying optimism. The atheism of the natural sciences is a methodological procedure insofar as it subjects the world to an objectivizing way of viewing things. It must necessarily disregard God, because God, as the supersensory, cannot be the object of an objectivizing way of seeing.[6]

Atheism which ends in nihilism is rather the consequence of the *secularization of the world*, of which the objectivizing way of viewing nature is only a partial symptom. Secularization can be characterized simply as the world being conceived by man as an object[7] and thus delivered over to technology as its object.[8] This secularization takes place in every sphere of life, in morality, in law, in politics. For the relation of man to a transcendental power has been abandoned in all spheres of life. Heidegger calls this epoch in which the world has become an object the epoch *of subjectity*,[9] i.e.

---

[6] Cf. Ebeling, The Nature of Faith, pp. 81 f.

[7] Cf. Heidegger, Holzwege, p. 236.

[8] Cf. D. Bonhoeffer, Prisoner for God: Letters and Papers from Prison, ed. E. Bethge, tr. R. H. Fuller, New York, 1959, p. 145: "Man has learned to cope with all questions of importance without recourse to God as a working hypothesis." (Widerstand und Ergebung. Briefe und Aufzeichnungen aus der Haft, ed. E. Bethge, Munich, ⁶1955, p. 215.) Further on the process of secularization, cf. Ebeling, Word and Faith, pp. 128 ff.; R. G. Smith, "A Theological Perspective of the Secular," The Christian Scholar, 43, 1960, pp. 11–24, pp. 18 f.

[9] Heidegger, Holzwege, p. 237. *Subjectity*, of course, is to be distinguished from *subjectivity*. The latter refers to the subjective mode of the individual in his judgments (e. g. judgments of taste); the former refers to the disposition of an entire epoch to the world and history, a disposition which has achieved the status of self-evidentness. [The reader will perhaps excuse the neologism subjectity, which represents *Subjektität*; the form is drawn by analogy: *Subjektität – Subjektivität* / subjectity-subjectivity. – translator.]

the era in which the world conceived as object | is subjected to the planning of man as subject, a planning which is controlled by the values which man himself establishes.

And religion? One must first of all reflect that *Christianity itself was a decisive factor in the development of the secularization of the world* in that it de-divinized the world.[10] The Christian faith, by de-divinizing the world, allowed it to appear in its pure worldliness. It disclosed and evoked the *freedom* of man from the world, freedom from all powers which can encounter man from out of the world.[11] It is the freedom of which Luther said: "A Christian is a free master over all things and subject to no one." This consciousness of freedom is the presupposition of the secularization of the world; the latter follows, however, only when the continuation of Luther's remark is forgotten: "A Christian is a servant in the service of all things and subject to every one," or, to put it differently, when it is forgotten that *freedom from* the world is at the same time *responsibility for* the world.[12] This forgetfulness increases the more man becomes conscious of the possibility, in pure objectivizing thought, of dominating the world through science and technology, of making it serve his purposes, evaluations and plans.

This process uses, so to speak, the rôle which *reason* plays in life. Freedom from the world is at the same time responsibility | for the world; that means, the world is delivered over to the reason of man.[13] For in order to be able to act responsibly, to come to decisions as they are required again and again, man must recognize the causal connection of events in the world, must gain insight into causes and effects, and arrive at jugdments about what serves the purpose and what does not. It is to this end that he has his reason. Indeed, in the power of his reason he grasps the laws under which

[10] Cf. EBELING, Word and Faith, pp. 135 f., 344; The Nature of Faith, pp. 80 f. Further, especially F. GOGARTEN, Verhängnis und Hoffnung der Neuzeit, Stuttgart 1953; R. G. SMITH, "A Theological Perspective," p. 21.

[11] Cf. GOGARTEN, Verhängnis und Hoffnung, p. 8: (the most remarkable thing transpires in secularization) "that the autonomy of man gains the radical sense which it has in the modern world only through the perceptions and experiences disclosed in the Christian faith." *Ibid.*, p. 12: Secularization is the "legitimate consequence" of the Christian faith, and insofar as it "is grounded in the Christian faith," it "makes the world the world (Verweltlichung der Welt)." Cf. *Ibid.*, 93 ff.

[12] On the interdependence of freedom from the world and responsibility for the world, cf. GOGARTEN, pp. 19, 24 ff. VAHANIAN makes the same point, Death of God, p. 61: "Biblical thought considers the world as man's sphere of action and pre-eminence. Man's responsibility to God and his involvement in the world emerge as polar elements attesting to the original goodness of creation." It is significant that both GOGARTEN and VAHANIAN make the distinction between a legitimate secularization (secularity) and a degenerate secularism (secularism). Cf. GOGARTEN 129 ff.; VAHANIAN 60 ff. Cf. R. G. SMITH, "A Theological Perspective," p. 21.

[13] Cf. GOGARTEN, p. 88.

man's actions universally stand, i.e. the moral laws, whose force alone keeps the human community sound and whole. Thus, according to the myth of Protagoras in Plato,[14] Zeus sent reverence and justice to the earth by Hermes in order that political community might be possible. But rational judgments and plans, without which human work and community are not possible, are threatened by the danger that they will be placed in the service of self-seeking and that the authority of the moral laws will thereby wane.

The more reason is conscious of itself, the more the laws which regulate the community will no longer be simply derived from tradition, but will be understood as the moral laws which reason sanctions. And thus heteronomy turns into *autonomy*. Autonomy is equivocal. In the genuine sense autonomy means self-legislation in the sense that the individual affirms the moral law as that in which he himself comes to win his authenticity.[15] But the recognition that the rational man is a lawgiver in this sense, turns into the delusion that the individual as subject arbitrarily determines what is good and evil, as was the case already in the 'Greek Englightenment' among the Sophists. And so today autonomy is unfortunately often spoken of as a self-legislation of the individual that understands itself to be free of obligations which transcend the individual level, and that determines value and valuelessness of itself. The outcome is nihilism.[16]

Religion was also drawn into the wake of "subjecticy." This is simply given with the fact that Christianity appears as a particular example of religion and is classified within the continuity of the history of religions (which, of course, is possible in any case). If in this context Christianity is acknowledged as the highest religion, then the capitulation to subjectity becomes evident at just that point. For the judgment about lower and

---

[14] Plato, Protagoras 322a–322c.

[15] Cf. KANT, Critique of Practical Reason, Part First, Book II, Chapter II, V: "In this manner the moral law leads through the conception of the *summum bonum*, as the object and final end of pure practical reason, to religion, that is, to the recognition of all duties as divine commands, not as sanctions, that is to say, arbitrary ordinances of a foreign will and contingent in themselves, but as essential laws of every free will in itself, which, however, must be regarded as commands of the supreme being,..." (Kant's Critique of Practical Reason, tr. T.K. ABBOTT, London: Longmans, 1923, p. 226).

[16] On autonomy cf. also R.G. SMITH, "A Theological Perspective," p. 18. EBELING puts it very well in Word and Faith, pp. 113f.: "But now, to the reality that concerns modern man there belongs ... the discovery of the autonomy of the reason and accordingly the inescapable duty to make use of the autonomous reason – not, be it noted, to make autonomous use of the reason; for it is not man himself but reason which, rightly understood, is autonomous, whereas to confuse the autonomy of the reason with the autonomy of man results precisely in a new heteronomy of the reason..."

higher religions can only be a judgment of the subject which evaluates. It is by no means the case that religion necessarily disappears in subjectity. The western world, which has been a 'Christian' world for centuries, today is in general not anti-Christian, but a-Christian, partly in the sense that Christianity appears to it to be antiquated and the questions to which Christianity proposes to give answers have become for it irrelevant; but partly in the sense that the questions as such remain living issues for it, but now modern man himself gives the answers. Thus there arise ideologies, which assert that they are able to reveal the meaning of the world and history;[17] or doctrines of salvation are propagated, often from exotic religions, the choice among which is left to the subjectivity of the individual; or again – especially in the U.S.A. – the biblical hope of a millenium is secularized, that is, converted into optimism which seeks to renew the world through the "social gospel."[18] But above all, there arises a *religiosity* to which men flee, so to speak, from the claims as well as from the bitterness or tediousness of profane everyday life.

"In the last analysis, religiosity is an expression of sublimated loneliness."[19] The pressing problem for man in a world which has been cut loose from ties to the beyond is to find himself, to become certain of his own being. For with the loss of reference to the transcendent, man's certainty of knowledge concerning himself has also been lost.[20] The question of God does not therefore die away; but the form of the question | suggests "that the deity is a missing link in man's unsuccessful attempts to grasp the meaning of his self and of the world."[21]

The question by no means completely dies away in decided atheism either, where atheism draws back from the abyss of nihilism and, even though it does not risk entertaining the ideas of the transcendent God and his revelation, would still like to speak in some way of the divine as somehow immanent to the world, whether it be as the world's creative ground or as the spiritual life which lives and evolves in the world.[22] Indeed, one can say that such "atheism" stands nearer the Christian understanding of faith

---

[17] Cf. R. G. SMITH, "A Theological Perspective," p. 19.

[18] Cf. VAHANIAN, pp. 28 ff.

[19] VAHANIAN, p. 4. Cf. also R. G. SMITH, "A Theological Perspective," pp. 20 f.; The New Man, London, 1956, pp. 62 f.

[20] Cf. VAHANIAN, p. 183. Further, BONHOEFFER, Widerstand und Ergebung, p. 258: "Man (*scil.* who is threatened by today's organization) is thrown back upon himself. He is ready to cope with everything, but not with himself. He is able to insure himself against everything, but not against man. In the last analysis, however, everything depends on man." (Cf. Prisoner for God, p. 178.) Further, R. G. SMITH, "A Theological Perspective," p. 12.

[21] VAHANIAN, p. 78.

[22] Cf., for example, what ROBINSON, pp. 127–29, says about JULIAN HUXLEY and ALBERT CAMUS.

than some institutional Christians who understand the transcendence of God as a Beyond which has nothing to do with the world.[23]

Religiosity abandons precisely that – at least according to the Christian faith – upon which genuine religion is based: the relation of man to the transcendent God as that which stands over against. Religiosity is conceived from the point of view of the subjectivity of man. In this sense Karl Barth once fought against Schleiermacher and the theology of experience inaugurated by him, in which religion is understood as a province of the human spirit, as the feeling of absolute dependence. To what extent Barth's criticism of Schleiermacher was justified I leave open.[24] In any case, it was justified to the extent that the relation to God was reduced to feeling. Vahanian takes up this battle against religiosity from the standpoint of the Christian faith with renewed vigor, as did Bonhoeffer before him. And they are followed by John A. T. Robinson.

Gone is *the relation of man to the transcendent* as that which stands over against man and the world and is not at their disposal, which is manifested only through encounter, only as gift, and cannot be reached by turning away from the world in a religious flight into a beyond. Now the word *transcendence* is ambiguous. It can be said that rational thought transcends all unmethodical and random thought. Reason is transcendent with respect to primitive-innocent opinions as well as arbitrary individual judgments and | evaluations. But reason remains in the sphere of subjectivity, while religion, particularly the Christian faith, abandons this sphere.[25] The Christian faith speaks of a *revelation* which it understands to mean God's act as an event which is not visible to the objectivizing thought of reason, an event which as revelation does not communicate doctrines, but concerns the existence of man[26] and teaches him, or better, authorizes him to understand himself as sustained by the transcendent power of God.[27]

---

[23] It is therefore understandable when ROBINSON, p. 127, produces a variation on Paul's formulation in I Cor. 9: 20f.: "I am prepared to be an agnostic with the agnostic, even an atheist with the atheists." Likewise cf. R. G. SMITH, The New Man, p. 109, on FEUERBACH.

[24] On this point cf. CHR. SENFT, Wahrhaftigkeit und Wahrheit. Die Theologie des 19. Jahrhunderts zwischen Orthodoxie und Aufklärung (BHT 22), Tübingen, 1956, pp. 1–46.

[25] I disregard here that and to what extent it can be said that the existential life (e. g. in personal relationships) transcends the sphere of subjectity.

[26] Here I disregard the paradox, which involves the revelatory event being at once a historical as well as an eschatological event, both with respect to its origin, Jesus Christ, and with respect to his constantly renewed presence in the church's proclamation.

[27] If one is persuaded that every man is basically moved by the question of God and that therefore the Christian proclamation may reckon with a preunderstanding, then one can ask whether this pre-understanding is not also concealed precisely in religiosity. Now H. G. GADAMER, in his book, Wahrheit und Methode, Tübingen, 1960, which is of greatest significance for theologians, has contested (in the

In this theologians like Tillich, Bonhoeffer, Ebeling, Vahanian, R.G. Smith and Robinson are one. But they are also agreed that *the transcendent is to be sought and can be found not above or beyond the world, but in the midst of this world.*[28] Allow me to quote some sentences of Bonhoeffer: "The 'beyond' of God is not the beyond of our cognitive faculties. Epistemological transcendence has nothing to do with the transcendence of God. God is transcendent in the midst of our life." "The transcendent is not the infinitely remote, but the nearest at hand."[29] The 'death of God,' according to Vahanian, takes place precisely in that the transcendent presence of God is lost if transcen|dence is conceived as purely otherworldly – just as in religiosity.[30] Or, to quote another formulation of Vahanian: "Religious authority does not entail the eradication of personal autonomy for the sake of blind assent to a system of beliefs claiming the sanction of absolute or divine authority. But religious authority... symbolizes a synthesis of subjective truth and objective reality... Faith is an attempt to reconcile subject and object, subjective truth and objective reality, without overwhelming either one of the terms."[31]

Faith permits the world to be the world, indeed, it gives back to the world its authentic worldliness; faith "recognizes the hidden unconditional ground even in the most autonomous of human pursuits. It needs to welcome those pursuits not for the hope that they may be violently 'baptized' into Christ, but for their own sake."[32] Dietrich Bonhoeffer formulates

context of the hermeneutical problem, pp. 313 f.) that one can speak of a pre-understanding for the understanding of the biblical texts, namely, a pre-understanding that is given with the question of God that drives human existence. I am of the opinion that the pre-understanding is given precisely in that experience which Gadamer designates as the "authentic experience," namely, the experience in which "man becomes conscious of his finiteness" (339 f.). This experience is certainly not always realized, but it surely persists as an ever present possibility.

[28] For R.G. SMITH cf. "A Theological Perspective," p. 15; The New Man, pp. 65–70, and especially 94–112: "This-Worldly Transcendence." EBELING, The Nature of Faith, p. 160 f.

[29] Widerstand und Ergebung, pp. 182, 255 (cf. Prisoner for God, 124, 175). On BONHOEFFER cf. especially R.G. SMITH, The New Man, pp. 96–106; EBELING, "The Non-religious Interpretation of Biblical Concepts," in: Word and Faith, pp. 98–161.

[30] VAHANIAN, p. 44.

[31] VAHANIAN, pp. 164 f. Cf. p. 11: "Now, as then, today and always, the Christian problem is to correlate the truth of Christianity with the empirical truths men live by, without confusing them: man cannot live by one or the other kind of truth alone." p. 169: "On the contrary, even as the meaning of existence lies outside existence, in the dialectical relatedness implied by the polarity between Creator and creature, so also the meaning of history lies above and beyond history." The formulation of TILLICH, quoted also by VAHANIAN, is in substantial agreement: "Theology moves back and forth between two poles, the eternal truth of its foundation and the temporal situation in which the eternal truth must be received" (Systematic Theology, Vol. I, Chicago: The University Press, 1951, p. 3).

[32] R.G. SMITH, The New Man, p. 69.

the discernment of faithful relation to the world very pointedly: "And we cannot be honest without recognizing that we must live in the world – '*etsi deus non daretur*'. And this is just what we do recognize – before God! God himself drives us to this recognition."[33] This is precisely what Robinson designates as the necessary revolution: the God above the world having become the God beyond the world, today it is a question of finding God in the midst of the world, in the present. The contrast between here and beyond, and thus the contrast between naturalism and supernaturalism, must be overcome. God must be recognized as the Unconditional in the conditional.

It is surprising how such theological perceptions are also taken up by sociologists. Eckart Schleth says in his book, *Der profane Weltchrist:* "The unity of Christian and world is found in the 'nevertheless' of the believer for the world, in his imperceptile eschatological existence here and now, in his freedom from the | world, in the world and for the world." Further: "Life in faith, the character of which is to be permanently in process of fulfillment, is life in the 'ultimate reality', which is always here and now and identical with everyday things."[34]

The relation of faith and worldliness is a dialectical relationship, as R. G. Smith especially has emphasized.[35] I will try to make the meaning of this dialectical relation clear by means of an analogy. The loving look into an eye which is loved and loving is fundamentally different from the objectivizing look with which an ophthalmologist examines the eye of a patient. But when the doctor who has to treat the diseased eye is also the one who loves, the two ways of seeing stand in a dialectical relationship; he has to examine the eye of the other in an objectivizing way precisely in his love. The objectivizing way of seeing enters into the service of those who love. Robinson endeavors, following Tillich, to make clear the relation between faith and worldliness in the dialectical relation between engagement with the world and withdrawal from the world. To this dialectic corresponds the dialectic in the relation of man to God, namely, as the relation between personal freedom and utter dependence, between ultimacy and intimacy.[36]

He who has understood the dialectic of the relationship between worldliness and faith in relation to the transcendent God, also sees that the

---

[33] Widerstand und Ergebung, p. 241 (cf. Prisoner for God, p. 163).

[34] E. SCHLETH, Der profane Weltchrist. Neubau der Lebensform für den Industriemenschen, Munich, 1957, pp. 114, 159. Cf. p. 8: The author is of the opinion "that the church as 'eschatological phenomenon' occurs where Christians without reservation take the profane world seriously, because only in the 'solidarity of faith and unfaith' can the new creation in Christ be recognized and the world served by it."

[35] The New Man, pp. 106f., also pp. 58–70; "A Theological Perspective," p. 22.

[36] ROBINSON, pp. 100, 130f.

recognition of God as the nearest at hand, as he who is in the midst of worldly life, *does not imply pantheism*.[37] For the dialectic is missing in pantheism, and it avoids the paradox that is given to man to conquer, the paradox of grasping the unconditional in the conditional in every now: that means, not in a theory, but in existential comportment, in the conscious or unconscious decisions of life.

The contrast can be made clear by saying that faith in the transcendent presence of God can be expressed in the phrase "transformations of God." Ernst Barlach chose this phrase in order to say that the paradox of the presence | of God in the world takes shape in ever new form, just as he himself wished to give expression to the suprareal and infinite in his works in ever new forms.

Ernst Troeltsch once also spoke of the "transformations of God," as he sought to hold on to the idea of God in his philosophy of history in view of the "pluralism of reality and its movement" and vis-à-vis the changes in the knowledge of truth and in the ideals.[38] These changes depend upon an "inner life-movement of the All or the Divinity," upon a "life-process of the Absolute," a "becoming of the divine Spirit."

Troeltsch saw the problem, but he sought to solve it not on the basis of the historicness (Geschichtlichkeit) of human existence, but from a standpoint which views history from the outside and speculatively postulates a transcendent deity, which has its life beyond my specific historicness.[39]

Hans Jonas represents the opposite extreme in his essay "Immortality and the Modern Temper,"[40] to the extent that he projects, so to speak, the historicness of man into God himself and speaks of the destiny of the deity for which man is responsible.[41] We men are experiments of eternity, as it were, and God's own destiny is at stake in our decisions, in the universe which he has left to itself. God's being at the mercy of the world does not mean his immanence in the sense of pantheism. Rather, there is the paradox that the deity has chosen a destiny which consists in the continuous elevation out of immanence into transcendence, for which we men are responsible. In such a process, in the succession of surrender and deliverance, the deity becomes itself.

---

[37] R. G. SMITH, "A Theological Perspective," p. 16, also emphasizes this point.

[38] E. TROELTSCH, Der Historismus und seine Probleme, 1922. The formulations in question, to which reference is made above, are collected by GOGARTEN, Verhängnis und Hoffnung der Neuzeit, pp. 112–114.

[39] For criticism of TROELTSCH, s. GOGARTEN, pp. 114–116.

[40] HTR 55, 1962, pp. 1–20.

[41] JONAS, of course, also sees the dialectic between the relation to the world and the relation to God, and says that we encounter the eternal in the temporal, especially in the decisions in which eternity and nothingness meet in one in that the now of the decision is always to be understood as the final moment of time granted us. That means in fact to understand the end in a light from beyond time.

Schubert M. Ogden understands God's being as historical being in another way.[42] God's eternity is not to be conceived as his timelessness following the metaphysical tradition, but rather | as his eminent temporality, his historicity.[43] God is a God who acts, as he is known in the Bible; his self must therefore be conceived in strict analogy with the human self, and anthropomorphic language about God is entirely appropriate. Just as man is not an isolated I, neither is God. Without the universe, without the world, his creation, God is not. To this extent he not only stands in relation to the world, but is dependent upon it. But this dependence is actual, i. e. it is actualized in his own free decisions as well as in the free decisions, which correspond to his own, of the creatures that constitute his world. As answer to God's decisions which arise from unbounded love, the latter themselves contribute to God's self-creation.

This all certainly sounds astonishing at first hearing. Is not God, as we learned from Psalm 90, he who was there before the mountains were brought forth and the earth and the world created, God from everlasting to everlasting? Indeed he is! But we understand Ogden when we comprehend how he endeavors to free the idea of the eternity of God from the metaphysical conception of God as the unmoved mover, the *"causa sui,"*[44] and to conceive the eternity of God as historical without giving up thinking of God as creator. If, according to the biblical tradition, God is a person, so is he historical. In support of the view that God is not, apart from the world, the creator is not, apart from the creation, Ogden is able to invoke John 1:1–3, that remarkable assertion that in the beginning was the word, and the word of creation at that, through which everything came into being. This word in the beginning was with God, indeed the word was God. That is no different from what Ogden intends to say. And when we reflect on the word "before" in the Psalm, it is to be said that already for the Psalmist the meaning of "before" is not exhausted in the chronological sense, but that it means the creative superiority, the creative origin. This origin did not occur once as *prima causa*, out of which world history then unfolded in time; on the contrary, this origin is always present.

With this we come back to the assertion that for modern man the idea of a God above or beyond the world is either no longer viable or is perverted in a religiosity which would like to escape from the world. By no means!

---

[42] JR 43, 1963, pp. 1–19.

[43] Cf. M. HEIDEGGER, Being and Time, tr. J. MACQUARRIE and E. ROBINSON, London, 1962, p. 499, n. xiii: "If God's eternity can be 'construed' philosophically, then it may be understood only as a more primordial temporality which is 'infinite.'"

[44] Cf. M. HEIDEGGER, Identität und Differenz, 1957, Pfullingen, pp. 70 f. (Cf. Essays in Metaphysics: Identity and Difference, tr. KURT F. LEIDECKER, New York: Philosophical Library, 1960, pp. 64 f.)

Only the idea of God which can find, which can seek and find, *the unconditional in the conditional,* the beyond in the here, the transcendent in the
present | at hand, as possibility of encounter, is possible for modern man.

It then remains to keep oneself open at any time for the *encounter with
God in the world, in time.* It is not the acknowledgment of an image of God,
be it ever so correct, that is real faith in God; rather, it is the readiness for
the eternal to encounter us at any time in the present – at any time in the
varying situations of our life. Readiness consists in openness in allowing
something really to encounter us that does not leave the I alone, the I that
is encapsulated in its purposes and plans, but the encounter with which is
designed to transform us, to make us ever new selves. The situation can be
heartening just as well as disheartening, can be challenging as well as
requiring endurance. What is demanded is selflessness, not as a pattern of
moral behavior, but as the readiness not to cling to our selves, but to receive
our authentic selves ever anew. This readiness can be interrogative, but it
can also be completely naive. For surprisingly God can encounter us where
we do not expect it.[45] |

We have thus perhaps come to an understanding of what is meant by
the "transformations of God." All of us are probably acquainted with sagas
and legends, pagan as well as Christian, in which the profound idea of the

---

[45] That is evidently also the intention of HERBERT BRAUN, whose avoidance of
the word "God" in his delineation of what the New Testament has to say to me
(Gesammelte Studien zum Neuen Testament und seiner Umwelt, Tübingen, 1962,
p. 297) has offended and evoked criticism (cf. especially H. GOLLWITZER, Die Existenz
Gottes im Bekenntnis des Glaubens [BETh 34], Munich, 1963, pp. 26–29). BRAUN's
purpose is to emphasize, over against an ideological theism, that God is not "the one
who exists for himself," but rather is "the whence of my being agitated" (p. 341;
= "The Problem of a New Testament Theology," JThC, number 1, pp. 169–183,
pp. 182f.). This being driven about is understood by BRAUN as determined by the
"I may" and "I ought." It might be asked how this dialectic (if it may be called
that) relates to the dialectic between worldliness and a believing relation to transcendence. But, in any case, the relation to transcendence is understood in the New
Testament, according to BRAUN, as an event, and indeed, as he formulates it, as an
"unexpectable" event (275). The believing self-understanding awakened in such an
event is not theoretical knowledge, but "an event which occurs again and again"
(277). The truth of the relation to transcendence understood in this sense is "bound
to its being perpetually proclaimed anew" (277) and to its being heeded (297), to its
being heard (298), respectively. The self-understanding awakened by such hearing
is actualized in concrete human community. BRAUN is thus able to put it very sharply:
"Man as man, man in relation with his fellow man, implies God" (341; = JThC, 1,
p. 183). – R. G. SMITH also emphasizes the importance of community, "A Theological
Perspective," p. 22: "Man is (scil. man) in so far as he receives. He is (scil. man)
only so far as he is whole. And this wholeness is found only in relation to others.
Man's being is being in relation. This simply cannot be arranged or planned. It
happens, it is an event in which man's being is disclosed in the presence of the
other." – The problem of the relation of law and gospel also belongs here; see
EBELING, e. g., Word and Faith, pp. 143 f.

transformation of God has been concealed in the mythological represen-
tation of the metamorphosis of the deity or of gods, who visit a mortal
incognito and unrecognized. How the one visited receives the god determines his destiny.

The New Testament contains the most striking proclamation of the
"transformations" of God, and oddly enough in the picture which Jesus
sketches of the last judgment (Matt. 25: 31–46). The judge of the world
assembles all men before his throne, some to the right, some to the left. To
those on the right he says: "I was hungry and you gave me food, I was
thirsty and you gave me drink, I was a stranger and you welcomed me..."
And when those so addressed inquire in astonishment, "When did we do
all this?" the Lord will answer, "What you did to one of the least of these
my brethren, you did to me!" The dialogue with those on the left runs
correspondingly: "I was hungry and you gave me no food, I was thirsty
and you gave me no drink, ..." And when they ask, "Lord, when did we
see thee hungry or thirsty... and did not minister to thee?" then they
must face the answer, "What you did not do to the least of these, you did
not do to me either!" This picture thus contains the two doctrines, which
belong together, of the "transformations" of God and of the presence of
eternity in time.

Theology and the Evidentness of the Ethical [*]

by

Gerhard Ebeling

Translated by James W. Leitch

I

The relation between the proper theme of theology and the problem
of ethics is usually discussed as the question of the *relation between dog-*
matics and ethics – the question whether the traditional division of systematic theology into these two disciplines is appropriate or, if not really
appropriate, is nevertheless expedient for external reasons, or whether it is a
characteristic symptom of the mistaken development of theology in modern
times and as such must be corrected by consistently taking ethics up into
dogmatics. Evangelical theology today mostly accepts, at least in principle,
the comprehending of ethics in and under dogmatics. It would be inviting
grievous misunderstandings if we sought to declare ourselves opposed to
this prevailing view – as if it were not the case that theological statements
about faith and works, about God's doings and man's doings (or however
else the difference between dogmatics and ethics may be interpreted [2]) form
in irreversible descending order an inseparable unity. Certainly, there
would be many questions to be put here: – Is the view customarily held
today of the origin, meaning, and surmounting of the old separation of
ethics from dogmatics completely watertight? [3] Does not the distinction, |

---

[*] "Die Evidenz des Ethischen und die Theologie," ZThK, 57, 1960, pp. 318–356.
[1] Guest lectures, delivered during the Theological Week at Greifswald on October 24 and 25, 1960, and at the Kirchliche Hochschule in Berlin on January 9 and
10, 1961. [2] G. EBELING, Word and Faith, London, 1963, p. 414.
[3] On the prevailing view cf. the remarks in RGG³, II, cols. 228 (G. GLOEGE) and
712 (H. VAN OYEN). The repeated assertion that the setting up of theological ethics
on its own feet over against dogmatics is to be traced back to G. CALIXT is a misjudg-
ment of the real fact that G. CALIXT constituted as a theological discipline the
ethics which till then had been studied as a philosophical discipline. On this point
cf. JOHANNES WALLMANN, Der Theologiebegriff bei Johann Gerhard und Georg
Calixt, (BHTh 30), Tübingen, 1961. | That from SCHLEIERMACHER on an
isolation of ethics from dogmatics made its appearance (RGG³, II, col. 712) ought
not to be so roundly asserted, considering what SCHLEIERMACHER himself says on
the question of division of disciplines in: Kurze Darstellung des theologischen Stu-
diums, ed. H. SCHOLZ, Leipzig, 1910³, §§ 223–231. He considers a separation of

even when it is made light of as an entirely extraneous matter or is taken up into the program of dogmatics itself, still betray a theologically meaningful duality of aspects which is not to be eliminated?[4] And are there not much more important problems at work in the modern twofold division of systematic theology than it seems when the foreground is occupied by secondary questions so prone to barrenness as the distinction of theology's disciplines and the ordering of its material? Let us therefore spend no more time on the customary question of the relation of dogmatics and ethics.

Vastly more provoking than the fact of theological ethics asserting its independence of dogmatics is the thing that is of such immeasurable conse-quence for the modern age: the *emancipation of ethics from theology* altogether, or to put it in still more fundamental terms, the secularistic emancipation of ethics from the Christian faith. The Christian church, it is true, has always been – more or less clearly – aware that the Christian faith is not by any means only a better kind of morals, and conversion to Christ is not *eo ipso* identical with a moral transformation. However closely the two things may belong together, so that there is an imminent danger of a moralization of Christianity and a corresponding moral defamation of everything that is non-Christian or even only non-Orthodox, yet (speaking in general terms) the specifically religious character of Christianity would be obscured if there were not morality to be found also outside of | Chris-tianity. Indeed, even the possibility of appealing to people with the Chris-tian message would be open to question unless a certain measure of moral consciousness, whatever the theoretical interpretation of it may be, could be presupposed also in the non-Christian. All the more so as the relation

---

Christian ethics from dogmatics "not to be essential," and emphasizes on the con-trary notable disadvantages attending such a practice. In spite of there being considerations also to the contrary, he declares it to be at least a desirable thing "that the undivided treatment, too, should assert itself again from time to time." To be sure, the fear "that in a very detailed treatment that might hardly be possible without the mass losing all shape" (§ 231, cf. also: The Christian Faith, § 26) is not entirely unfounded, as is shown by KARL BARTH's imposing attempt to put the idea into practice. That among the protagonists of the interconnection of dogmatics and ethics MARTIN KÄHLER is singled out among others for honorable mention (RGG³, II, cols. 228 and 712) seems to me not to have adequate foundation in the mere uniting of apologetics, dogmatics, and ethics as three fields treated one after the other in a single volume (Die Wissenschaft der christlichen Lehre von dem evange-lischen Grundartikel aus im Abrisse dargestellt, Leipzig, 1883, 1893², 1905³).

[4] That could be shown also in K. BARTH's Church Dogmatics, both in the execu-tion and also in the methodological reflections on the point. Notice, e.g., the following remark (I, 2, New York, 1956, p. 794): "That dogmatics has always to be ethics cannot alter the fact that it is first and foremost and in itself dogmatics. As such it is concerned with the Word of God. Only in subordination to this is it also concerned with the Christian life. Only in this subordination and dependence can this second theme be properly treated. Therefore in dogmatics there must always be room for the explicit recognition of the precedence and independence of the first theme."

of the Christian faith to morality does not merely display peculiarities in matter of detail but differs in structure from the relation between religion and morality as found elsewhere. Roughly speaking: on the one hand, the relation of Christian faith and morality is incomparably close, on the other hand, it forms a distinction of outright antithesis.

Since the beginnings of the encounter between Christianity and Graeco-Roman antiquity there has therefore been at least a limited reception of extra-Christian philosophical ethics which has played an important role in Christian theology and has influenced to a high degree the formation of Christian ethics. Over a wide field – think of the teaching on the moral virtues in Scholasticism – the exposition of ethics in theology was a reproduction of the ethical heritage of the philosophy of antiquity. Incidentally, the Reformers' criticism of the influence of Aristotelian ethics on theology referred not so much to the field of ethical questions as such, but rather to the interpretation of faith in the categories of Aristotelian ethics.

In spite of everything the ethical was so closely interwoven with Christianity – also, of course, in the Reformers' view – that it seemed unthinkable to separate the ethos from the authority of revelation and from faith's urge towards fulfilling the commandments or from the examples of Christian living. Abandonment of the Christian faith caused *eo ipso* fear for the dissolution of ethics.

But now, there arose from Christianity itself the compulsion to give ethics a standing independent of the Christian faith, at all events in its confessional form. Naturally, the process of secularization and its most important result in the emancipation of secular ethics is not by any means derivable solely from the fact of confessional conflict. But the latter had no small influence on a more deeply rooted process going on at many different levels – at first indeed more of a retarding influence but for that very reason one that called out all the sharper a reaction. The confessional split pressed with all urgency the need to make morality independent – | to be sure, not necessarily independent of any religious basis at all (as indeed right up to the present, Western man today is still likeliest to feel his ties with Christianity where morality is concerned), but certainly independent of any basis in doctrines of the faith bearing a confessional stamp. For in that form the Christian faith had *de facto* surrendered its validity as universally binding truth. The fact that being a Christian is identical with being a man, which had earlier seemed self-evident, became questionable once what it means to be a Christian had itself come into dispute. Morality, however, as what is absolutely binding on everyone, as the guarantee of corporate life, and as the basis of common culture, had necessarily to be of a universal kind. Its validity could not be limited to membership of a particular believing community. Just as science had necessarily to find its basis in general principles of knowledge which were independent of the disputed principles of faith, just as jurisprudence had to appeal to natural law in order to create a new order out of the chaos of confessional disputes, so there had also to be a natural ethic binding upon every man, the validity of which was independent of the individual's religious views.

This emancipation of ethics from theology, however, was not by any means understood as a makeshift by the thinkers who became its standard representatives, but was combined with the claim that in this way the phenomenon of the ethical came to light in its purity for the very first time. Not necessarily in the form of a new definition of the content of the ethical – it came to that too, of course: one need only think of Nietzsche – but certainly in the sense that the real nature of the ethical was held to appear in sharp focus now for the first time, unobscured by other motives. And it is quite true that – despite the pattern provided by the philosophical ethics of antiquity – it was only in modern times and as a result of its emancipation from the Christian faith that the nature of the ethical attained completely clear consciousness. The reason for that is, that the bond between the Christian faith and morality was a much closer one than that between the religions of antiquity and ethics, and also that Christianity, even when ethics was emancipating itself from it, provided a more radical grasp of the ethical. For the fact that the ethical now manifested itself to critical thought in its own specific peculiarity with unusual sharpness one need only point to Kant. The relation which exists precisely between Kant's view of the ethical and the tradition of the Reformers has been much discussed, and has admittedly also remained controversial. But that there are important cross-links here is indisputable. I would only draw attention, without further interpretation, to the following point: | whereas Luther – seemingly as an outward, rough definition of the ethical – equated *moraliter* with *civiliter* and *politice* and restricted it to the aspect of *opus*, i. e., in Kantian terms understood it as mere legality, Kant took up what for Luther fell under the *usus theologicus legis* – namely, the radicalness of the demand confronting the conscience – and included it as the peculiarity of morality in his definition of the ethical, i. e., he used a secularized theological aspect to de-restrict the ethical.

Moreover, the actual development of the course of things has itself seemed to justify the setting up of secular ethics alongside the Christian variety. In close interchange with the revolution in the realm of thought, the world of modern man has assumed a completely new face. Wholly new facts, problems, and tasks have come into view. That has brought up for ethical definition a mass of material that could not be mastered at all on the basis of traditional theological views, and therefore left nothing more to be expected from theology. It has seemed that the reality of modern man could not be brought within the field of the reflections of theological ethics – except in a negative, condemnatory sense, yet not in such a way as to do justice to this new reality, and to help it in its difficulties. Where Christian ethics was not reduced altogether to an ethic of the individual inner life, it has nevertheless been understood as teaching on how the believing Christian is to behave in the world. Reaction to the process of secularization has even brought a further hardening of this limitation to a special Christian ethos. With that, the really burning ethical problems of the modern age have fallen outside the competence of theology. Already for the simple reason that, at all events for a large percentage of our contemporaries, the prerequisite of Christian "believing" just does not exist any more and therefore the offer of a special Christian ethic in their case comes to the wrong address. But also, and above all, for the reason that these newly presented problems have their roots in a field which lies far removed from the traditional realm of Christian living, and belongs to secularized man – i.e., the ethical problems as posed above all by the technological world of industrialization and its sociological consequences. It was secularized man in the modern age who brought up these problems and now he must also cope with them on his own. In this verdict on the situation Christians and non-Christians have often enough joined hands, though with opposing evaluations: the non-Christian with the superior feeling of having to do with questions about which theology, because it comes from another age | and is essentially backward, understands nothing; the Christian with the surprise that can oscillate between feelings of inferiority and superiority, and that expresses itself in the idea that all these new-fangled problems do not really come within the Christian field of vision; they can concern theological ethics at best in the particular form of whether and how the Christian, without detriment to his being a Christian, can and may have dealings with things so foreign to his Christianity – yet not in the form of what is to be said in principle about the particular problems themselves, in ways that are everyone's concern. The emancipation of secular ethics from theology is at all events also an expression of the fact that reality has split into separate fields – those in which Christian ethics might still be as competent as ever, and those in which secular problems foreign to the Christian tradition have seemed to require also a correspondingly secular ethic with its back turned to the Christian tradition.

Now, however, we can see clearly enough, without need of further illustration, that today we are involved in a moral crisis of vastest dimensions – a crisis not merely of ethics, but one that goes very much deeper: a crisis of the ethos itself.[5] The eman | cipation of ethics from Christian faith seems to be turning into an emancipation from ethics itself.

---

[5] We cannot enter here into more detailed illustration and analysis of this situation, on which there is such an infinite amount of discussion today. Let me quote only a verdict in which FRITZ HEINEMANN sums it up: "A reliable and universally binding answer to these questions [viz. – the 'inescapable questions' 'which lead

Yet is that really possible? An emancipation from theology, from Christian faith, from religion altogether seems, as experience shows, to be quite within the bounds of possibility. From the West, where it had already had a long history and been able to draw upon the Christian heritage also in positive ways, secularism has burst like a springtide suddenly and without preparation upon the whole world as an accompaniment of Western civilization. We have still no idea of the full extent of the revolutionary results of secularism where morals are concerned – no idea how (or whether) humanity will solve the problems secularism poses in regard to the evidentness and bindingness of moral obligations. But one thing we can surely say already: it appears very questionable whether there can really be an emancipation from ethics altogether. It can naturally take place as a dissolving of obligations, as light-hearted or criminal disregard of moral principles, yet surely only in the form of revolt, of attack upon something which then only makes itself the more obvious in its powers of resistance and its incontrovertible necessity for human life in society. That indeed is why the moral crisis of today is so deeply disturbing: it is a question of something which we cannot somehow also manage without if need be. With the ethical, human nature itself is at stake.

These reflections convey a disturbing impression of the relation between the ethical and – to put it in general terms for the moment – the religious. What took place under the slogan of the emancipation of ethics from religion had the appearance of reducing what was not absolutely necessary to what was absolutely necessary: – Where religion is concerned, each may do as he likes; the ethical, however, at all events up to a definite point,

---

perforce to ethics and make it everyone's concern'] is rendered more difficult today by the crisis which has overtaken not only ethics but the moral consciousness itself. Both crises belong together as symptoms of the more deep-seated crisis of man, but must be clearly distinguished. The crisis in moral life is closely bound up with the social, economic, and political revolutions of our century. The rising proletariat thought it could reject the traditional values as bourgeois, and could reject values in general as ideological superstructures of social and economic interests. NIETZSCHE attempted a transvaluation of all values: he sought to replace the plebeian Christian morality of sympathy, of the mass, of decadence, by an aristocratic morality of power. The dictators finally declared with brutal openness that *good* is what serves the interests of the party, the state, or the race, and thus engendered among individuals and groups a complete uncertainty about values. Anyone who sought to examine today the rules which govern the moral behavior of individuals in different countries and gather them together in *national ethics* would be faced with almost insuperable problems in consequence of the deep-going differences. Much the same is true of *philosophical ethics:* not only does it not exist in a generally accepted form, but there is not even unanimity as to the nature of its problems. Indeed, it is even a mark of the crisis in that discipline that the primary ethical questions | are supplanted by secondary ones." (Die Philosophie im XX. Jahrhundert. Eine enzyklopädische Darstellung ihrer Geschichte, Disziplinen und Aufgaben, ed. FRITZ HEINEMANN, Stuttgart, 1959, pp. 450 f.)

cannot be left to the discretion of the individual. From the point of view of concrete living, of human society, the relevance of religion is, it seems, secondary to the relevance of the ethical, as far as the question of elementary necessity is concerned. For that reason the ethical became for modern man the criterion of religion and, if there is one at all, the approach to the understanding of religion. Religion must accredit itself by showing whether it is of service to morality – or alternatively, it must be content | to be considered a mere ornament of morality and as such superfluous, or even to be attacked as a hindrance to morality.[6] And the fact is, that life does go on even when religion has shrunk to a *quantité négligeable*. Life is in mortal danger, however, if it disintegrates where morals are concerned. That is the difference between the two historical turning points of the modern age: – The *emancipation of ethics* at the beginning of the modern age went hand in hand with optimism, progress, and undeniable advancement of life. The loss of religious tradition might be painful – yet the moral foundations were still preserved. On the other hand, the aspect of the moral crisis of today which conveys the impression of *emancipation from ethics* is incomparably more menacing because it touches the most elementary foundations of life and threatens to rob mankind of all hope.

It would spell the end of our existence as Christians and as theologians if the movement from Christian faith to morality were in fact one of climax from merely hypothetical necessity to categorical necessity.[7] And

---

[6] It is misleading to take the theology of A. RITSCHL, W. HERRMANN, and others, as characterized simply by this tendency and to speak of ethics here being given precedence over dogmatics (thus VAN OYEN, RGG³, II, col. 712) or of dogmatics threatening to dissolve into ethics (thus GLOEGE, *ibid.*, col. 226). Even KANT's hermeneutical instruction that the mysteries of the divine nature which are included in the doctrine of religion "must first be transformed into moral concepts" (Religion within the Limits of Reason Alone, translated by THEODORE M. GREENE and HOYT H. HUDSON, Preface to the second edition 1794, Chicago and London, 1934, p. 13), ought at least to be reflected upon before it is dismissed. Cf. ERNST FUCHS, "Bultmann, Barth und Kant," ThLZ, 16, 1951, cols. 461–468.

On W. HERRMANN's view of the hermeneutical significance of the ethical for theology cf., e.g.: "In order to understand Christian faith and the mental processes in which it develops, we must set out from the understanding of the ethical." "The understanding of the Gospel is hindered among us by nothing so much as by the prevailing confusion on the simplest ethical concepts. Only a morality which rests upon independent knowledge and therefore seeks to be nothing more than service to society, i.e., self-denial, brings men into the inner frame of mind in which they can understand that the appearance of Jesus Christ in this world, their encounter with him, is for them redemption" (Ethik, Tübingen, 1913⁵, reprinted in 1921, pp. 6 and V).

[7] That would mean in the first case: *if* you wish to take the question of religion seriously, *if* you wish eternal blessedness, *then* faith is indispensable to that end. In the second case, one cannot speak so hypothetically but must declare categorically: as the man you *are*, you are subject to the demands of morality. You lie, if you seek to dispute that and to evade it.

yet it will not do to meet the situation we have indicated simply by stating dogmatically that the present moral crisis is of course just the natural and long-prophesied result of the Western world's | religious crisis, of its emancipation from Christian faith. However true that is in the last resort, there would nevertheless be several questions to ask. For one: what failure on the part of Christianity allowed things to reach this stage at all? Further: what is actually the ultimate significance of the possibility of this dual phenomenon of a religious crisis, on the one hand, and on the other, a moral crisis which is at least temporally separated and certainly to be distinguished from it? And lastly: how can our proclamation establish the supremely helpful necessity of Christian faith precisely in regard to the concretely pressing problems of the present moral crisis? We must be clear about this: that the phrase "moral crisis of today" is a pale slogan masking a grim reality, and describes something which constitutes the utmost challenge to theology to give a theological account of itself – by no means only in regard to ethics either, but also precisely, and primarily, in regard to dogmatics.

In *one* respect Christian faith, too, must certainly grant the ethical an indisputable precedence: that the ethical has the character of concreteness, of what can be experienced, of the indubitable, the indispensable, and the evidently helpful, although, judged from the standpoint of faith, in a very limited and provisional sense. Even a neutral analysis of the ethical problem would confirm that it contains at heart the question, "What is man?" and therefore builds one way or another on definite ideological presuppositions and shares in their controversiality. Nevertheless the observance of a precedence of the ethical remains correct. The ethical problems do not allow of being shelved until there is unanimity on the other basic question.[8] They have the prerogative of what lies to hand, of what is concrete and realizable, of what may perhaps be only a very limited, imperfect, provisional help, but nevertheless a real one. One could even describe the special dignity of the ethical as the necessity of the preliminary, the inescapable task of giving first aid. That, however, is not by any means to say that the ethical problems thus characterized are no concern of theology. On the contrary, they are the decided concern of theology, as surely as the man who is exposed to these problems is the concern of theology. And theology is affected in a twofold way at that.

| For one thing, theology has to consider the problem of ethics precisely in the above-mentioned sense of first aid, i. e., in the sense of what the Reformers' theology comprised under the concept of the *primus usus legis*. For although the ethical has the prerogative of what is most immediately to hand and to that extent evident, yet we see again and again that men

---

[8] Cf. what R. Descartes says in the Discours de la méthode, Part III, admittedly on the basis of a different approach, about "provisional morality."

can be blind even to the immediate and evident. It is the business of theology also to care about the immediate and evident if need be, by bringing it to expression as such. The power of faith must show itself precisely in making us free also to such service. Hence to that extent theology's participation in the problem of ethics arises out of what in the narrower sense is the business of dogmatics. Yet let us beware of the simple step of letting this theological conception of the problem of ethics be narrowed down to a presentation merely of the fruits of faith, or of a revealed law. We would leave aside here the questions suggested by these stock phrases! On no account, however, may the theological treatment of the ethical problem be restricted to what concerns Christians alone and what can only on the presupposition of Christian faith be seen to be true and binding. Rather, theology must enter into the full range of the ethical problem, and thus also into the questions which exercise and trouble Christians and non-Christians alike, and on which a certain measure of agreement must be reached even in relative independence of the difference where faith is concerned – i. e., on what must be done, however provisionally, to maintain the humanity of human life.

Secondly, however, theology has to consider the problem of ethics from the standpoint of what is the real business of theology. To that extent the ethical problem has its place in the doctrine of the fundamental principles of dogmatics. For man, in his actual givenness as the object of demands and always the subject of past action, is a condition of the understanding of the message of faith. That must not be misconstrued as if man and his surrounding reality were first of all to be interpreted quite apart from the message of faith, in wholesale and uncritical acceptance of his own particular secular understanding of himself. If the message of faith is to have any meaning, then it must demonstrate its meaning, and therewith its necessity, precisely by illumining that given reality. That, however, demands that proclamation and reality should meet. Dogmatics is not keeping to its subject matter and must remain unintelligible, if the given reality which confronts our proclamation and without which | the proclamation would beat the air, lack concreteness and indeed an object, is not also present to dogmatics as a given fact; for with its presence or non-presence the truth of theological thinking and the intelligibility of all theological statements are at stake. To that extent ethical reflection on man in the reality which concerns and surrounds him has a hermeneutical function for theology as a whole. Here, to be sure, as always in the problem of understanding, we come upon the hermeneutical circle. Theology has no other means of making intelligible what it has to say than by seeking and reaching man in the ethical reality in which he finds himself. Yet it can seek and reach him there only if it is guided by the proper theme of theology and confirms its truth precisely by in fact reaching man in his reality.

Or to put it in the terminology of the Reformers: that which is the proper theme of theology – the Gospel – is expressible solely in relation to the *lex*. For the Gospel shows itself as Gospel solely in reference to the *lex* – namely, in the way of not becoming an unrelated supplement to the *lex* but entering in liberatingly upon the *lex*. Not the least of the confusions which blind and fetter man under the *lex* is that he cannot distinguish between an *usus civilis* and an *usus theologicus legis*. He cannot do so because he does not distinguish between law and Gospel. We could also say: he perverts ethics and does not grasp what theology is about, because he does not distinguish the two fields of what is valid *moraliter* and what is valid *theologice* and so set them in true relation to each other.[9]

I do not wish to enter here into the difficult problems of method which this sketchy exposition of my approach involves. I will rather, with the same unguardedness over against methodological criticisms, take the risk of embarking on an analysis of the phenomenon of the ethical, in order to make clear what is the business of theology. Perhaps that will open up a basic understanding of Christian mission, not in the propaganda-ridden sense of the self-assertion of an ideology and institution, but in the sense of being sent into the world to selfless service where the fires are hottest. |

II

If in what follows I speak of *compulsions toward an understanding of moral demands*, then I do not mean compelling proofs – these essentially cannot exist where it is a question of understanding and therefore of freedom – but I mean the indication of conditions of understanding which are given with human existence and have the character of creating need.

Let us start with what is plainly the most elementary basis of our being morally challenged: *the compulsion to act (Nötigung zum Wirken)*. To interpret this as an urge to activity caused by the bare necessity of maintaining an existence, would be superficial. If man did not act – and that in the ultimate sense includes even the seeming opposite, namely, reflective thought, prayerful contemplation – he would fall victim to the throes of boredom. Thus what compels man to action is time. That is indicated also by such expressions as putting in the time, passing the time, or even killing time. Here we come upon a most notable basic experience: time as empty time,[10] as pure potentiality, but therefore as an inescapable demand

---

[9] I must here refrain from an excursus on LUTHER's fundamental distinction between *"moraliter"* (*"civiliter"*) and *"theologice"* and the corresponding distinction of a *duplex iustitia (activa* and *passiva)* and a *duplex usus legis (civilis* and *theologicus)*. Cf. meanwhile my essay, "The Necessity of the Doctrine of the Two Kingdoms," in: Word and Faith, pp. 386–406.

[10] That is naturally a completely different thing from the view of time which

upon man, as a pressing basic law of his existence. If we dot not satisfy this demand in one way or another, if we do not now and then still the voice of this law, if we do not stop the maw of this voracious monster, then we ourselves are slain by it. For boredom kills. That of course is an extreme experience of time, but for that very reason an informative one. For the most part, time is thought of as definite possibility, as permission, as authorization, as a gift. The usual complaint is that we have no time, because it invites us to a thousand things at once. The desire to have more time, of course, likewise betrays the pressure of time. Not only as empty time in which freedom becomes a burdensome constraint, but also as time that is always already booked up and disposed of, in which freedom likewise turns to compulsion, time is a summons, a claim upon man. It is also possible, of course, for a man to live in harmony with the time that is given him, so that its character as a gift is brought out in thankfulness for time. But even then time is welcomed for the sake of the summons he is ready to accept. To be sure, we must look a long way to find a man who not only occasionally passes his time in such composure, but | also maintains it when time assumes the character of painful pressure. Even the very fact of its running out gives time a face man feels to be hostile. The radical disappearing of time is the disappearing of man himself. When its summons ceases, then precisely thereby its claim grows so radical and irresistible that it becomes the final summons to man and makes him so completely one with itself that he passes away along with time.

This character of compulsion about time has still to be considered explicitly in regard to how far it compels to action. We do not need at the moment to review the whole breadth of the field that comes into view here, but only to catch sight of the ultimate depth of this summons to act. Man is summoned to action for the reason that he is summoned to himself. For it is still an open question who he really is. Man has not come to grips with himself. He must therefore go beyond himself, as one who outwardly acts and forms. In all his forming, his own form is at stake, in all his action *(Wirken)* ultimately his own reality *(Wirklichkeit)*. As subject to the summons of time he is summoned to the realization *(Verwirklichung)* of himself. But can that be done by works *(Werke)*? And has it not a suspicious smack of the idealistic cult of personality, as if it were man's task to turn into a realization of his own image? That the summons is aimed at man himself certainly must not neutralize the fact of the summons to works. The claim which is constitutive of existence itself must not reduce to the vanishing point the individual claims, each of which demands something of man. The value and relevance of works must not be detracted

---

remains neutral towards any material definition and takes it as physically measured time.

from in favor of the radicalness of the summons which means the end of all works and therewith death. Throughout life the radical summons remains open and unfulfilled, however surely it is *this* summons which causes man to pay attention to the manifold claims addressed to him, to the abundance of opportunities for works. It is simply a fact that to take life seriously means to take works seriously. There is an aspect of human nature in the light of which one cannot speak urgently enough of the significance of works. They are the lasting tracks of man. They cleave *(haften)* abidingly to him as the past with which he himself is to be charged *(behaften)*. He does indeed build himself a memorial by them. The only question is, what is the "memo" which works as a literal "memo-rial" set before us for our reflection. Surely it takes the form of querying whether works answer to the summons, whether they have done justice to it, and indeed whether they ultimately can do justice to it at all. The radicalness of the summons points back behind the works to the mystery of the person. The self-realization to which man is compelled is more accurately | understood not as the erection of a memorial but as a consuming of himself, as a candle consumes itself in burning. That is why it is so natural that man, confronted by the summons to cope *(fertig werden)* with his life and himself, should try to meet the challenge by accomplishing something *(fertig bringen)*. The fear of annihilation drives him to creativity. In creative action he seeks consolation for his creaturely transience. But since the demand is made on man himself, it is one which, however much it is a compulsion to act, nevertheless cannot be satisfied by works.

That takes us a step further by bringing us now to consider the *compulsion to surrender (Nötigung zur Hingabe)*. If we have spoken of the claim *(Anspruch)*, we must now speak of the answer *(Entsprechung)* – and that, too, in such a way as to keep in view at one and the same time both the elements into which the compulsion to act divides itself: the fact of the summons to man himself as also of the summons to works – we can also say: the radical demand and the limited demands.[11] For the togetherness of these two aspects is manifestly decisive for the ethical problem.

That brings us into the wide field of the so-called material questions of ethics. However necessary it may be to follow Kant in thinking the ethical problem through to the uttermost on the point of its formal definition, and however confusing the situation becomes when we enter into the material questions of ethics, yet the important thing is precisely the transition from the claim, as compulsion to act, to the manner of the response. The two courses most commonly adopted here both seem to me inadequate, *viz.* –

---

[11] I refer – also for what follows – to the book by K. E. Løgstrup, Die ethische Forderung, Tübingen, 1959, to which I owe individual suggestions. The far-reaching material agreement between us arose independently of each other from a parallel theological approach.

to let oneself be guided either by a legal codex written in man's heart or by
a hierarchically ordered system of values. The first course does at least bring
out the basic ethical phenomenon as a being summoned, called, claimed, even
if it would be more appropriate to interpret that not in the sense of codified
laws but as the question mark branded on the heart of man.[12] On the other
hand, in so-called value ethics there lies the correct reflection that the
demand is never the primary thing: it would become meaningless if
nothing preceded it. If I may be allowed a word-play which is etymologi-
cally not unjustified: a thing can be *geboten* (i. e., demanded) only where
something is *geboten* (i. e., tendered, given). The problem of material ethics
must take its bearings on the gifts | which constitute the reality of human
nature. The commandments are the call to observe responsibility for what
is given. The commandment to honor our parents is preceded by the gift
which is committed and entrusted to us in the form of father and mother.
We must avail ourselves of that gift and take responsibility for it, that is,
let father be father and mother be mother. Or if the demand is negative,
e. g., "thou shalt not kill," then the starting point is the life of my fellowman,
which as a piece of fellow-humanity is so far committed and entrusted to me
as to be put right into my hands. It would lie in my power to kill it. Yet in
doing so I would destroy not only the gift itself but – what is ultimately
still more serious – the trust shown towards me in committing it to me.[13]
The way in which man responds by his action to the claim made on him is
thus careful handling of what is given, responsible use of the gifts.

The phrase, "compulsion to surrender," *(Hingabe)* points to that. It could
be taken simply as an obvious reference to the fact that existence is action
and as such goes on in alternate giving and taking. The man who wishes to
have and achieve something must pay the price. The man who is unable to
give up anything will not gain anything. There is no success without effort,
no victory without sacrifice. But these slogans do not reach the basic
moral fact. For in place of the gift bestowed on man they put the gift
which man himself chooses to give – and thus in place of the claim made
on man the claim man makes. Surrender, however, properly understood, is
not the paying of a purchase price in order to get something else in exchange, but the way man takes the part of his fellowman, of a thing, of a
task, of what is entrusted to him, the way he accepts responsibility for it
and takes care for the well-being of what is entrusted to him. Surrender
means dedicating oneself to what is given into one's hands. That this
phrase "compulsion to surrender" brings to expression a fundamental
evidentness of the ethical can be plainly exemplified by the mother given

---

[12] Cf. my essay, "Theological Reflections on Conscience," in: Word and Faith,
pp. 407–423, esp. p. 420; also pp. 278 f.

[13] Cf. LØGSTRUP's remarks (pp. 7 ff.) on "Trust and its elementary relatedness
to human existence."

over to the care of her child, the child given over to its play, the craftsman given over to his work. Here we see compulsions so strong that it seems absurd to seek to command explicitly what is urged by the gifts themselves (i.e., the child, the plaything, or the piece of work): the gift arouses surrender.

| But now, this characterization, which has enabled us to see conscientiousness, responsibility, gratitude, joy, trust, and love as basic phenomena of ethics, was attained on the basis of the undisturbed gift–surrender (*Gabe – Hingabe*) relationship. The moral problem, however, becomes a burning one only when the gift–surrender relationship is disturbed in some way and the compulsion to surrender does in fact demand the paying of a price, the bringing of a sacrifice, in order to have the gift (in the double sense of "preserving" and "attaining" it). That poses the problem of the limits of surrender – on the one hand, as the lower limit below which its moral character disappears, on the other hand, as the upper limit, to surpass which appears to be going beyond morality.

I would elucidate the problem of the lower limit with the help of a fact by which life in human society is largely determined today: the disappearance of the phenomenon of morality as a result of impersonalization. Human life is dividing up more and more into various fields in which relationships are reduced to definite rules of play, dictated by technical and impersonal considerations. The supplanting of the ethical by the merely conventional has always existed. And it is not without reason either that wide fields of human relations are regulated by prescribed forms. They are a sort of precautionary measure, not merely against the possibility of moral failure, but also against our being too intensively challenged. One could hold that today there have only arisen new forms of convention in order to master the effects of the technological world upon human relations. It is plainly a peculiar feature of this modern development, however, that the human element is ever more strongly edged out or neutralized by technical necessities. To be sure, even today the smooth functioning of the gigantic machine of human society is dependent on an incalculable factor, man himself, who happens to be not merely a functionary but occasionally of his own accord exercises responsibility, or lets that kind of independence be found wanting precisely at the few points at which the system of automation still depends on the factor of moral decision. The ethical is today being edged out more and more forcibly into the realm of private life. And even there the field within which the manner of answering claims is left open is shrinking. The possibilities for the human element are shriveling to the scantiest. But apart from the sphere of private life moral problems are dissolving into technical questions which only the specialist can answer. For others it seems impossible here to reach their own responsible judgments and decisions. One of the most urgent tasks of the study of ethics | today is therefore to examine how amid the so-called self-contained laws of the individual realms of life the specifically human aspect, i. e., the responsibility for man, presses for recognition, so that attendance on machines is regulated from the standpoint of the service of man. The compulsion to surrender contains within it the distinction between person and thing and the dominance of man over things.

That raises the problem of the upper limit of the compulsion to surrender. How far does man's responsibility reach, extensively and intensively? Admittedly it can sometimes also be necessary to focus a man's moral responsibility within narrower limits than he likes to believe. Man is capable not only of exercising too little responsibility but also of laying on himself or taking to himself too much. In general man appears to have only a narrow circle for which he bears responsibility and in which he can thus be addressed as morally involved. Yet it would be worth considering whether responsibility is not after all measured by what affects man himself and involves him. We are all too painfully aware that we are indeed involved today by global decisions in the face of which, it seems, we are nevertheless completely powerless and relieved of all share of responsibility. But is it not the case that, in spite of everything, the fact of our being involved gives us also a share of responsibility, and that contrary to all outward appearances there are things that make it possible and necessary to exercise our own responsibility even in world-wide problems? Even if it is in an entirely different way from the few who hold the reins of world events, we too in our outward impotence are summoned by those events to a responsibility which, if we rightly recognized it, would let us recognize also the limits of our impotence. But that gives rise to the question as to the measure of surrender on the intensive side. If surrender means surrendering oneself – how does that take concrete shape? Certainly, by answering to the summons to works, primarily in surrender of something that falls within the realm of possession and ability, and thus in surrender of values or in giving up time. But how far can that be expected? Where does the compulsion to surrender take its bearings from if in the last resort it is to be vindicable as surrender of oneself?

We now carry our reflections a stage further from the standpoint of the *compulsion to put right (Nötigung zum Zurechtbringen)*. Only here do we enter the field of the distinction of good and evil which is fundamental to ethics. To that extent in referring to the compulsion to act and the compulsion to surrender we were | still in the forecourt of ethics and it was only the observations on the disturbance of the gift – surrender relationship that pointed us beyond it.

If the phrase, "compulsion to put right," is to help us further at this point, then that means: the knowledge of what is good is not inferred from abstract ideas, but is experienced in the encounter with evil. Let us leave aside the question as to where it is appropriate to ask about the good in itself and about a hierarchy of values, and therefore also about the relation of good and being. At all events, it is hardly appropriate where we ask what can force itself inescapably on every man. The question as to what is morally good is experienced concretely under the compulsion of evil, and thus in compelling need. Good is then primarily a qualification not of being but of happening.[14] Good is what makes good, i. e., what is superior to evil, is able to overcome it, to make good again the disturbance or even destruction caused by evil, to set wrong right. There is something immediately convincing about the understanding of "good" as the power of making good. Anyone can see that vigorously taking the part of the man who has fallen among thieves and effectively countering the evil done there, is a good deed. And it is surely equally convincing that the person whose mere presence itself makes good and banishes evil is truly to be called good. We know of at least analogous experiences: a cheerful man is a man who makes cheerful, a free man one who makes free, or *e contrario*, a perverted man is a perverter of men.[15]

In order to discover the basic things which compel an understanding of the ethical, we must take our bearings on what in actual fact happens and necessarily has to happen. What is morally necessary becomes evident from what threatens man in his human relations. In order to expose ourselves to the problem of ethics, we must | keep our eyes on the concrete threats to human relations and remain constantly in contact with the sort of situations in which the problem of the ethical is painfully felt. That accords with the structure of responsible action as it comes to light in the basic professions: the farmer wards off hunger, the doctor sickness, the judge injustice, the teacher foolishness, etc. Likewise there is significance in defining the ethical in the light of the need that has to be met.

But what is the need which makes the ethical necessary? What is it that I am morally summoned to put right? At bottom nothing that requires putting right is exempted from finding its way into the realm of ethical problems and becoming an object of moral responsibility, so far as man is

---

[14] This alternative is formulated with an eye on the prevailing ontological tradition. M. HEIDEGGER's way of inquiring into being, of course, rightly calls in question this usual distinction of "being" and "happening."

[15] The structural kinship with the interpretation of *iustus esse* as *iustificari*, which was so significant for LUTHER's basic discovery at the Reformation (e.g. WA. 56, p. 172, 4 [Scholion on Rom. 1:17, 1515/16]: '*Iustitia Dei*' *non ea debet accipi, qua ipse Iustus est in seipso, Sed qua nos ex ipso Iustificamur, quod fit per fidem euangelii*, i. e.: The "justice of God" is not to be taken as that by which God is "just" in himself, but as that by which we are justified by him, which happens through faith in the Gospel. Cf. RGG³, IV, cols. 498 and 500) raises questions regarding the relation of theology and ontology which cannot be further discussed here. – Cf., however, also Plato's definition of ἀγαθόν (good) as σῷζον καὶ ὠφελοῦν (salutary and beneficial), and of κακόν (evil) as ἀπολλύον καὶ διαφθεῖρον (destroying and corrupting), *Polit.* X, 608e.

affected by it. Every need that affects man becomes a moral summons to remedial intervention. Yet we must inquire explicitly into the scope of that statement: which man under a threat has so much to do with me that I am summoned to remedial help? The approach of natural law has usually been content with the negative formula: *neminem laede* – do nobody wrong, stand on no one's toes. Yet that sets out from a completely abstract view of reality, as if man were first of all something on his own and the relation to his fellowman were a secondary addition. Rather, man existing on his own, apart from his fellowmen, is an unreal ghost of a man. And it is likewise a sign of an abstract conception of reality when the principle *"neminem laede"* simply presupposes inviolateness as a given fact. As if any man ever found himself in the state of unviolated human relations! The true and only serious urge to ethical reflection is the fellowman who is already wronged, the one already humiliated and offended, whose toes we have stood on perhaps precisely by failing to allow him to come near us, to encroach upon us, hurt us, drag us into his suffering. Hence it accords with the evident fact of human relations having been already impaired, when we set out from the compulsion to put right and interpret that compulsion as the call to love our neighbor. The fact is, that the command to love our neighbor, in the radical sense of love also to the seemingly furthest off, to our enemy, is to be asserted and upheld as the obvious and the truly reasonable thing. Otherwise it would be robbed of its stringent bindingness and its elementary significance. Thus to the man who did not understand what love of our neighbor means, Jesus held up nothing else but a picture of life itself, i. e., of what everyone has a chance to see if he | opens his eyes: take your cue from the man who has fallen among thieves – he knows who his neighbor is.[16] By this means we are helped to see the self-evident. And likewise by the assurance: "What ye have done unto one of the least of these my brethren, ye have done unto me."[17] That Jesus identifies himself with the needy is certainly not to say that only for this reason is the latter worthy of help.[18] Rather, Jesus appeals to the evident-

---

[16] Lk. 10: 25–37.   [17] Mt. 25: 40.

[18] The "blessed of the Father" have as little idea of having done something to Jesus as those who are "cursed" for their failure have any idea that they have been guilty of failing Jesus. Those who took the part of the hungry, homeless, sick, and lonely had done so simply because they saw the need as a plain opportunity to intervene remedially. They did what impressed itself on them in this case as reasonable, because necessary. The interpolation of the idea that it was to be done for Jesus' sake would threaten to ruin the whole. The others, it is true, thought themselves excused by the fact that they had not been aware of meeting Jesus in their poor afflicted fellowman: had they known that, then they would naturally have found it another matter; then – not because of the obvious need of a fellowman, but because of the obvious future glory of the Son of Man – they would of course not have failed. But that would be a complete contradiction of what Jesus is after. The criterion is

ness | attaching to the claim of the person in need, and uses that evidentness to verify himself. This claim of my fellowman is the claim of Jesus himself. The intelligibility of this claim makes the claim of Jesus intelligible. The man who has no eyes for his fellow's need can have no eyes for the claim of Jesus.

We have been reflecting on the compulsion to put right, from the standpoint of the question: which man under a threat has so much to do with me that I am summoned to remedial help? We were driven to the insight that the demand to love our neighbor is simply true, i.e., expresses what is demanded by the reality of human relations as everyone has occasion to experience it. At all events, as one himself in need, every man understands the love shown to him by his neighbor (or the absence of it) and – rightly – considers it reasonable that the man who can help also does help. It belongs to the essence of this demand that it is radical. It goes beyond all given relations to our fellowmen as decreed by kinship, friendship, comradeship, nationality or the like, and summons us to pure cohumanity. It likewise goes beyond all given forms of convention by leaving open the question as to what manner of putting right, what degree of surrender, is demanded from one case to another. The demand is radical because it requires that what is right – right because it puts right and thus is necessary – be done in personal responsibility.

With that we come upon a tension peculiar to the ethical. The radical

---

not whether greatness and glory, but whether wretchedness and need, are so plain to us that we let ourselves be concerned and involved in them. Thus the historizing interpretation is not valid either – that the people in question naturally could not yet have known what an exalted personality had met them in the guise of the poor; that the one group was lucky without knowing it, whereas once the secret is known it is of course not enough simply for the need alone to be an impulse to help; that the lustre of a good work now attaches to such action only as a pious work done explicitly for Jesus' sake. Religious argumentation of that kind is a grotesque distortion of moral necessity. Then of course it would be up to the righteous to say instead of Mt. 25:37–39: "Lord, we were fully aware of that, and indeed we were counting on it: if it had been a case not of you but merely of our fellowmen, then of course we'd not have done it!" Cf. here W. HERRMANN's cutting remarks: "Morality is poisoned at the roots the moment a certain thought which is admittedly sacred in the eyes of every religious man is made the *ground* [my italics] of moral conviction, *viz.* – the thought that the moral law is the law of God. It is a thought which we Christians of course would not wish to live without. If, however, we really see in it the ground of our moral conviction, then we have no moral conviction at all. On the contrary, our conviction has then a twofold content which has nothing to do with morality but can be an expression of profound immorality. Then, in the first place, we are possessed by the idea that we must bow before an omnipotent Will, and secondly, we imagine that we are told what this Will demands of us. The first can be a cowardly idea, the second one of self-deceit. Yet that is the attitude millions of men who think themselves truly moral and pious have inwardly adopted." (Gesammelte Aufsätze, ed. by F. W. SCHMIDT, Tübingen, 1923, pp. 407 f.).

demand as it arises from his co-humanity exceeds what man is able to do. Without being exonerated from it, he is yet at the same time dependent on ordered social relations and ways of behaving, on given forms of community, of custom, of law, which are not for him to decide, but in which at any moment the depth of the radical demand can make itself felt and beyond which it can call to action that is non-standardized, extraordinary, of a kind that must be freely discovered and embraced. The phenomenon of the ethical comes properly into view only when attention is paid to both of these factors in their tension with each other. If the ethical phenomenon were restricted to action on the lines that are already laid down by given rules and regulations, then the decisive thing would be passed by as surely as if it were limited to the radical demand of co-humanity. Only the respecting of both these dimensions of the ethical phenomenon accords with the compulsion to put right. The radical demand, upheld in isolation, would destroy the forms of man's common existence, and therewith man himself. The definite and limited demands of social | life, likewise taken in isolation, would cause the human element in man to waste away. The radical demand can hold us to deeper and more conscientious, more personal, and more loving observance of the limited demands, and these in turn can train us to more concrete observance of the radical demand. Yet conflict is inevitable. The limited demands have the tendency to obscure the radical demand and to consider the putting right completed when the accustomed order is preserved. The radical demand has the tendency to relativize the limited demands and to be misconstrued as if the thing to do were to follow in fanatical disregard of them the compulsion to put right, instead of upholding the limited demands precisely for the sake of the radical demand and assuming responsibility for their correct observance – or else, as the case may be, for their remedial transformation. The radical demand is undoubtedly misunderstood when we relegate the ethical problem entirely to the sphere of the so-called questions of individual ethics and do not take up the problems of the shaping of law and custom, of social and economic forms – that is, when we inquire merely into man's conduct *(Verhalten)* in the individual moral decision, but do not also take responsibility as well for the ethical relevance of the shaping of his circumstances *(Verhältnisse)*. But even thus associating the two with each other does not exempt from the conflict as to how the radically interpreted demand is related to life amid the social necessities of every day.

What is the source of the conflict? And why does the ethical phenomenon split into these two dimensions of radical demand and limited demands at all? That leads us to the root of what really requires to be put right. If it were a case merely of threats to man from without, then (so far as human fellow-feeling can be the object of a summons) ethics ought to be no problem. Then everything would be done that can be done by men in order to help the person in trouble. And what is not in man's power to alter would be borne as such in compassion. But now we have above all to do with the trouble that arises through man himself, and indeed from his failure in co-humanity *(Mitmenschlichkeit)*. It is here that the chief problem of ethics comes to be concentrated: – What means is there of putting right not only the consequences of failure in co-humanity, but also the failure in co-humanity itself? How is man, so deeply threatened by himself, to be put right? How can co-humanity put right the failure in co-humanity? How can man put man right? The real root of the moral problem is man – and that, too, not | merely in so far as he is summoned to action, called to surrender, compelled to put right, but above all, and in the midst of it all, because he falls short of his summons and his calling in manifold ways and is therefore in the first instance himself one who requires putting right, who leaves undone what he is called to do, who cannot be depended on, who becomes a menace to his fellowmen, but, before that, has all along become a menace to himself and got into contradiction with himself.

The reason why there is a radical demand is, that the troubles afflicting man from without and within arise from a source that is inexhaustible, and grow to immeasurable dimensions, so that man has to be put right from the roots. That, however, is why there is also the whole range of limited demands, which seek to enable men to live together in spite of broken co-humanity and in the midst of it – which thus, in ways that are provisional and not by any means thoroughgoing, but nevertheless temporarily effective and to that extent very necessary and up to a point also salutary, restrain and partially put right the consequences of the menace man is to himself. The fact that the split between the radical demand and the limited demands is a source of conflict points, however, to the fact that the problem of the ethical is manifestly not ethically solvable. For how should man when he is a menace to himself be able to free himself from that menace? How should man at odds with himself be able to put himself right and come to grips with himself? Yet how, either, should man when he is a menace to himself fail to feel the compulsion to put right, and refuse to let himself be summoned to a task which, when we look at the immediate circumstances, is not by any means void of meaning and of success, yet when we probe to the bottom is an apparently hopeless, impossible task? We ought not to underestimate what man can achieve in the way of self-discipline. But it would be an illusion to imagine that the man who is a menace to himself will be more completely put right the more he takes pains with himself. If anything could put him right, it must come from without, from his fellowmen. Indeed, the most important way for a man to become neighbor to another, to take his part, to care for him and take responsibility for him, would be to yield to the compulsion to put right his fellowman who is a menace to himself and his fellows. The truly good work, because the one that makes good the source of evil, would be for a man to take the part of another in such a way as to free him from the menace he is to himself. At this point there opens up first of all the wide field of our daily, mostly unconscious influences on each other, even to the length of education and spiritual guidance. Though | ultimately we may be skeptical of success, penultimately the thing to do is to give ourselves over completely to this very task. What is here neglected, or even made worse than ever, contributes decisively to the moral crisis of today. The fact that here we come upon a limit to the effect one man can have on another, the fact that man who has such unprecedented capacities experiences the impotence in which he stands helpless before the helplessness of a fellowman, who is helpless because he is at odds with himself – that must not become a reason to despair of putting right here and now whatever is humanly possible. But it should give ground to reflect on the causes of such impotence.

Just here, where the problem of ethics and the theme of theology are but a hairbreadth apart, we must beware of prematurely discarding moral responsibility – e. g., on the pretext that, of course, it is self-evident that no man can really help another, since *each* is surely man and as such a menace to himself. There would first of all – penultimately, of course – still be much food for thought regarding the causes of the inability to put our fellowman right. Instead of merely complaining, say, about his obtuseness, unconscientiousness, and obduracy, we might ask whether particular circumstances contribute towards making a man unaddressable, and even de-humanize him to such an extent that he can no longer be addressed on his own account and as his own self. Our impotence in face of our fellowman can, of course, also have its cause in the failure to consider what must be the nature of the power that can avail here. What we usually understand by "power" can only do the opposite of what would here be required. To be sure, there are dreadful techniques of molding men by which, it seems, men can be made into anything. But to force a man to rights according to a particular plan is the very opposite of putting him right. Methods of physical and mental violation can indeed achieve a great deal, but the one thing they cannot achieve is precisely this: to put a man right as man. For to that end it would be necessary to give him freedom – not merely to allow him the freedom he has (that alone can sometimes also mean a great deal for putting right human relations!), but to give him the freedom he does not have. That is essentially impossible by means of compulsion and force. For that there is no technique. And for that the consciousness of impotence is more promising than the will to power. Here we put our finger on the sorest point. Who has this freedom, that he can give freedom to another? It is a question here not merely of the method, but of the thing itself. It would not be enough to say: man must be put right *in* freedom. Rather, the essential thing is: | man must be put right *to* freedom. Precisely that is what is meant by "putting him right." That, however, is a matter for the power *(Macht)* which is called authority *(Vollmacht)*, and which is often closely akin to impotence *(Ohnmacht)*. The lack of authority is lack of freedom. But is that not to leave the sphere of what is morally binding and can be morally expected? Perhaps. But at least does as much liberating co-humanity take place as lies within the bounds of what can be expected?

That question leads us finally to include in our reflections also the *compulsion to render account (Nötigung zur Rechenschaft)*. This aspect is not tacked on as a supplement to the ones already discussed – the compulsion to act, to surrender, and to put right – so that one could well recognize these, yet deny a compulsion to render account. Rather, it is of the essence of compulsion, as we are discussing it in this whole context, that it is not taken as coercion in the causal sense, but as a compulsion to the exercise of freedom, and thus not as something which relieves of responsibility, but as something which is to be responsibly embraced. Only what is done in freedom, and what man therefore also assumes responsibility for, is action, surrender, putting right. The fact that responsibility is an essential part of human nature, and that without the compulsion to render account human society would be impossible, is beyond dispute. That can be made clear (superfluously enough) from the concept of accountability. Only the manner and measure of human responsibility can be controversial. From our experience of accounting as one man owes it to another, we know only graduated and limited obligations to render account. No man owes an absolute account of himself to another. Yet it must not be inferred from that that responsibility is limited to the concrete encounter with a fellowman to whom I have to render account of myself. Man's responsibility extends further than the field within which it is possible for one man to call another to account. The standpoint of ethics is strictly affirmed only when man's responsibility is not confined within the limits of rendering account between man and man.

The universality of responsibility is shown by the fact that we know ourselves urged to conscientiousness even when we are subject to no one's control and no one could call us to account. To be sure, how far conscientiousness does in fact carry weight with us apart from the supervision and inquiry of a fellowman, is another question. Yet there is an indisputable tendency toward it in the compulsion to honest exercise of the reason. For my own sake I am compelled to distinguish between truth and falsehood, and | to render myself critical account of the fact that I am not deceiving myself. Man is dependent upon certainty, however often he may sin against this elementary compulsion to clear-cut thinking. Thinking means rendering oneself account. Reason itself has the structure of responsibility.

Between man's rationality and morality there is a close connection. That, on the one hand, he is the ζῷον λόγον ἔχον [the animal having the power of *logos*, i.e., of both "reason" and "word"] and, on the other hand, the being who is compelled λόγον διδόναι [to give reason], to which λόγον αἰτεῖν [to ask reason] appropriately corresponds, are facts which arise from one and the same root: as one who has the power of *logos* he owes word and answer *(Antwort)*, he is answerable *(verantwortlich)*. Morality is thus not a supplement to reason. We could rather ask whether what is called moral accountability does not materially precede what is usually designated as mental accountability. Thinking manifestly belongs in the realm of morality, so that it is a moral obligation to think, while thinking is also bound to be morally responsible.

That brings us to the fundamental definition: man has his existence in the word-event. It is no chance that precisely the fundamental ethical category "responsibility" with its implied forum-structure of being compelled to render account – whether to oneself, to another human authority, or to God – brings us to the linguisticality *(Sprachlichkeit)* of man. The addressability of man and his own power of speech, which from the abstract point of view precede every word-event, would nevertheless be nothing without participation in the word-event. Man, it is true, is endowed by nature with the power of speech, yet he must first learn to speak by having speech spoken in front of him [*vorgesprochen*, i.e., in the sense in which, e. g., a teacher speaks words to be repeated and so learned by a child] – or more correctly, by being addressed in definite language by his fellowman. For that reason man is addressable, accountable, and responsible only thanks to the actual fact of having already had experience of his fellowman. Or what is the same thing: man's historicness always derives from history that has already happened to him. To that extent co-humanity is a condition of the possibility of responsibility.

If it is to be meaningful to speak of responsibility to God, then that cannot be a case of a new and isolated kind of responsibility, but only of the truth, depth, and radically concrete form of man's single responsibility. Responsibility to God is intelligible only *in*, and not *alongside*, responsibility to ourselves and therefore only *in*, and not *alongside*, responsibility to our fellows – although this unity in turn is understandable only in virtue of the correct distinction between "*coram Deo*," "*coram hominibus*," and "*coram seipso*." If the *distinction* is necessary, then it is in the interest of the | proper grasp of the *one* responsibility, the *one* linguisticality of man which is at stake amid the maze and multiplicity of languages. Man would lose his responsibility if he lost that unity absolutely. He would become speechless as it were, or would at least fall into a barbarification of his linguisticality, if he were content with a plurality of unrelated languages – a language of reason, a language of inter-human relations, and a religious language. For each of the separate languages would then become an unintelligible language, and man, ultimately condemned to unintelligibility, would cease to find it a language at all.

It may cause surprise that with the compulsion to render account our reflections on the evidentness of the ethical should issue in observations on the problem of language. In the realm of ethics – so it is usually thought – the movement is exclusively from word to act in the sense of the realization of the word. Words appear to be things which need realization. Now, however, it has been shown that in the ethical itself there takes place a reversal of this, the only relation usually considered between word and act: act necessitates word. Certainly, words seek to be done; but deeds must be answered for. From the standpoint of the compulsion to render account, the word – namely, the word of justification, excuse, or as it may be of accusation and condemnation – follows the act which has been done, or possibly left undone. Word now becomes necessary precisely because what has happened can no longer be altered by any deed.

That of course is not the only way in which act and word belong together from the standpoint of responsibility. If action is the way in which man replies to the challenge of a multitude of claims, then action, too, has itself to be understood as a response. Man's deeds have word-character. It can be learned from them whether he has understood something of the situation in which he finds himself, or whether he completely misunderstands it. It can become plain from a man's deeds – more clearly and more convincingly than by words – what is in the man. A very ordinary deed can be uncommonly eloquent and significant. It can awaken hope and plunge into despair, it can – not in its immediate effect as a deed, but in its effect on the understanding, and thus in its word-effect – open up a whole world, but also destroy a world. For deeds give food for thought. They interpret, but also require interpretation and show themselves in this their hermeneutical character to be, like everything that bears the stamp of man, a form of the word-event. As response to | a claim, action is thus itself observance of responsibility as required at the moment in question.[19]

---

[19] As an example, take a simple story like that of the Good Samaritan (Lk. 10: 30–35). Quite appropriately it is only at the end, in the instruction and promise to the innkeeper, that the style of direct speech is employed. All that precedes can have been done without a word. The act of the robbers may, of course, have been accompanied by the strong language of gangster jargon; but that was non-language of non-men. That the passing by of priest and Levite took place in silence is as much part of the situation as that the half-dead victim could do no more than groan. The Samaritan's action will not have been accompanied by talk. What need is there of words when one is doing the obvious?! The rescued man will have been able at most to reply with a look. Thus an encounter in which the one and only important thing was the helping, rescuing deed, and words of any kind were not only superfluous but out of place. A wordless event – and yet pack full of word-event! We could lose ourselves in an inexhaustible task of interpretation: framing and expressing in

But now, this identification of act and word can also be reversed. Words can be deeds. Not just as a shameful substitute where deeds might be expected, but in such a way that in special cases a word can be a deed in a far deeper sense than outward deeds can be. Thus on occasion a word can be the greatest blessing and help. In the light of | this its highest potentiality, however, everything we say has a special measure of responsibility imparted to it, in accordance with Jesus' saying: "By thy words thou shalt be justified, and by thy words thou shalt be condemned."[20] In the fact that this measure of responsibility devolves on our *word* of all things, so that the compulsion to render final account is the compulsion to render account of what we have said, and it is not our acts but our words that here appear as the factor by which the judgment is determined, this much becomes plain: words are the most significant acts of man, because they are the means by which the claim which at the present moment has to be replied to and answered for, and thus the response character of human conduct, can be quite conspicuously fulfilled or quite disastrously missed.

---

words what was uttered here. As one who was impotent and no longer capable of speaking, the victim was an unprecedentedly powerful and unequivocally intelligible summons to every man. Those who passed him by heard it well enough. They belong to the story only as those who failed to respond to the call. The man who obeyed the call, on the other hand, made clear not only that he had understood *(verstanden)* but more than that: that he gave his consent *(Einverständnis)* to the man who constituted the call. The act of mercy was done wordlessly, not because it meant nothing *(nichtssagend)*, but because it was so obvious, so human, so encouraging, quite apart from offering practical first aid. It was entirely word. It spoke for itself. Any talk could only have weakened and endangered the word-event that was taking place in this deed, not enhanced it. That is confirmed also by any attempts at interpretation. We may of course on occasion employ psychological feeling for the situation to *express* what it really is that so *impresses* us about this story. Far beyond what we have said, however, the word-event enshrined in it evinces itself in the fact that the story has become a text that will never lose its appositeness and power as long as there is evil and suffering, hard-heartedness and a glimmer of a hope of sympathetic love. Yet such a text in its tendency towards becoming present word-event in the proclamation can hardly be done justice to by that kind of descriptive interpretation, whose additions threaten rather to destroy what gives the text its linguistic force, *viz.* – the very fact that it does not make everything explicit but expects us to hear the language of this text as a language of facts *(Tatsachen)* – not abstract, "bare" facts, but concrete and eloquent "matters of doing" *("Tat-Sachen")*. It is here indeed that the real word-character of such a story lies. Its words do not aim at registering the facts of what has happened, but at making room for the word-character of what is reported. Because the recorded event itself speaks such a powerful language, the narrative must be | as sparing as possible in its own use of language, so as not to point in some way to the past but to let the forward-pointing language of what has happened come to expression. To do justice to such a text in the sermon would mean, not to elaborate it in some way, but to let it authorize us to respect its complete clarity as well as its stringent silence in such a way as to charge the hearer with the question who his neighbor is, to show him the obvious and lead him to see it as a matter of course to love one's neighbor.   [20] Mt. 12:36f.

The exercise of responsibility in the sense of the response given in the course of a man's existence to the claims that challenge him, and thus in the sense of the present observance of responsibility, sometimes takes place in its purest form by means of the spoken word. Of all the things one man owes another, word is in one respect the foremost. There can be situations in which a man longs for nothing so much as a good word, and in which consequently one man can give another nothing greater than a word and incurs no greater guilt than by failing in that respect. Indeed, in everything one man does to another the decisive, the really human thing, is the word that takes place, possibly unspoken, in such action.

Yet however much act and word belong together in present observance of responsibility, there still remains a difference between that and the subsequent compulsion to render account of how man on each occasion has in fact observed responsibility. That is made peculiarly impressive by the fact that it is not only in regard to action that there is a compulsion to render subsequent account, but also more than ever in regard to the words we have spoken. The word that has taken place must still be completed by the word of accounting as another aspect of the word-event. No deed, not even a deed in the form of a spoken word, can be left to itself. It becomes complete only through | what follows it – and indeed not only through the consequences of the deed in the usual sense of the often unforeseeable effects occasioned by it, but above all through the accounting that follows it, through the word in which what was done is answered for in consequence of man's being summoned to a responsibility which now cannot possibly be observed by acting, but only by word – or by its negative mode silence, if we have nothing to say in justification. What a man has done is not over once it is done: rather, it only now becomes really relevant through the man's being compelled to adopt an attitude towards it, to identify himself with it. For what has really and ultimately to be accounted for is man himself. He is summoned to answer for himself in his selfhood. That is the bracket joining the two modes of applying the concept "responsibility": in the sense of present observance or exercise of responsibility by means of deeds that are also words and words that are also deeds, as also in the sense of rendering account, the vehemently compelling character of which lies in the fact that while life lasts it never comes to an end but is still also future. No definitive declaration by a human tribunal is able to crush the compulsion to render account and put it finally to silence as it can be voiced again and again in the conscience. The suit in which man is involved as one called to responsibility, as one summoned to render account, never comes to an end during this life. For the court of conscience there is no statute of limitations, and no discharged cases. Because man himself is the object of responsibility, the responsibility suit, including also that of responsibility for the past, goes on as long as he lives.

III

In examining the phenomenon of the ethical we occasionally came upon a boundary which it did not itself take us beyond, but did point beyond. It manifestly belongs to the essence of ethics that its problems stretch into dimensions in which it is not competent, into the realm of questions which cannot be mastered from the ethical standpoint.

We must be cautious of concluding from that without more ado that the business of theology is thus legitimized by ethics. The existence of unsolved problems does not justify the acceptance of any solution that offers itself. Pointing out religious needs does not *eo ipso* prove the truth of faith. It might well be that beyond ethics | there remains nothing else to be said but to declare an insoluble ethical aporia which we are not permitted to veil behind religious illusions. The last thing we can say might well be that man must cope with himself, and in fact cope precisely with the experience of being unable to cope with himself. It would be an apologetic illusion if we were to hold that by showing the need which the above-mentioned compulsions in the ethical realm not only point back to but also lead into, we have already proved the necessity of theology. A postulated necessity is not enough, but it requires a necessity which happens and establishes itself, a necessity *(Notwendigkeit)* which shows itself to be need-meeting *(Not wendend)*. The reality of what meets a need must be verified by the reality of the need.

In what we have said of the compulsions toward an understanding of the ethical there are above all two places where theology must show its justi-fication in terms of the problem of the ethical. Our reflections on the com-pulsion to put right showed that man himself as the ultimate source of menace requires to be put right by means of the love that springs from freedom and opens up freedom. If theology has to do with what is absolute-ly necessary to man, and consequently with what concerns him not apart from morality but in the midst of the moral compulsions and thereby shows its supreme necessity, then the authority and the freedom to exercise liberat-ing love will be included in the business of theology. But can this necessary element, then, be presented in any other way than by liberating love actually happening? However mistaken the moralistic reduction of Chris-tian faith to practical love may be, it contains in spite of abysmal misunder-standing this one element of truth: that faith must certainly be charged with being the herald, the κῆρυξ, of love. And in a much more profound sense than the above moralistic one, it could be true that believing is the occurrence of liberating love. Then, however, would the only meaningful thing not be to *live* faith as authority to exercise liberating love? Or is it meaningful, and indeed absolutely necessary, for that very reason to *speak* of faith?

It was a help here that we had pursued the analysis to the point of indicating the compulsion to render account. That indicated the second place at which theology must show its justification in terms of the problem of the ethical. The concept of responsibility opened up the many-sided connection of act and word, and we learned that man himself is the object of responsibility. That implies something more. I will venture to make it explicit by saying: man has to answer for the world, indeed he has to answer for God. Thus theology, if its business is to be what is absolutely necessary, must | have to do with the word-event, which is bound up in so many ways with the phenomenon of the ethical and yet is not itself a thing to be mastered by ethics.

But what is supposed to be meant by answering for the world, or indeed answering for God? If God is to be answered for at all, one would presume he would have to answer for himself. And it would likewise be up to God to answer for the world. Would it then perhaps be necessary to go on to say that it is really up to God to answer for me? Would that not in actual fact have to be asserted if it is to be a responsible thing to speak of God without merely pushing to its extreme the moral aporia, my failure to answer for myself – namely, to speak of God in such a way that something other than the ethical thereby comes on the scene, *viz.* – the thing that is superior to the moral aporia and capable of meeting it? Would speaking of God not be meaningful, and thus hopeful and necessary, only if it were the countermove to my answering for myself? Thus in such a way that God's answering for himself relieves me of having to answer for him, but thereby also relieves me of having to answer for the world, and indeed even relieves me of having to answer for myself? If, at all events, there is a word in which God answers for himself, then that cannot be something that has no relation to answering for the world and answering for man himself.

But let us consider from still another standpoint the responsibility to which man is summoned. We began by saying that the reality *(Wirklichkeit)* with which man has to do summons him to action *(Wirken)*. We were led to the concept of responsibility first of all by the compulsion to render account of what he has done *(das Gewirkte)*. But now, man undoubtedly cannot by his action alone do justice to the reality he has to do with. And that, too, not merely because his action remains far behind what he is really summoned to. That is of course also true. But the point at the moment is that the reality with which man has to do cannot possibly be done justice to by action alone. It does not summon him by any means only to action. Rather, it summons him also to speech. To a great extent the reality with which man has to do is one he cannot correspond with, and so do justice to, by action at all, but solely by word.

Once again it is confirmed that problems arise in the ethical field whose solution is not a matter for ethics. The fact of our being summoned to word and the fact of our being dependent on word are not simply an aspect of the ethical and no more. That becomes clearer | if instead of "summons" we say "question." "Summons" evokes the idea of an achievement that is expected of man, of an act he has to perform. Now it is certainly true, as we made clear already, that in particular circumstances a word, too, can be a deed. Here, however, it is a case of being asked questions the answering of which does not fall under the category of acting. Man is questioned in manifold ways by the reality with which he has to do. It gives him not only things to do, but also things to think about. He is addressed and questioned with a view to his understanding. From the wide range of phenomena thereby indicated I can only single out a few major points.

1. Being questioned lays hold of man like a kind of powerful suction. The suction of this being questioned has the tendency toward totality. There is no stopping at partial and isolated questions: how this or that in the confusing abundance of phenomena is to be understood. These questions have *a priori* a coherence which is not indeed perceptible as a matter of course, yet powerfully forces itself upon us. It is not merely this or that that becomes a question, but the whole of reality. And probably one would have to say: it is the whole that is primarily questionable. Under the pressure of the comprehensive questionableness, the individual parts also become questionable. On the other hand, the fact of the individual part's becoming questionable is already the result of a certain illumination which makes the individual part separable and perceptible in its individuality. So, too, the storm of being questioned is more readily withstood at individual points than as a whole. Yet by concentrating on the individual point there is no evading the suction toward the whole. The effort to give an answer to individual questions is constantly threatened and called in question by the comprehensive questionableness of the whole.

Whatever the word "God" may mean, at all events it points in the direction of this radical questionableness of reality as a whole.[21] Speaking of God in the general terms of religious or philosophical language is an interpretive naming of the unintelligibility of reality as a whole, and can therefore be interpreted as speaking of the absent God, the *deus absconditus*, whose absence is precisely the troublesome thing and to that extent is present as radical questionableness. That of course is not by any means how the religious or philosophical talk of God thus characterized understands itself, but is rather a definite interpretation and as such a particular form of answer, not a description of the point in which all religions and world-views are united, but on the contrary, a statement of the ground of their disunity, a | declaration on the controversiality of God, and one

---

[21] Cf. my essay, "Rudimentary Reflections on Speaking Responsibly of God," in: Word and Faith, pp. 333 ff., esp. 347 ff.

which charges the theistic, deistic and atheistic answers with radical questionableness. For to hold our ground in face of the idea of the *deus abscondi-
tus* is possible only under the promise of the word which frees us from the
radical questionableness because in it God encounters us as pure word, so
that the God who is present as pure question, and consequently absent,
can no longer trouble us.

2. This tendency toward the questionableness of the whole has its
counterpart in the tendency toward the questionableness of man himself.
For one thing is characteristic of the sharply marked question structure:
however much man may appear to himself at first to be the questioner, he
is yet himself the one who is questioned. In all his reflections man comes to
questioning in such a way that he knows himself questioned as one who
must give answer. And the suction of the radical questionableness now
shows itself again in the fact that the man who is questioned is himself the
person who is called in question, who thus does not remain himself an
onlooker spared from questionableness, but on the contrary is most deeply
affected by it. Whoever is radically exposed to being questioned experiences
thereby the questionableness of his own self as the real sting of *all* questionableness. Hence in thus being questioned man is summoned to vastly
more than merely answering this or that question, adopting an attitude to
this or that problem, and thus merely giving individual answers. Rather, by
his radical questionableness he is summoned to be an answer himself. To put
it tritely: man is not called to exist as a question mark all twisted up in
itself. He is called to be pure, clear word, to exist, so to speak, as an unambiguous sentence, as a clear confession, as a testimony, in the word-event
whose origin and future is God.

3. This way of speaking of the radical questionableness is already determined by the specific word-event which overcomes the radical questionableness and does not suffer us to be struck dumb before it, but rather
allows us to exist in face of it as an answer in the unquestionableness of
the unequivocal and truly self-evident, and *that* means, of the word of God.
And precisely this is the business of theology: by answering for faith in
Christ to answer for reality in its radical questionableness. The fact that
our analysis of the ethical pointed us into the problem of the word-event,
but thereby pointed us also beyond the horizon of ethics, marks the decisive
connection between the themes of ethics and theology. To expound this
would be the task of a theological doctrine of the word as the manner of
God's coming and of faith as the coming to its goal of that word. However
true it is that theology is thereby assigned its place in answering for the
Gospel of Jesus Christ, yet it must not for that reason | remain unnoticed
that man still always finds himself in a twilight between questionableness
and word-event. What that means can be grasped only in giving a responsible
theological account of reality. A responsible theological account of reality,

however, *must* address itself to this fact. Man may be ever so much exposed to questionableness and a victim of it, so that his words are questionable, deceitful, undependable, empty words. Even then he is not without the word that would be God's word to him if he would admit it. Man may be ever so decisively, or indecisively, or even in hypocritical piety, godless; he is nevertheless not without God, because he is not without a reflected glow, be it ever so deformed, of light and life. That would have to be modulated, as it were, through every key in major and minor as the doctrine of the preservation of the creation in spite of man who is a menace to himself, and therefore to his fellowmen and himself; but at the same time also for the sake of this same man, who, in spite of the menace he presents, is still man, kept within bounds or forced back within bounds and consequently, to those who know the reason for that, not by any means completely hopeless man but on the contrary, man for whom there is the greatest hope, who has promise, for whom it is worth entering the lists and expending oneself. The theological doctrine of the preservation of the world has its focal point in the fact that, and the manner how, word still takes place in spite of everything. To those whose heart is awake the very birds of the air and lilies of the field preach a sermon. Still more, everything true and good that has come to expression and been handed down among men reminds them what the word could actually achieve if man did not only partially make a right use of it, but gave full room to it and became, so to speak, a word-bearer, a messenger of true word, and that means a witness to the word of God.

For that reason a twofold word-event has to be distinguished: on the one hand, the word-event that is always already taking place in the historic existence of man, whereby, to be sure, word takes place only partially and fragmentarily and at best in a provisional sense salutarily, but in the last resort hopelessly and perditiously – word without a future and therefore at bottom annihilating word –; on the other hand, the word-event which makes word take place completely and truly, and that means truth-bearing, salutary, hopeful, future-shaping, life-giving, abiding word. Both forms of the word-event have in common that they take place correctly only as received and gratefully acknowledged word. That this is true of the word of proclamation may be easier to see than that it holds of every right word among men. Yet even in this general form it ought | to be plain that truth can never be invented but only perceived, heard and gratefully acknowledged. Even the general word-event is, rightly understood, testimony to the fact that the questionableness in and behind everything is not by any means the true face of reality; and that neither is the summons to act the last and profoundest note in the language of the reality with which we have to do. Both things – the questionableness and the summons – derive their power from the gift that proceeds ever anew from the never bygone, never silenced word of the Creator. For that reason both forms of the word-event, different as they are, are nevertheless most closely related to each other and dependent on each other: the language of the proclamation engages with all the languages of reality; and all the languages of reality find in the language of the proclamation their true interpretation. To shut the one off from the other would mean failing to give the word of God its due. The most serious of all failures in theology comes about when the range of the word of God is narrowed down instead of giving room to the freedom of the word of God in the encounter of both forms of the word-event and participating in its linguistically creative occurrence.

4. Since man's being man is at stake in it, the word-event is always to be considered in terms of co-humanity. Man is essentially co-human. That he is inexchangeably himself and to that extent an individual, not a mere example of a species but an Ego, a person, and that for that very reason he is exposed to the compulsion to act, to surrender, to put right, and to render account, is rightly understood only in view of his co-humanity, for only in relation to co-humanity can the real nature of word and language be grasped. If, however, there is a very close connection between what is word and what is called "God," then it will be possible to speak rightly of God, too, only in view of man's co-humanity, and not in any way apart from that in some isolated relationship between God and the abstractly conceived individual – conceived, too, even in the further abstraction of mere soul. For that reason, precisely the reverse is also true: if God concerns man in his co-humanity, then his co-humanity is to be understood as granted by God, claimed by God, and dependent on God. In theology, too, no less than in ethics, our co-humanity is the thing which is at stake. That is why theology has to do with a church; for that reason to be sure – for the sake of the church – with a critical eye on what by and large in unhappy obtuseness and resignation is usually called "church."

That language and word-event are indeed one with co-humanity, | should be obvious from the phenomenality of speech. Speech exists only in virtue of language that has been mediated, handed down, spoken in front of us by others. It is not thanks to himself that anyone speaks, but rather thanks to those who have addressed him and spoken a language in front of him. Speech is always already a sign of love. Even speech that is misused to express hatred is only possible because the man who utters it once experienced the love that taught him to speak. Speech is a sign of being dependent on community – not merely community of conversation but also community of the same language. The man who has the power of speech participates in infinite riches, stands in communication with countless men of countless generations. But of course speech is aimed at concrete encounter. What really is the meaning of "word" in co-humanity and for co-humanity? What is it required for? What can it do? What is its highest potentiality? What we said of speech as a sign of love gives a pointer also to the meaning of concrete word-event. A small child who is not spoken to perishes. The adult may be less sensitive, because more hardened. But for him, too, communication, being loved and loving, is decisive for his existence – even, as all too often happens, in the negative mode of clouded or even broken communication, the perversion or the extinction of being loved and of love. In all this the word-event is not by any means merely an expression and symptom of what is in man and what is the state of his co-humanity. It is certainly that as well – and indeed in a way that has most significant consequences for our fellowmen: "How can ye, being evil, speak good things? For out of the abundance of the heart the mouth speaketh." [22] Yet the thing is above all, that it is in the word-event that communication takes place in the purest and most necessary form, but therefore in it, too, that the profoundest and most significant cause of defective communication and broken communication can lie. On a superficial view, it is true, the maximum of communication seems to lie in the greatest possible immediacy, the wordless merging of one person into another. The word-event, on the other hand, as a mediated form of communication seems to be an expression of still existing separation, an imperfect form of co-humanity. In actual fact, however, the very distance preserved and granted by the word is the condition of the possibility of a communication that reaches the ground of existence. The only reason why particular ways of behaving which take place in silence can speak for themselves and touch the depths of a fellowman is, that the encounter takes place in an atmosphere already determined by the word-event. | So the silent act, too, can become the communication of what is not communicable by action as such. For word-event is communication-event. It must not be imagined, of course, that the highest form of communication is self-communication. On the other hand, neither must the word-event as communication-event be reduced, say, to mere information in the sense of a particular technique of signifying – unless of course we were to go to the root meaning of signification between men and understand "*informare*" with the help of the Aristotelian concept of form. Then (though it would certainly be deviating from the Aristotelian definition of *anima* as *forma corporis*, or of the *virtutes* as *formae* of the *potentiae animae*) we could say: word is the *forma* of man, who is the *materia* of word. On that basis it would be understandable that Jesus Christ as the *verbum Dei* is, according to a remark of Luther's in the 1531 Lectures on Galatians, "*forma mea*," "*sicut paries informatur albedine*" [my "form," as a wall is "formed" by white color] – although this stock illustration of *forma accidentalis* is out of place, since Luther, strictly speaking, understands Christ and therefore word as *forma substantialis* of man: *vita, qua vivo, est Christus* (the life by which I live is Christ). [23]

---

[22] Mt. 12:34.   [23] WA 40/1, p. 283, 7–9, on Gal. 2:20.

Word-event is always communication of what – normally, of course, not in the radical sense just indicated – lies *extra nos*. What takes place in the word-event is characterized by the formula that I speak to you about something. Perhaps the corresponding Latin preposition *de* ("down from") or the Greek περί ("gathered round") can bring out more clearly the significance for the word-event of the thing *extra nos* which comes to be communicated in it. The thing spoken of (German: *über*) is the source from which the word comes down to me. It is the thing around which the word gathers. It is therefore, however, also the place to which the word leads, or the thing which arrives in the word. Or if we may interpret the German *über* ("over") as a reference to the ground underneath, the thing spoken of (= *über!*) is the ground of the word-event, which releases word-event and causes me to have something to say. In the word-event as communication between men there is thus always world present. Word-event is communication of world. Co-humanity is not to be abstracted from co-worldliness.

But now, it would have to be asked in what respect word in its co-humanity and co-worldliness is absolutely necessary, and thus what it is that word alone is able to communicate. One could attempt to indicate that by phrases like "reality as a whole," or "the future," or "the ground of existence." To understand all that, however, | as communicable by word alone is possible only if it is understood as dependent on the theological truth which could be termed the *fundamental statement (Grundsatz)* of theology, *viz.* – that *God alone comes in word alone;* and if this fundamental statement *(Grund-satz)* of theology in turn is founded on faith's confession that the word in which God comes *has happened,* that as σάρξ it has become man and thus co-human.

We have seen the dimension of the theological break out in the ethical, on the one hand, with compulsion to put right as the question of freedom and authority to exercise love, and then further with the compulsion to render account as the question of freedom and authority to exercise word. Both indications point to the same thing: the remedial word which as liberating word, and that means as word that gives freedom to exercise word, opens up freedom to exercise love because it communicates love as being loved. The middle term between word and love is faith. For faith, as reception of love addressed to me, is freedom to exercise love.

This word-event does not disclose itself within the realm of the ethical, however much it is at work therein. Ethical discourse, the *verba moralia,* cannot give faith as authority and freedom to love. That is the business of the word whose observance is entrusted to theology – the *verbum fidei* which is true, pure word because it is *verbum Dei.*

Man in the Open Situation

A Question Concerning the Relationship of Ethics to the Christian Faith in Our Day*

by

Dietrich von Oppen

Translated by Merlyn E. Satrom

I. A Fruitful Question

In one of his articles,[1] Gerhard Ebeling raises a programmatic demand which deserves the greatest attention. This demand relates to the question which is central to all active thought and work of the church today: the question of the relationship of faith and world, indeed the world we know as our modern world, the concrete world which surrounds us. Ebeling focuses the general question concerning faith and the world today in the question concerning the relationship of the proclamation of faith to that aspect of reality which we experience in a deeply disturbing way as our "ethical crisis," that is, that we have become uncertain in our ethical norms and even in our moral awareness.

It is not, however, the direction of his questioning alone which deserves special attention. Rather, the way the subject is approached is decisive, and it appears that this is done in a particularly fruitful way. Ebeling asks, "How can our proclamation establish the supremely helpful necessity of Christian faith precisely in regard to the concretely pressing problems of the present moral crisis?" (p. 103) Shortly thereafter he expresses it more succinctly: "If the message of faith is to have any meaning, then it must demonstrate its meaning, and therewith its necessity, precisely by illumining that given reality which, however, demands that proclamation and reality should meet." (p. 104) Here weighty truths are encountered: proclamation and reality – and here in particular the reality of our ethical crisis – are indissoluably related to one another; they have to meet so that reality becomes illuminated and so that the proclamation proves its meaning and its necessity. This is most certainly | the meaning of the Gospel of Him who is the light of the world. This illumination of the world from His light is, however, a perpetually new task for the proclamation of faith.

---

* "Der Mensch in der offenen Situation: Zur Frage nach dem Verhältnis der Ethik zum christlichen Glauben unserer Zeit," ZThK, 59, 1962, pp. 315–345.

[1] G. EBELING, "Die Evidenz des Ethischen und die Theologie," ZThK, 57, 1960, pp. 318–356; Eng. tr. see above, pp. 96–129. The quotations are taken from the English translation.

Nonetheless, this task must be accomplished and must not remain merely a programmatic demand. We must allow ourselves to be involved in reality if reality is to be met by the proclamation and illuminated by it. Today there is more virgin land than ever to be broken, for in the upheaval of the past decades and centuries "the world of modern man has assumed a completely new face . . . that has brought up for ethical definition a mass of material that could not be mastered at all on the basis of traditional theological views." (p. 99).

We are obligated to work toward the meeting of proclamation and reality. At the same time we must be aware of the radical upheaval of our times. The programmatic demand, in the form in which Ebeling has expressed it, can prove both helpul and fruitful in this connection. In this article an attempt will be made to allow ourselves to be involved in reality in the sense in which Ebeling demands it, and to show that the statement of faith can in fact illuminate our situation, or, as Ebeling expresses it in another place, that it can bring "clarity into the maze of reality which concerns us." [2] As another result of this encounter we will perhaps find indications pointing to the reverse effect within the proclamation-reality relationship. In the same context and on the basis of his whole approach, Ebeling anticipates this reverse movement as well: "Ethical reflection on man in the reality which concerns and surrounds him has a hermeneutical function for theology as a whole . . . Theology has no other means of making intelligible what it has to say than by seeking and reaching man in the ethical reality in which he finds himself." (p. 104). It is in this conviction that the following effort is made.

II. Two Central Elements of our Reality:
The Technological-Organizational "State of Life" * and the Open Situation

It is not possible here to scan our present reality in such a way that we gather and compile empirical facts from a wide spectrum. We can only proceed from central, given elements which are clear and generally known, and on the basis of these | make important empirical facts – in the greatest possible number – discernible and accessible.

The article referred to above also calls attention to these central, given elements in two ways. It adduces the "ethical crisis of vastest dimensions" in which we find ourselves today and it points to the double step by which this crisis came about. The first part of which was "the emancipation of ethics from the religious," which then led to the second, an "emancipation

---

[2] Cf. G. EBELING, Word and Faith, Philadelphia, 1963, p. 387.

* [The German word *Daseinsverfassung* (translated "state of life") is used by the author to describe the objective and thought world as it is presently constituted. Our social, cultural, technical, and language forms as well as the way we think and work are part of our *Daseinsverfassung*. Tr.]

from ethics altogether," whereby now "human nature itself is at stake." (pp. 100ff.). In other words, the ethical question in this context is not a timeless question but a question which is asked in the concrete historical situation as a question concerning an upheaval effecting all of history, which is to be mastered here and now. The historical change is not merely one which has often occurred and which people have often been called upon to master. Rather, this is a historical change of singular weightiness which radically poses the question, "What is 'human existence' *(Mensch-sein)*?" This in turn has its basis in the fact that the question of faith has been decisive in this upheaval from its very beginning, because the upheaval came by way of "emancipation from the religious," that is, leading through secularization to secularism (Gogarten).

We can and must begin here in order to ask further about reality today. What occurs when an entire age is secularized in its thinking and finally becomes "secularistic," i. e., when an age disregards faith as a decisive power in life? This secularized age manifests that it has learned to "disregard" particular aspects of things, persons, events and relationships, and to concentrate exclusively on others. That is, the basis of secularization and secularism is a general capacity for *abstraction*. Abstraction is the limiting of observation or of treatment to particular aspects of things, persons, or relationships by excluding and disregarding all other aspects. Abstraction is a process of the reckoning which proceeds toward goals and which, from these goals, determines the choice of the points which it considers important enough to be taken into account. Western man has developed this capacity of abstraction through many centuries.

Objectification, i. e., the detachment of the observed or manipulated object from the observer or manipulator, must be singled out as a particular accomplishment of abstraction. Through this act of force — since that's what it is — the existential separation of an "object" from a "subject" is achieved. Thereupon, we, as subjects, try to deal with data im | personally and without attaching value judgments, assuming these data at first to be neutral in meaning.

By abstracting and objectifying in this way, we occidentals have developed a thoroughly "mechanistic and constructivistic way of thinking" (Yorck von Wartenburg) which determines our "state of life." Our technical world as well as our forms of life, that is, our technology and our institutions, are built on this way of thinking. This principle has penetrated the breadth of our existence. It has penetrated the liberal arts with particular intensity and has been developed especially in the natural sciences. It now supplies the structural law not only for our technology but also for our social institutions: "It is as if the way of thinking of the exact sciences in their modern form had become reality through some means of magic. Only a minimum of rules *(Setzungen)* and only those things which can be constructed from them are valid – the way it is thought there (in the natural sciences), is the way it is built here."[3]

However, with this new, earth-shaking principle of construction it is true, to use Ebeling's expression, that "a mass of material" has come up for "ethical definition" which not only "cannot be mastered at all on the basis of traditional theological views" but which demands a re-examination of *all* concepts – of the legal no less than the political, the educational, the economic, the military, the linguistic, etc. We are as yet preoccupied with these fresh orientations on every hand. In this article, however, we are concerned solely with the ethical questions and with their relationship to the assertion of faith.

But it is in fact extremely important for the "ethical definition" whether we are dealing with *"things"* – Rilke calls them "dark and wise" – or *objects* and *wares*, which are neutral in meaning. Today even "things" approach us as neutral. Similarly, the limited obligation of *convention* or *rule* has taken the place of the deeply binding *mores*. An *office* has become a *function*. Today we are no longer embraced by *"orders"*[*] from which we cannot withdraw, but are members of *organizations* which we can join or from which we can withdraw as we wish. The *destiny* of a person meets us as a *case* of legal advice, of social welfare, of administrative responsibility, or of medical care. In our world, which has become more and more dependent upon science, *language* is more and more permeated with rationally manipulated *terminology*. This list could be extended indefinitely. If one wishes to summarize it in one word, however, one can say that we no longer live in a *"world"* – this word being used in its former dark and full sense – | where people, things, events and circumstances had their exact and given place and thereby had and found their meaning in their mutual relationship. This world has been resolved into a *conglomorate of facts*. This conglomorate can be analyzed and systematized from various points of view but no longer yields a whole in which man feels at home. Faith, too, has lost its former place in this conglomorate and has become just one aspect among many.

The disintegration of this former "world" and this loss of given place and meaning is observed and lamented on all sides today. In it, one observes a deadly impoverishment and depletion of our life. This lament forms the actual content of a widely diffused cultural criticism which appeared in the nineteenth century at the same time as the new "state of life" erupted. This cultural criticism was oriented primarily to the catchword "mass" (*Vermassung*).

---

[3] HANS FREYER, Theorie des gegenwärtigen Zeitalters, Stuttgart, 1955, p. 83.

[*] [The German word *Ordnung* calls to mind the "orders," both religious and secular, which existed in Europe until the nineteenth century and were typical of cultural life in all parts of the world before that time. *Tr.*]

But laments about the past and wishes to restore it do not help. They fail to see that the transformation of this way of thinking cannot be retracted; that the technologically and organizationally formed "state of life" cannot be removed. Such a criticism of culture fails to master the new "state of life," i.e., to see and encourage its vital forces which point to the future. The accomplishing of this task is all the more important because our technological-organizational "state of life" will and must be rapidly accepted by the rest of the world. If the rest of the world does not accept it, the world will not be able to take care of the mass of humanity which is increasing with equal rapidity. And if *we*, after all the catastrophes, can no longer share the optimism for progress which is still impelling the *rest of the world*, we must, on the basis of our previous experience with the modern world, encounter their optimism with more than a weary skepticism.

As long as we notice only the depravation of our present "state of life" in contrast with the former "world," our "state of life" will not be mastered. Expressed in another way, as long as we are still in search of and fail to find sense and meaning where it was previously found – *in* the objects, *in* the functions, *in* the organizations, *in* the events, *in* the facts, etc., our "state of life" remains unmastered. The immanent neutrality of meaning of these objects, functions, organizations, etc. cannot be removed, their "re-animation" is an idle wish.

The liberating movement away from a merely negative cultural criticism comes about when we recognize another reality which is inherent in the "state of life" formed by abstraction and objectification. This is the *situation* of the thinking, experiencing, and acting | human being. Indeed, this situation in our day is basically an *open situation*. But what does that mean?

Man has always lived in situations and he has always had to respond to them. But in the old "world "they were to a great extent pre-formed from the traditional "orders" and ways of thinking, and the responses to these situations had already been shaped by those same energies and had been handed down from generation to generation in the form of mores and law. Contemporary man lives in an infinitely complex and changing world, and experiences this world in the form of perpetually new situations. The new-fashioned, abstract "forms of being" can only give him partial solutions and partial help for such situations. From the most complex political situation to the simplest everyday situation, new responses are constantly being demanded of man. His situations are predominantly "open" in contrast to the former situations which were predominantly "pre-formed."

For contemporary man, however, this open situation is the element in which things, events, or circumstances – in themselves neutral in meaning – are connected *for him* with his existence in a new way. Here the things, events, and circumstances again obtain their meaning, their place, and find their meaning *for him* in their mutual relationships – but now in a different manner than before. In finding their new meaning and their new place, they unfold a multiplicity, an abundance, and a wealth of meaning all their own which leaves behind the former wealth of meanings handed down by the institutions. Seen from this viewpoint, our age is not an age of poverty but of richness in meaning, indeed of overwhelming richness in meaning which must be unrelentingly and independently recognized (*wahr-genommen*).

We now have two basic materials for "ethical definition": the open situation and the technological-organizational "state of life." Each conditions the other and yet stands in an indissoluble tension to the other. Since man withdrew from the "orders" and rebuilt his being according to this double, tension-laden principle of construction, he has been thrown into an ethical crisis, even a crisis of moral awareness as such.

This break-up has found expression in contemporary efforts, among others, to consider ethics as "situation ethics" rather than, as was formerly the case, as "normative ethics." We do not intend here to go into the farreaching problems which are connected with this attempt, but this much should be said: one will only be able to make progress under the following circumstances. First, the fact of this historical break-up must be consciously established as a presupposition, | i.e., the current epoch must be considered separate in very principle from former epochs. Secondly, the concept "situation" must be understood precisely in the sense of an *open situation*. Thirdly, the insoluble relationship of this open situation to the technological-organizational "state of life" must be seen. Here the "norms" continue to appear – but in a new way and with basically limited validity.

So much for the attempt to state the conditions for our ethical conduct on the basis of a few central and given elements. This is the kind of reality which the Christian proclamation encounters in our times, and everything depends upon whether the proclamation in fact meets reality. The Christian proclamation meets reality when it enlightens reality. Therefore we have to ask if and in what way this occurs.

The confrontation of the Gospel and modern reality will be discussed in this article under four rubrics which represent central assertions of faith. The point of departure is the statement which stood at the beginning and in the center of the Reformation: freedom from the law and justification by faith alone. This affirmation offers a central formula which can disclose to us our relationship to our modern "state of life." And conversely, the modern "state of life" gives us a new approach to this expression of faith which has already become so peculiarly remote to us.

When we consistently ask other questions in this same manner, we will discover that the first article of the Apostles' Creed, the words of Christ in the "great commandment" and the eschatological expectation can also prove to be statements which enlighten existence for contemporary man. At the same time, it is also true that modern reality on its part can reveal and sharpen our ability to see the "reality for faith" (*Glaubenswirklichkeit*), or – to say it in Ebeling's words – it can have "a hermeneutical function in relation to theology."

III. Free from the Law: Man in the Organization

The task of proclaiming the faith is to make the old Biblical words contemporary in the reality which meets us. This is also true for the concepts of the doctrine of justification as it is expressed in the key text, Romans 3:28: "For we hold that man is justified by faith without the works of the law."

In this text we find the basic anthropological fact that man – in contrast to plants and animals – is a being who | is not "right" from the beginning, but must be made right. This *justificari*, this being-made-right, has two different sides which are clearly distinguished in the doctrine of justification. We speak of the "forensic" and the "effective" nature of justification and mean both that man must be declared free of all sin by Him who confronts him and that his actions must in fact be made new and right. Man becomes "right" not only when he has been freed from acting wrongly but also when his reputation has been restored.

During the greater part of human history the "law" has had this double power of justification. The "law" was the entire complex of binding norms which surrounded man as "order," law, and mores, and which directed his life. In those times the "individual" was neither recognized as a legal nor as a sociological entity. The reality of society consisted in super individual institutions.[4] The institutions, i.e., their mores and their law, made man right "before gods and men." He who "did the works of the law" was justified whether these were the laws of an Egyptian ruler, of the Greek city-state, of Confucian ethics, of the Celtic clan, or of the Germanic tribe. These "laws" lasted for a long time and lent solid support to these tribes, peoples and domains.

The "Law" of the Old Testament was of another kind, and, since Christ could be called its "fulfillment," pointed beyond itself. In "fulfilling" the "Law," Christ broke up the traditional support of man's world. Through Him who was and is "the end of the Law," all legal norms were revealed to be temporary and not final. It now became clear: works which institutions had thrust upon man from the outside were insufficient to justify man before the one, eternal Father-God. In this way an upheaval occurred which deeply shook the foundations of individual and community life. To this day this upheaval has been experienced by the world of norms

---

[4] Cf. below, p. 144, n. 7.

– the world which has been challenged – as a shock and a menace, the response to which has been persecutions. The One who brought the Gospel and who time and again told His believers in simple words that the Gospel was a shock and menace to the world and that they must await persecution, was Himself executed in the name of the broken "Law." But the believer now knows that the power of the "Law" was finally taken away with His resurrection.

To be sure, Christianity has itself relapsed into legalism time and again, and has cre|ated in turn sacred institutions and venerable, extensive and durable forms which were awesomely inhabited and preserved: the Holy Roman Empire, the church itself, monastic orders, brotherhoods, and congregations. The battle between the Law and Gospel which was begun by Christ did not diminish, but flared up time and again, stirring and transforming the world – in St. Francis of Assisi, in St. Elizabeth of Marburg, in Luther, in Pietism. Out of these and many other upheavals, the world finally emerged in a new form in which the "law" (i. e. the institution) took on a new appearance. The "law" appeared now as the "organization," which dominates the scene in the Western World and is well on its way to rule the entire earth in a short time. Within the organization, Christianity succeeded in taking the power away from the law, and since that time the proclamation of the Gospel no longer takes power away from the institution, but makes factual statements explaining the very character of the institution. Where the institutions sustain the belief that they alone are able to make man right, the challenge of taking the power away from the institutions will always be present. But taking the power away from the institutions in such a case does not shake the modern institution at its core; rather it calls it back to its real self. For the modern institution lives to be placed in question and to be of limited validity.

The present-day "organization" is distinguished basically from the earlier "order" in that it is not able to produce a form of being *(Daseinsgestaltung)* which is capable of existing on the basis of its own power. For the organization as modern state law, as club rules, as company regulations, as work rules, or as traffic regulations has been thoroughly secularized. The organization comes in contact with man as some abstract figure affecting only certain aspects of his life and always excluding all others. The organization is only the framework of activity that can no longer follow the multiplicity and changeability of modern life in its particulars. But since it is an open framework of action, it requires more performance and commitment than can be enforced. Under compulsion of the open situation, it time and again demands even sovereign and responsible violation of the laws and rules of the organization itself. Thus the law, now in the form of the organization, is still valid, but it is no longer unconditionally valid; it is valid only within limits.

The distinction between the old and the new law will become clear in the following analysis: Where a man submitted willingly and without objection to the old law in the form of the "order," he became a pious, formed figure – a farmer or a burgher or whatever, determined by mores and the law. It is self-evident that the "order" was slightly or even greatly violated in numerous cases, and that the people in those days were not by any means all "pious." Today, however, where a man submits willingly and without objection to the law in the form of an "organization," | he becomes a disfiguration of a man and, in extreme cases, inhuman. In the most harmless instances he becomes a pedant who inverts the benefits of the "order" into a plague, in that he makes himself and others slaves to his exactness in the letter of the law. The bureaucrat is more dubious. He, being true to his office, sees and handles "cases," but he sees *only* the cases and forgets the people behind them and their fate in their ever new and open situation. He does not venture to use his discretionary power, be it ever so necessary. Similarly, the "functionary," being devoted only to his own organization, enters proceedings with blinders on and is not in a position to think himself into the situation of his fellow man. Further, the legal fanatic who insists on the letter of the law, thus damaging the justice which he sought to protect, works toward the disintegration of the organization. But the pinnacle is reached in the present day by the absolutizing of the institution in the form of the totalitarian state and in its inhuman instruments. The principle of construction of the organization (that is, abstraction and objectification) denies itself by its total claim upon man because it has in effect only a partial claim and allows man to be free in all other areas.

The groups which produce these disfigurations of man have in common the belief that the organization can be perfected and that it is possible to subdue man to full obedience to the organization. This is simply no longer possible. The law as organization is no longer in a position to "justify" man, and this is not only true in the light of final standards, as was the case in the Gospels' opposition to the old "orders." Rather, that the law as organization can no longer "justify" man is obvious and clear. This is what we meant when we said that the Christian proclamation of the Gospel no longer takes power away from the institutions but makes factual statements about the nature of the institutions. The disfigurations of man referred to above make this clear. What is right *(recht)* is no longer only decided by the law *(Recht)*, but is decided in the concrete situation which today is always an open situation. The man of the "order" could not attain his real "self" *(Dasein)* – according to the standards of those days – if he withdrew from the law. The present day man would not attain his real "self" *(Dasein)* if he were to remain under the guardianship of the law.

Thus the Christian "freedom from the law" becomes an interpretive and revealing formula for the ethical situation of modern man in his specific institutions, that is, in the organizations. This is not to be understood in its obvious liberal sense of contrast between freedom and obligation ("as much freedom as possible and as much obligation as necessary"), but in the sense of a sovereign position both in and above the organization. This is the Christian "freedom to do and | leave undone"[5] as formulated by Luther. For it is only possible for the modern organization to exist when people serve the organization in this way. Unconditional obedience is its ruin. Modern law depends upon "freedom from the law" understood in this way. It is built up from this standpoint and with this objective.

But our statement of faith says not only "free from the law" but goes on to say "justification through *faith* alone." What does *that* mean for us in the modern world? What approach is available to us who live in the modern, technological-organizational world?

An approach opens to us when we ask, "Where does the unconditional perceptibly meet us?" Is there such a thing in our modern world? For, with the disappearance of the old "orders," the established horizons of being have disappeared. These horizons offered clear lines of conduct and were the horizons from which the holy took its form. The form and norms of existence are now only valid in a limited way; they have become mobile and are at our disposal *(verfügbar)*. Where is that which is not at our disposal *(Unverfügbares)* – that to which faith can hold – in our voluble world? Does it exist at all anymore, or is the only course left to the believer that of his own inwardness?

No, it is not only the course of our own inwardness which remains open to us. In our mobile world which has been relativized by individual forms, the unconditional does meet us. It meets us in a threefold way: First, in the form of *the actual situation* in which we must act. The situation is given us in just this way and in no other – with all of its helps and limitations, its harmonies and conflicts, its consistencies and inconsistencies. It is senseless to wish that the situation were other than it in fact is. In our ordinary everyday activities, this majestic relentlessness of the situation usually remains imperceptibly in the background. But now and again there are moments when it greatly and powerfully, fascinatingly and shockingly touches our heart and thought.

Secondly, the unconditional meets us *in the form of other people*. Imbedded in the actual situation there appears another power in the form of the particular person who meets us. He is apparently easy to shake off when he is an inconvenience, but he is nevertheless placed there as a reality in our lives whose inescapability becomes obvious to us in one way

---

[5] Cf. GUSTAV WINGREN, Luther on Vocation, Philadelphia, 1957, pp. 94 ff.

or another. Just as the situation is given in this way and in no other, the person is also given to us in this way and in no other.

Finally, the unconditional meets us *in the form of the approaching future*. This has become a somewhat | alien thought for modern man. He believes that through his planning and power he is able to command the future. We occidentals and particularly we Germans should have become somewhat more reflective as a result of our experiences with suffering. One fact about the future which we had repressed to too great an extent should have been particularly forced upon us and should have become more intimate to us: death. But death is only one of the unavoidable destinies. We deal just as awkwardly and ineptly with these things of the future as we do with the situation and with other people. Precisely through these three elements in the "labyrinth of reality which meets us" it becomes clear that this labyrinth is in need of illumination and that we need to receive directions for our way through it. The Christian proclamation of faith in fact has something to say here which can bring illumination and give us directions. In relation to these three things which are not at our disposal, it is clear in what way our modern life is "made right" by faith.

For the relationship to these three unconditionals is different from the relationship which once existed to the unconditionally valid holy "orders." In living under the "orders," one simply had to obey them, but we have *to respond* to the open situation. This response exists in the tension between that which confronts us as that which is not at our disposal, and an extraordinary power to possess and control *(Verfügungsgewalt)*. This is, however, a situation in which we often badly falter, not least because we are not able to recognize it. Here the Christian proclamation has something to say which decisively illuminates the way for us.

IV. The First Article:
Our Dual Relationship to and in the Open Situation

When, in our day, we ask what faith is, we find it easy to look to that venerable formulation which has been the summary of faith for the church throughout the centuries – the so-called Apostles' Creed. Upon examination we find that the interrelation of the post-Christian eras is thereby, in fact, not denied. For just as our modern era has evolved under the influence of the Christian faith through many centuries, we also find the outlines of our era already present in the ancient formula of faith. We notice that our two-fold relationship to and in the open situation is sketched already in the first article: the abstract-objectivizing one and that which surrenders to it. Both of these have grown out of the ancient formulation, "I believe in | God the Father Almighty, Maker of heaven and earth," and hence it is still possible to find both elements present in these words. What do we mean by that?

The second half of the formula, "I believe in God . . . Maker of heaven and earth," contains the encounter which has made man the knowing subject who can possess and govern with respect to a factual world. "The Christian orientation of the consciousness (of radical transcendence) made the modern mechanistic constructivistic way of thinking originally possible through its freedom from* the world."[6] We have already adopted the concept "mechanistic constructivistic way of thinking" from Yorck von Wartenburg to describe this specifically technological-organizational attitude which we are no longer able to give up. In the above quotation he establishes this important connection.

The Christian faith, in the relationship it has engendered to the world, has been decisive in establishing the modern technological-organizational way of thinking and the "state of life" produced and supported by this way of thinking. For faith in God, who, as Maker of heaven and earth, stands beyond the heavens and the earth, was the basis of the "Christian orientation of the consciousness of radical transcendence." The cosmos had been holy up to this time. By directing the believer's vision beyond the cosmos – or however one might describe the holy cosmic order – to the Creator-God, who was alone holy, the world was made profane. In this way man acquired a "freedom from the world" because within faith he found an Archimedian point outside of creation. The idea of an "Archimedian point" fits here because the occidental Christian has subsequently really made use of this "point" for the purpose of which Archimedes dreamed. That the Christian has "moved the earth" from this point is to say that he lifted the form of existence *(Daseinsgestalt)*, which had been created in the form of "orders," off its hinges, and to a great extent the activity of the natural elements themselves off its hinges; this led to a new situation – one in which the form of existence could be objectively created and manipulated.

This unheard-of power to make and possess things has become our fate today. We can no longer renounce it. In the lesser | as well as in the more

---

* [*Weltfreiheit* contains both the idea of freedom "from" the world and freedom "to" the world. The former is the more prominent and will be used throughout this article. *Tr.*]

[6] YORCK VON WARTENBURG as quoted by KARL LÖWITH, "Der Weltbegriff der neuzeitlichen Philosophie," Sitzungsberichte der Heidelberger Akademie der Wissenschaften, phil.-hist. Klasse, 4, 1960, p. 5. The article begins with this quotation as its motto and, in broad outlines, shows the relationship of the consciousness of radical transcendence to the modern mechanistic constructivistic way of thinking by means of numerous historical references. Also see F. GOGARTEN, Verhängnis und Hoffnung der Neuzeit, Stuttgart, 1953, where this same relationship is treated, using the concept "secularization" which "has its beginning in faith itself."

important circumstances, we must initially always coolly confront things with an unconcerned remoteness; we must logically calculate and conclude; we must construct, arrange and organize; we must classify and systematize. The durability of our technological-organizational "state of life" depends upon the fact that we proceed in this way, that we even continue to refine our "mechanistic, constructivistic way of thinking." Thus, to an ever greater extent, our "state of life" presupposes the "freedom from the world" out which this way of thinking arose. The necessary reduction to mere things *(Versachlichung)* is always in danger where any inner-wordly values, powers of forms, whether they be a social class or a nation, the economy or success, prestige or income, seek to become unconditionally valid. They are all to be questioned and to be shown their proper place and position so that the "state of life" as such might continue to exist. We are thereby referred back time and again to the source from which our freedom from the world at one time arose and from which source alone its life can be maintained: "faith in God . . . the Maker of heaven and earth." This alone transcends all other forces and values. This faith and the reality which grew from it and hence is connected to it, refer reciprocally, revealingly and illuminatingly to one another. Reality offers a new approach for the statements of faith, and the proclamation of faith illuminates and sustains reality.

That we confront an objectivized factual world aloofly as a knowing, possessing and governing subject is, however, only one side of our relationship to the open situation. As necessary as this one side is, if we exclude the other side, our conduct in this situation will be inadequate *(unsachlich)* or, to put it in other words, our conduct will be inhuman. There must also be another entirely different relationship to the world if our world is to have durability. It is that relationship which is expressed in the first part of the first article, "I believe in God the Father Almighty . . ." Here we see nothing of aloofness, nor of human power to possess and govern, nor of arranging and systematizing the objective world. Here we are concerned with that which is not at our disposal, an All-Powerful, against which there is no resistance but before which there can only be an obedient surrender. Here we are concerned with an All-Powerful which is not blind, but is a loving Father who loves me here and now, who is concerned with my salvation and "has numbered the hairs of my head." But this is the deepest and most comprehensive experience available to us in the open situation of life. This experience occurs indeed only when faith enlightens, fills and makes a living whole of that which has been learned through reason and understanding. |

An "Omnipotence" in fact meets us in the situation in such a way that that which is not at our disposal must be accepted. Here an absolutely superior power is at work, a power which places things, people and circumstances around us here and now – in this way and in no other. One cannot bargain. Desires to change the situation are powerless. It does not help to close our eyes to the situation. Instead, everything must be accepted as it is. A calm inexorableness meets us.

From still another standpoint, however, an al-mighty encounters us in the open situation. It is the might of the universe *(Mächtigkeit des Alls)* itself which meets us. For the open situation is no more and no less than the entire world converging here and now upon the acting person and offering him the conditions of his action. The animal lives, as J. von Uexkuell has shown, in an "environment" which is only a small part of the total world. That which doesn't belong to his "environment" is irrelevant for the animal. But man always lives in the total world, and this horizon has been frighteningly shattered before him since he can no longer live in sheltering "orders." Everything is important to him, even if only in perspective gradations of importance. The earth and plants, the animal world and human world with their natural conditions, the economic, the technological and the political conditions, the present achievements of medicine and the natural sciences as well as the entire future, all flow together in the here and now of the present situation. There is nothing which does not have a connection with, or an influence upon, the conditions of man's action. Thus the situation generally – but particularly the open situation – is the form in which the world converges on man. The former views of the world had a place for the earth and for man in the center of a cosmos. These former views of the world have been broken down by scientific discoveries and man has lost his place in the middle of the world. Today the universe becomes powerful for man in the here and now of the open situation.

But faith knows even more. It knows that it is not really a powerful, impersonal universe which encounters man, but that it is a personal Almighty who addresses himself to the believer, who calls the believer and loves him. This second important concept of the creed points this out in the word "Father," Almighty Father. It is a concept which encompasses far-reaching content: the begetting and acceptance as a son, lovingly raising him according to his own image and protecting and disciplining him – and all of that is comprised by the fact that Jesus Christ knew him as his father. The first article of faith thereby anticipates as well as embraces the second.

"I believe in God the Father" is the formula of the encounter which at one time led man into a new status, | or better, which led him into his proper status as a lonely and singular person before God. This formula, through the centuries and in all parts of the earth, has made man a person ever anew. It is the formula by which man knows himself to be begotten, to be called into life, and to be called to "eternal life." This knowledge encounters an actual exterior reality more directly today than in previous periods of history. For, whether we are believers or not, in the final analysis, all of us are, through the modern "state of life" and its open situation, placed in the world alone and unable to have anyone else take our place. He who, in one form or another, administers, gives advice or works in social welfare, has his greatest burden in that every "case" has its own particular character. In the last analysis, the concrete situation is such that it relates only to one single person and no one else can ever completely take his place. Even he who is closest, one's wife or husband, can never completely share the situation, nor can he ever fully participate in the other's situation.

This has not always been so. The old "orders," which placed man primarily in pre-formed situations with pre-formed answers, did not recognize individuals as either legal or social entities. That which was real and which upheld society was the group with its corporate situations and corporate "order."[7] Even when Greek philosophy began to consider the individual at the time when the "orders" of the city-states were being shattered, it was not the lonely individual who had his reality as a result of his particular singularity; rather, he received his reality through participation in eternal superindividual and supertemporal laws. Justification through the law had therefore not been left behind. |

The proclamation of the Gospel brought the "decisively other." The Gospel produced a basically new knowledge of man concerning himself

---

[7] This should be evident in the following two examples. Additional examples could be cited from every former epoch and area of life. JACOB BURCKHARDT writes in his book, Griechische Kulturgeschichte, I, (Kroeners Taschenausgabe, Bd. 58, 1952, p. 78): "The Greek city-state . . . was based upon the totality, which was regarded to be prior to the particular, as the individual home or as the individual person. We can add to this on the basis of an inner logic that the totality will outlive the parts; the concern was not only that the group had precedence over the individual, but also that the continual had precendence over the momentary or temporary. The surrender of his entire being was demanded of the individual not only on the battlefield and in special moments, but at any time in his life because he was indebted to the group for everything. He was indebted to the group even for the security of his existence, which only the citizen enjoyed in those days, and that only within his own city state and as far as its influence extended."

WILHELM GROENBECH describes the basis of life among the Germanic tribes in a similar way in: Kultur und Religion der Germanen, 5th ed., Stuttgart, 1954, vol. I, p. 63: ". . . in this state of immediacy there is no difference between me and you, as far as family relationship extends. If it is peace that establishes the foundation of the soul, it is a foundation of the soul which everyone within the family relationship has in common. It is here that the members of the family stand in such proximity to another that neither the will nor reflection can act as a buffer between them. The relatives strengthen one another. It is not as though they were two or more individuals who combine their strength. They act rather in exact harmony because deeply within each of them there is a secret power which knows and thinks for them. But even more than that, they are so bound to one another that the individual can draw power from his fellow tribesman."

and his relationship to the world. Man was called to be a completely differ-ent being. Or better, the cloak that had been drawn over him by the "orders" was withdrawn from his real being in that he was now called away from the dominion of every type of unconditionally binding "law," whether it be a concrete historical form or an eternal, universal law. Instead, his new and actual reality was revealed and established so that he knows that he, alone and singularly, has been called by God and before God – into his "upper room" behind the closed door. He knows that he has been called into a lonely responsibility which should no longer need the guidance, the control, and the ratification of his environment: "Beware of practicing your piety before men in order to be seen by them; for then you will have no reward from your Father who is in heaven" (Mt. 6:1). The Father-God calls individuals to responsibility. He takes away the power of the "order" at its decisive point. He no longer allows the "order" to exercise final control over its members. The Bible is full of instances of how God's call drew men out of the "order" and placed them in really open situations. As early as Genesis we find Abraham who understood the call that radically changed his life: "Go from your country and your kindred and your father's house to the land that I will show you" (Gen. 12:1). The prophets experienced what it meant to be called out from their people and to be placed in opposition to their people – for the sake of the people. The New Testament is full of instances of how the Father-God breaks up "orders" and places man in the open situation in which the previous wealth of experiences is no longer sufficient. There are examples of this kind in the New Testament, from Jesus' birth in the stable, his baptism in the Jordan, the call "follow me" extended to his disciples, Paul's Damascus road experience to the shattering of the old world with the dawning of the coming of the kingdom.

Since then, Christians have never completely given up considering them-selves a nomadic people of God in a transitory world, | even where their existence became anchored in tradition-bound "orders." And when today, in the process of this historical journey, the "state of life" has become basically transitory so that the open situation and the individual – who, in the last analysis, is alone and unable to be represented by another – have also become the external reality for everyone, then this is a reality in which faith must be at home because it is its own reality. The believer's faith permits him to recognize the depth, the background, and the contours of this reality. Faith encounters a reality which, as it stands, faith no longer has to question. Rather, faith fulfills this reality because this reality itself has grown out of faith and refers back to faith as its source.

More directly than in previous times, man will perceive in the open situation – which in the final analysis encounters him alone – the ever new call of a singular secret. We call this secret, "Person," who wishes to call man himself into life as a person – as a father his son. Whenever new circumstances call him to new, creative responses, man hears himself called to his father's image, as a son hears his father call. And again, as a son's experience with his father, man, in faith, knows that a future is lovingly kept ready for him in all situations, even where the situation is completely open and the results are unforeseeable, where the situation is outwardly chaotic and catastrophic.

"I believe in God the Father Almighty . . ." is, as we have already said, the formula of the encounter which in the past made man, who was encompassed by the law, a person. It is the formula of the encounter which, since its formulation, has tried again and again to make man a person. In a world built upon it, there is an approach to this formula which was not available in previous epochs: the particular reality of our "state of life."

It may appear as a self-styled understanding of this ancient formula of faith when two entirely different encounters – though necessarily closely related to one another – are pointed out: the encounter which made man a person and the second encounter by means of which he confronted the objective world as a knowing, possessing and governing subject. But each age has to find its own approach to the ancient measures of the creed. Each age must find its approach from the center of its existence.

Without referring to the first article of the creed, Dietrich Bonhoeffer described the relationship of the believer to the present world in a similar way. He wrote a letter from prison on February 24, 1944, from which the editor selected as a title (in the German edition) for the entire collection of his letters these words: resistance and submission. The passage may be put at the end of this section of our article as a testimony representing twentieth century Christian piety. | "Here I have often thought about where the boundaries lie between resistance to 'fate,' which is necessary, and submission to it, which is equally necessary. Don Quixote is the symbol for continued resistance to the point of absurdity or to the point of madness . . . Sancho Panza is the representative of satisfied and cunning compromise with things as they are. I believe that we really have to attempt the great and all that it is possible for each of us as individuals to do; at the same time we have to do the obvious and that which is universally required; we must be just as determined to take a stand against 'fate' – I consider the fact that the word is neuter (in German) to be important – as we are to submit to it at the proper time. One can only speak of 'guidance' beyond this two-fold process. God encounters us not only as the 'Thou' but also 'disguised' in the 'it', and in my question I am basically concerned with how we find the 'Thou' in this 'it' ('fate'), or in other words how 'fate' really turns into 'guidance.' Basically the boundaries between resistance and submission cannot be fixed. But both must be there and both must be grasped with determination. Faith demands this flexible, versatile action. Only in this way is it possible for us to endure the actual present situation and make it fruitful."[8]

This thought, having been developed and formulated in a boundary situation, has a fundamental significance for our life in the modern world. We are all constantly called to "flexible, versatile action" in the "actual present situation." Or in one word, we must "respond." This is the reality which our faith encounters.

V. "Love Your Neighbor":
The Present-Day Relationship to Others

'Love for your neighbor' appears to have such a universal validity that it has no special reference to present day circumstances. This is not so. Between each epoch and the ancient Biblical words there is a "special relationship" and it is the task of exegesis to find it and present it. A relationship exists between loving your neighbor and the modern world in that here the same thing is present as in the foregoing discussions of justification and the first article. That is, in the beginning and for a long time thereafter a breakup of tradition took place, which was outwardly almost unnoticeable yet extremely powerful. At the same time, however, there occurred a transformation of the "state of life." This "state of life" is, in the final analysis, so constructed that the original | attack has become a necessary presupposition for its continued existence. This change is a characteristic of the post-Christian era and it expresses itself also in the concept of love for one's neighbor. The most important factors have already been mentioned above. There remain only a few conclusions to be drawn.

The key texts in the Synoptic Gospels dealing with the command to love one's neighbor (Mt. 20:36–40, Mk. 12:28–34 and Lk. 10:25–37) make this command parallel to the love for God, giving both equal value and designating them the "great commandment" (Mt. and Mk.): "'Teacher, which is the great commandment in the law?' And Jesus said to him, 'You shall love the Lord your God with all your heart, with all your soul and with all your mind. This is the great and first commandment. And a second is like it. You shall love your neighbor as yourself. On these two commandments depend all the law and the prophets.'" (Mt.). Thus the Gospel itself places love of one's neighbor in the center of the proclamation.

The command to love one's neighbor does not stand alone at the center, however. It is most closely connected with the command to love God, and the two are parallel. In the Lukan account, both have been drawn together

---

[8] DIETRICH BONHOEFFER, Widerstand und Ergebung, ed. by E. BETHGE, München, 1955, pp. 150f.; cf. the Eng. tr. by R. H. FULLER, in: Letters and Papers from Prison, London, 2nd ed., 1956, pp. 104f.

into one sentence in that the predicate "You shall . . . love" appears only once. This gives the commandment to love your neighbor an extraordinary content, which now discloses itself especially to the contemporary man. Here the "particular relationship" of which we have already spoken becomes evident.

In view of the fact that God is the Wholly Other, that He is the Impenetrable Mystery, the One before whom it behooves us to be still and listen, to love Him means to say "Yes" even where I don't understand Him and where I wish His action were completely different. Only in connection with this "submission" do I have to "resist" (Bonhoeffer). Only in connection with "submission" and "resistance" can I discover "guidance" and give a "reply."

But is this valid in the relationship to my neighbor? Can this be the nature of my love for him? It is certainly not valid for community life in the traditional, well established "orders," since their life and stability depended upon the opposite. Their life and stability depended upon prior agreement and upon those things which were known, recognized and established as validated by both parties. Under these circumstances, the double movement of consciously making room and conciously responding, which brings about a new solution, was not necessary.

This, however, is an exact statement of things as they are given and demanded today. The neighbor exists, as we have seen, in our mobile, pluralistic world in a lonely situation and, in the last analysis, one in which nobody can take his place. It is impossible for anyone to understand him completely. | Therefore, in dealing with him, one must respect the secret of the person. This secret comes to light in his situation, his impenetrability, even though it is not confined to that. In dealing with the neighbor, one must try to come as close as possible to him by carefully listening to him and by thinking through his problems with him. To love your neighbor today means inwardly to say "Yes" to him even where he so acts in his situation – this situation which is accessible to him alone – that we do not understand him, or even where we believe him to be on a dangerous and erroneous path. Only in this way will my "response" in word or deed approach carrying out my responsibility toward him. I can never, with certainty, do him justice.

Living with one another today demands that we respect the secret of the other, that we lovingly make room for him and do that which is necessary. That is what modern 'togetherness' requires of us, and the parallel construction, love God and love your neighbor, says the same thing. The modern organizations can exist where this occurs. Because of their structural principle, they are not designed to embrace or encompass man completely. But where this does not occur, the modern companies, administrations, organizations, schools, hospitals, etc. become sick and man feels himself overrun, oppressed and degraded within them. Thus modern man, in his own way, discovers that "all the law and the prophets depend" on the great commandment; said in a modern way, that the total "state of life" depends on the great commandment. Note, however, that it is *all* the law, the *total* "state of life"; to understand the demand to love your neighbor only charitably, as is often the case, is an unbiblical narrowing. Loving one's neighbor by making room for him is a contradictory relationship, as is everything which the Gospel instigates, and it stands in profound contrast to the former existence which was constituted in "orders."

However, if one reads the words of the great commandment as we have just done, further consequences must be drawn. Here again, these consequences meet the given elements of modern life in a deeply meaningful way. For along with the command "you shall love your neighbor . . .," the closely associated command ". . . as yourself" has also been placed parallel to the command to love God. This love for self cannot be understood as egoistic self-love. If the solemn and inexhaustible secret of the other person discloses itself in the love of neighbor, this must also be valid – from the close grammatical connection of the two statements – in relationship to one's own self. With Augustine Christianity first really learned to recognize and to respect with amazement and fear the profound depth of the inner self. It is all the more valid for us who today no longer find ourselves interpreted by binding "orders" but rather have to master our own, ever new situations. This | can, to be sure, lead us to ever new discoveries about ourselves and in ourselves, and can always lead to ever new understandings of ourselves. This tension-laden and concernful dealing with one's self is indispensable for leading a responsible life and is entirely different from a self-satisfied self-love.

It should also be kept in mind that loving encounters with God, with our neighbor and with ourselves are not only grammatically parallel, but are also interrelated in terms of content in the summary of the "great commandment." This is also important in understanding them. For the love for God becomes concrete and practical in dealing lovingly with the neighbor and with one's self. And this love for God thus does not remain a spiritual relationship which might be considered unfruitful. Both of these human relationships receive their real depth and basis again only in love for God: that which is important here is neither my neighbor nor myself, with our dubious characteristics, but – and above all – what the creating and loving God has in mind for us. Since God loves our neighbor just as he is and wishes to build him up from where he now is, we too should love this person, make room for him, and with great care assist in his edification. But, understood in this way, the loving of self without loving the neighbor would be a fatal and unfruitful self-contemplation. Loving our neighbor cannot be characterized by carefully assisting or making room for one's neighbor without a corresponding attentive and loving but critical relationship with ones's self and one's own destiny. "Self-forgetfulness" leads only to a too intimate, too unpleasant and too destructive "love of neighbor." Thus, loving our neighbor – with which this section of our article is concerned – is enmeshed in a skein of personal relationships between God, my neighbor and myself. This sphere of personal relationships sustains and supports itself in itself and an entire "state of life" can "hang" upon it. This section proceeded from the statement that the neighbor is one of the three ways in which the unconditional meets us even today. We have expanded this statement by noting that behind this unconditional *the* Unconditional stands and that the self is also one way in which the Unconditional meets us in the interdependence with the encounter with our neighbor.

Finally, there remains the obvious question which, according to Luke, was asked of Jesus: "Who is my neighbor?" He answered the question with the parable of the Good Samaritan. There are a number of features to be gleaned from this parable which correspond to our modern condition, or better, which profoundly expose our modern condition.

First of all, it is a fact that the crucial conduct in this parable was carried out | by a person who was in no way called upon, under those social circumstances, to help the one who was in need. The Jews had nothing to do with the Samaritans. The gulf between these two groups, which, as bearers of two types of the same faith, were constantly accusing each other of heresy, was deeper than that between the Jews and the Greeks. By thus selecting a "Samaritan," Jesus emphatically expressed that political-social relationships are not the decisive element in constituting the relationship of love for the neighbor.

What, then, is decisive? It is the open situation which calls for a solution. In this case, it brings two people together who otherwise have no association with one another and who have no need to associate with one another. And the situation contains its evidence within itself. Here no norms, no traditions, no principles of any kind are needed in order to know what should be done. The bleeding and helpless victim along the path is call and indication enough.[9]

Thirdly, however, the conclusion of this parable takes an astonishing turn: "'Which of these, do you think, proved neighbor to the man who fell among the robbers?' He said, 'The one who showed mercy on him.' And Jesus said to him, 'Go and do likewise.'" The situation alone, according to this story, does not establish the relationship to the neighbor. The priest and Levite came across the same situation. The situation is only the chal-

---

[9] Cf. G. EBELING, "Die Evidenz des Ethischen," pp. 337 f.; Eng. tr., above pp. 112 f.: ". . . the evidentness attaching to the claim of the person in need."

lenge and this challenge must be taken up and accepted. The relationship to neighbor is a true relationship only when it is recognized (*wahr-genommen*). Man is placed in this personal relationship and exists differently in it than in the relationship of the binding "order" of the former type. In the latter, the homogeneity was understood and self-evident. In the former, the homogeneity exists primarily as a challenge and a demand, and is actualized only through the response.

Fourthly, in the open situation, the demand of the relationship to neighbor is not a total demand, but one which is meaningfully limited through the demands of the situation itself. The Samaritan did not take the injured man into his house to live with him the rest of his life, but bandaged him, took him to an inn, left money there for his care, and promised to stop on his return. He then went on about his business. It is clear that this limitation, which is contained in the situation itself, does not diminish the importance of the demand.

The importance of the demand is emphatically accented elsewhere: "As you did to one of the least of my brethren, you did it to me" (Mt. 25: 40). This is to be said in the last days by the "King" before whom all people will be gathered to be judged. In other words, even if the concrete de|mand and its solutions be ever so limited, that which is involved is always the totality of the world and of history; that which is involved is their goal and meaning.

In all of this, however, the framework and background which are actually present in our man-to-man dealings under modern conditions are demonstrated. In our mobile and universally coherent world, the politico-social conditions no longer establish a decisive basis for responsibility toward one another. Real responsibility again and again goes beyond all of the constituted groups to which we belong and the boundaries which they establish. These responsibilities emerge from the most manifold situations in which we are placed by the troubled and rapidly changing events of our day. The open situation, however, in which we find another person in his lonely singularity, is always the way in which the total world – the entire present, past and future world – converges upon this one person. The world with its meaning and final goal is involved here whether we know it and recognize (*wahr-nehmen*) it or not. It depends upon our ability as believers to recognize the depth of the situation, if we are to become for another person that which this far-reaching content encompasses – that is, his neighbor, here and now.

From whatever side one might approach it, the proclamation of faith always reveals our present reality to us. This is also true here: the word about the "neighbor," as it was first preached, was considered shattering and therefore offensive because it devaluated the established class lines and boundaries between the free and the slaves, the Jews and gentiles, the

Greeks and barbarians, and between the nobility and the peasants. Up to that time the world had rested upon its adherence to these established class lines and boundaries. Where the boundaries had already been blurred, as in late antiquity, this was considered to be a sign of decadence and not a promising path leading to new foundations. Today, within a history penetrated by the knowledge of "neighbor" as yeast leavens dough, a world has been shaped which can no longer renounce this knowledge of neighbor. Absolute divisions, such as those between the Jews and Samaritans, can no longer provide footing for the world, but have become deadly dangerous!

VI. "*Thy Kingdom Come*": *Our Relationship to the Future*

The third way in which that which is not at our disposal meets us in our mobile world of relative forms, is in the approaching future. Here, too, the Christian proclamation of faith has something decisive and revealing to say with its entire complex of statements about the eschatological expectation. |

It is difficult to understand why contemporary theology is so hesitant to connect these statements with the concrete events which fill our newspapers and history books. Where this is not done, we forfeit an extremely important message for our existence, and theology is guilty of not supplying its age with one of the most helpful illuminations. These events are then empty and without depth for us, and the eschatological proclamation loses its claim upon us.

The question is not whether the curious pictures of the Apocalypse will occur exactly as they are related. What is pivotal is our relationship to the present age, in which mankind ever more anxiously sees one crisis after another approach, in which everything appears to be tottering, and in which many things, which previously looked unshakeable, have already collapsed. And pivotal is our relationship to the future which, on the one hand, we await with secret or open fear, and, on the other hand, we try to anticipate with bold planning. The question is whether we have our own *certainty* of the future (*certitudo, Zukunftsgewißheit*) with which to oppose the presumptuous *surety* of the future (*securitas, Zukunftssicherheit*) of the communist world and of other young industrial lands which think the future is at their disposal. The question is whether our certainty of the future is not only able to hold its own, but is stronger and more durable. We will be unsuccessful, however, if the Christian thinks only in the context of his own personal existence. The examination of the total course of the world and the examination of the actual happenings of history are *also* important at this point. Since theology for the most part doesn't risk making this examination, it is difficult for contemporary man to find an approach to theological statements. One of the essential reasons why theology can only painstakingly "make itself understood" (Ebeling) to modern man is that it fails to take this risk. But modern man himself is left without the knowledge that even the most horrible events can form the basis of a certainty for the future, and that this in turn permits a calmness which does not seek to be anesthetized, but which can look everything soberly and factually in the face:"Watch, be not afraid. For this must take place, but the end is not yet." (Mt. 24:6).

Everything turns not only on calmness in the face of catastrophes which affect all of history, but on the mastery of our present day "state of life." Even here, in the simplest everyday events, the proclamation concerning the last days necessarily encounters contemporary events. For the modern world is – in contrast to a world of "orders" – a world oriented toward the future. Traditional "orders" were erected upon the past, on their founders and their foundations. They were based upon the traditions and upon the deeds of fathers and forefathers. An "organized" world proceeds by establishing goals and planning, that is, with a glance toward the future. In | the "organized" world, everything depends upon the fact that, on the one hand, the past never becomes too powerful and inflexible and, on the other hand, that the planning does not become so bold that it believes the future to be at its disposal. The organized world is in need of knowledge about the beckoning and challenging future, but a future which, in the last analysis, is not at our disposal. For the future is one of the things which confronts us in a way similar to the open situation and our neighbor. It challenges us to self-reliant action, but is not at our disposal and brings our self-willed actions to nought. This is what is being said in the proclamation of the Almighty God as Lord of the future and the proclamation of the coming of His Son, who "will come to judge the living and the dead," and in whom the course of history shall be completed.

That the drama of history circles about this "coming" is clearer today than ever before. It has become clear in what we have already said, precisely in the point which has emerged from a variety of perspectives: the Gospel began as an attack upon the existing foundations of the "state of life," but then, through its influence over a longer period of time, brought forth a new "state of life"; this new "state of life" now points back to that same power which brought it forth (the Gospel), as the presupposition for its existence. With each decade we are farther removed from the old, holy "orders"; the powers which bear their imprint may still live on, but they are slowly dying. Our direct dependence upon the power of the Gospel and upon the vitality of faith grows in the same measure. The theme of history – "*Ecce homo*" – becomes ever clearer in the perplexing clamor which surrounds us.

But this process is not a quiet flowering and not growing pacification. It is not an "evolution" from one stage to another. On the contrary! It is just at this point that the metaphor of "labor pains" interprets our age in its deepest undercurrent. And here it becomes clear that one misinterprets the Gospel if one awaits a progressive calming of the world through the increased activity of the Gospel. The Gospel *has* been effective to the greatest extent and it *has* qualitatively changed history, profoundly so – even so-called profane history – since the time of Christ. But its own sober prophecy has itself proved, that the shock and horror will spread more widely and more deeply. For the holy "law" as a viable option has been directly or indirectly abolished among all peoples and the established foundations of life have thereby been shattered. This occurred when it was disclosed that, as foundations of life, they were only provisional and thus, in the last analysis, not dependable. However, since the gate and the way which lead to the new life are narrow, those who find it are few (Mt. 7:14). Man remains bound to the "law," but the laws of our age no longer assist the strictly obedient, | as at one time, to achieve a provisionally viable and pious form of life; they rather make him a disfiguration of man if not inhuman. For the laws of our age are abstract laws which depend upon "fulfillment" in order to be able to stand at all. This point has been more fully discussed above. Thus the world goes through ever deeper crises the more the former "orders" disappear. These "orders" had deep potency for life even if this potency was not ultimately valid. "Watch and be not afraid . . ."

But it would be all too innocuous if one were to see here just the shock and disintegration. What is here revealed, what takes form and brings the real conflict into the drama of history, is evil itself. The former "orders" usually charitably covered and bridged the gulf of evil in man. The Gospel has removed this veil and has destroyed these bridges. We shudder today and are deeply moved when we see what man can do to his fellow man; we shudder even more at how he can do it. Evil itself has been awakened. But ultimate evil is not thinkable without ultimate light. Bonhoeffer says, "Apostasy *(Abfall)* is infinitely more serious than the fall *(Fall)*."[10] The New Testament in many ways describes the reality which is summarized by the one word "Antichrist." We have to guard against understanding this figurative language as historically concrete. It could be an unhealthy delusion to see the antichrist directly embodied in distinct historical persons. The result would be a crusade-ideology in which the cause of one's own party would be mistaken for that of Christ's. Rather, the power of the antichrist is at work everywhere and shows up in all of us. It is thus a sign of our times. How can it be otherwise if, as already stated, the theme

---

[10] D. BONHOEFFER, Ethik, München, 1953, p. 11; cf. Eng. tr., Ethics, New York, 1955, p. 4.

of history comes ever more clearly to the fore: *Ecce homo*! Where Christ is near – and "near" need not be understood temporally – the antichrist is not far away.

But the antichrist's essence is not only the satanic in the form of evil but also the power to do wonders: "For the coming of the lawless one by the activity of Satan will be with all pretending powers and signs and wonders . . ." (II Thess. 2:9). The powers unleashed by faith work the unheard-of and the wonderful even where they have been separated from faith. The apostate, in his relationship to the world, retains the powers which he, as a man of faith, has received and has discovered in himself.

Therefore the power of the antichrist exists not only in compulsion and destruction, but precisely in seduction. "For many will come | in my name, saying, 'I am the Christ,' and they will lead many astray" (Mt. 24:5). That which is of the antichrist becomes, by its power, even a bearer of peace: "And the authority was given it (the beast) over every tribe and people and tongue and nation" (Rev. 13:7), so that an idol was erected to it and it was worshipped. Our age has had a great deal of experience with such longing and readiness to worship.

Thus, in many ways the antichrist is a hellish counterpart of the true Christ. This is by no means least obvious in the persecution of the faith. "It (the beast) was allowed to make war on the saints and to conquer them" (Rev. 13:7). In an era of great persecution, the Christian cannot ignore this interpretation. For along with it, the certainty is given that "the lawless one will be revealed, and the Lord Jesus will slay him with the breath of his mouth and destroy him by his appearing and his coming" (II Thess. 2:8).

"That which has not been promised cannot be fulfilled. All life which has not been prophesied is under a curse and must be repeated, since an unannounced era cannot bring forth fruit. He who experiences the event does not know what he should say about it. It has to be interpreted for him." [11] We find ourselves in this situation as long as contemporary theology withholds the eschatological interpretation of our era. And all history since the Easter event must be considered the "last times." The difficult and depressing mode of our existence has been "announced," but it cannot bear fruit if the announcement is not made to those who are affected by it.

To summarize, the satanic has become an open reality in our age more than ever before. He who is aware of the even deeper and more real reality will not close his eyes and will not despair in facing this present reality, since he knows that the boundaries of this reality are set by the more real reality – in due season. "The time is come and is already here,"

---

[11] From a lecture by EUGEN ROSENSTOCK-HUESSY.

– the future is here and is given; it is not at our disposal. But the future will not be awaited passively. How we place ourselves in relationship to it depends upon us – in the certainty of hope.

Conclusion: What is Sin?

The Biblical proclamation turns around the concepts of sin, the sinner, and the forgiveness of sin. In the encounter of the proclamation with modern life and the question which faith asks | concerning ethics, it is important that the word "sin" be clearly understood. It is not clearly understood today. The word has taken on a moralistic tone and its horizons have been reduced. One no longer feels that this word represents a powerful and shocking reality. For modern man the word "sin" appears outmoded. It seems not to have a place in his life. He thus feels himself unaffected and unmoved by it.

This evacuation of meaning and power from the concept is most closely associated with the disintegration of the former "orders." Sin was at one time understood, from the viewpoint of piety, as a breach of the "order." As long as the "orders" of life were valid as something majestic, holy and inviolable, sin was a powerful and startling reality. The Ten Commandments were heard and understood in this sense. They were a holy law and whoever repudiated them was a sinner. The established "orders" were understood as an unfolding of the Ten Commandments. But as the established "orders," sustained by tradition, died out, the reality of sin, as it was then understood, died with them, and belief in the holiness of the Ten Commandments died too.

The Ten Commandments, too, are a law whose "works" no longer justify. For they are all, practically speaking, an unfolding of the first commandment, "I am the Lord thy God. Thou shalt have no other gods beside me." On the basis of our reality, we find a new approach to the fact that this first commandment is the one and only true commandment. For it is not really a commandment but a revelation of a reality for faith (Glaubenswirklichkeit), from which our historical reality to a great extent has emerged. The Gospel created a new relationship to the world. This new relationship was freedom for him who believed in the one and only God and His Son. Out of this freedom a new "state of life" issued which points back to the faith and freedom of the believer.

This necessitates a new version of the concept "sin." Sin is always a failure to attain the true self (Daseinsverfehlung), just as faith is a fulfillment of the true self (Daseinserfüllung). Fulfillment of the true self, like the failure to attain the true self, takes on another shape as the "state of life" changes. For they are not only spiritual events, but also concrete events. At the time when the "state of life" was decisively determined by a world "order" (that means by the "law"), sin was a breach of the "order." But that which today has become determinative for sin, as a failure to attain the true self, has been stated above: the "law" as the sustaining "order" of being has been torn down; a new-fashioned form of law is now effecting being in that it no longer unconditionally surrounds man in a binding and protecting | manner. As one called upon, who in the last analysis is alone, man is responsible to the three great unconditional challenges through the situation, through his neighbor, and through the future. This is the horizon of being which has surrounded man at all times, but which was covered by the "orders" and which has been uncovered by the Gospel's invasion into the world. The Gospel has not left man helpless in facing these superpowers. Just as the former "orders," on a smaller scale, offered their pre-formed answers and had the power to "make man right," the Gospel, on a new and final scale, offers three answers. These are faith, love and hope. The Gospel is now the power which "makes man right." Thus faith, love and hope, which once aggressively and transformingly entered the lives of men, have become the presupposition of their existence. To miss this presupposition is "sin."

For in the new "state of life," life and death, existence and extinction are dependent upon really holding this great "openness" open. This means: no institution is to be granted total validity; we are to meet every situation as openly as possible without falsifying the response to the situation through self-love or by absolutizing any particular values; in the situation in which we are placed, we are to know how to recognize *(wahrnehmen)* who our neighbor is, even when nothing binds us outwardly to the other person, or even when he meets us as a bitter enemy; we are not to obstruct our personal and corporate future by closing our eyes. This and much more is the practical side of a deficiency in faith, love and hope. And deficiency in faith, love and hope is sin since it is remoteness from God. The Christian proclamation has always known this. Sin shows itself to us from a new side, however, as an attack on the foundation of our present day being, as separation from the source and the postulate of our modern world. Sin, as remoteness from God, frees the way for demonization of the powers which are unleashed through faith, love and hope. The freedom which began as a freedom of those believing, loving and hoping, and which created its own form of life, threatens to become satanic if the powers of its source are taken from it. Freedom *has become* satanic in many places in our midst. But even this the Gospel foresaw and predicted. The uncovering of that which is of the antichrist is one of the Gospel's tasks in its course through the world and history.

The warning against sin is not a warning with which one can confront the non|believer. For a knowledge of sin exists only where there is faith. There is no logical compulsion to believe. But faith needs a *"Sitz im Leben"* in order to bear fruit. And correspondingly, faith needs an express knowledge of the concrete form in which "sin "actually shows and expresses itself.

The thin, moralizing atmosphere which surrounds this word "sin" today is unbearable and will not do justice to the shocking reality which is intended. Theology, where it speaks of sin, "has no other means of making intelligible what it has to say than by seeking and reaching man in the ethical reality in which he finds himself." [12]

---

[12] Cf. G. EBELING, "Die Evidenz des Ethischen," p. 328, and above p. 104.

Preparation for Preaching —
The Route from Exegesis to Proclamation *

by

Manfred Mezger

Translated by Robert A. Kraft

I. Presuppositions

The person who has to prepare theological students for the central task of their future ministry, namely, for preaching, finds himself in a peculiar position. He knows that scripture, which provides the commission for and the content of our proclamation, as discourse out of the past, ought to be spoken today audibly, sensibly, so that it comes to be understood, works faith, and produces life. He realizes that there are helps available for him and for his students: (1) *Historical*, in the form of history of preaching, from which we distill examples of how the task of preaching has been pursued and mastered at various times in the past; (2) *Systematic*, in the form of doctrine of preaching, which formulates for us the principles of its substance and of its form; (3) *Practical*, in the form of sermon outlines, sermonic reflections, or collections of sermons. He finds that the place from which preaching originates, and the destination towards which it moves have received exhaustive examination and treatment. But who has mapped out the route?

In this matter we find that we are, in a unique way, left to our own devices, and the number of books and articles worth mentioning which today provide basic as well as practical instruction for the route from scripture to preaching is so small that one can count them on the fingers of both hands.[1] To be sure, there are many series and helps in the form of "meditations," the significance of which should not be ignored. But their

---

* "Die Anleitung zur Predigt," ZThK, 56, 1959, pp. 377–397. The article is dedicated to R. BULTMANN on the occasion of his seventy-fifth birthday. – [Throughout the translation, *Anleitung* has been rendered by "preparation," which is intended to carry a semi-technical connotation, including the ideas of guidance and instruction. But the literal meaning should also be kept in mind: *Anleitung* should put one on the course, give sound direction. *Tr.*]

[1] The instructive example of HERMANN DIEM, Warum Textpredigt? Munich, 1939, has not been followed up by anything which would be precisely analogous. See, however, W. BERNET, "Probleme der Predigt," Schweizerische Theologische Umschau, 29, 1959, pp. 36 ff.

strength, which lies in the quest for an exposition of scripture which is peculiar to them, always exists side by side with their weakness – the danger of the subjective approach, which does not do justice to the text or even does violence to it. Moreover, such meditations are drafted with a particular congregation in view – a congregation which, therefore, is not my own – or they are produced without any view to an actual congregation, because the author had none, or perhaps had | only an idea of one in his mind. In general, he who knows the literature can only say that, with respect to aids for preaching, we stand (for the most part) in a unique no man's land. When they are solidly done, to be sure, exegeses and meditations keep quite close to the text which is to be expounded. But they do not show, or they do not show concretely enough, how they become preaching and how this preaching looks. Sermon outlines or published sermons are *exempla practica* (practical examples) which essentially say only this: "Here is how I have done it." In which case it must be said of both efforts that a great deal is lost on the route from the result of exegesis to the sermon; and secondly, that by comparison with its textual origin the form in which the sermon appears seems to have passed through a mysterious underground process of filtering, like the Danube River, whose water, it is true, re-appears – but then it is flowing into the Rhine!

But preparation for preaching, which comes about in the form of instruction, can at no point shun the control of its steps. It is activity in the market place, where everybody can look on. With exegesis, it shares the interest in exposition *sine ira et studio* (dispassionately); therefore it does not ask how that which is learned may be made practicable. But it shares with the "meditation" (one should rather say, "sermonic reflection") the interest in concretion, thus in the destination – in man – at which it is intended to arrive. Therefore it encompasses and probes the entire route by which the translation travels across the hiatus between what is necessarily remote and our life, and, as it takes care that what was spoken long ago will not merely be repeated, but will be spoken anew, it must demonstrate what understanding means, and must make clear how that which is understood is brought to expression *(zur Sprache kommt)* – that is, how it can become communicable today to men who listen.

Preparation for preaching, then, is movement from the text to the actual act of proclamation. If exegesis aims at telling what is *there*, perceptive preparation wants to say what is *therein*. It should not be said that this takes place on another plane, for it is concerned solely with a consistent furthering of exegesis – admittedly, in such a way that its result is thought through with the congregation in mind, and is expressed not as a popularized academic lecture, but as an unambiguous invitation to belief. Exegesis expresses what the text is all about. The sermon addresses what the text is all about *to* the listener. The closer the correspondence between exegesis and preparation for preaching, the more integrally and convincingly is the text disclosed to the listener. All the preliminary preparations – text criticism, finding the key to the text, exposition of the text, and application of the text – are brought to "their most extreme condensation in the act of preaching."[2] Therefore, in one direction, preparation for preaching involves the inquiry of the sermon into the means of exegesis; for indeed, preaching is not only prepared, but | also obliged to make answer exegetically. So exegesis calls preaching to account with reference to its presuppositions. In the other direction, however, preaching reminds exegesis of its consequences. It does not do this in such a way as to harass exegesis with the question about the "practical applicability of the exegetical endeavor,"[3] but it will remind it continually that "the ability to become practical is the real basis of all scientific knowledge" (Dilthey).

Luther has left us no systematic treatment of homiletics. What he has expressed in propositions and statements about his own experience concerning exposition and proclamation, however, would almost be sufficient for compiling a section on preparation for preaching. But precisely in this connection is Luther himself the model for the free interrelationship between exegesis and proclamation. That is due, on the one hand, to his utterly theological existence in which exegetical and homiletical endeavor flow back and forth internally as in intercommunicating tubes. On the other hand, it is due to the vocational unity of professor and preacher which is achieved in his own person, and in which these disciplines not only come into contact, but even overlap. In his academic lectures, his exegesis often extends to the sphere of preaching – indeed, it enters right into that sphere. And in wide stretches, his preaching consists of subtle exegesis, by which is not meant so-called "practical exposition," but the demand for conceptual distinctions or the regard for theological connections – in relation to the listening congregation.

Within systematic homiletics (insofar as it appears in the textbooks), therefore, preparation for preaching belongs not to the technical aspects of the doctrine of preaching, but to its theory – although it is not itself doctrine of preaching but is *practice* in preaching, thus *presupposing* the doctrine of preaching. If preparation for preaching were simply a "practice of execution" *(Ausführungspraxis)*, it would not have any particular subject of its own. We will have to demonstrate that it does have such a subject of its own, even though we may have to have recourse to some propositions from theoretical homiletics in the practice of preaching. Doctrine of preaching necessarily deals with general theses. Preparation

---

[2] G. EBELING, "Die Bedeutung der historisch-kritischen Methode für die protestantische Theologie und Kirche," in: Wort und Glaube, Tübingen, 1960, p. 48; cf. Word and Faith, Philadelphia, 1963, p. 60.

[3] *Ibid.*, p. 42; cf. Word and Faith, p. 54.

for preaching necessarily deals with special theses. It bears (this seems especially true today) the burden and also the conflict over current problems of the proclamation, at times even before these problems have come into the forum of theoretical homiletics, there to be given a hearing or solved. This is what makes it exciting. And it has a deep-seated pedagogical passion for its task – which, in the shadow of Luther, is obviously beyond reproach. This is connected with the conviction that the crucial factor in preaching, just as in art, cannot be taught because it must be "given" to a person; | but also with the conviction that a great deal *can* be taught, and that the position as well as the situation of the sermon can be changed for the better, if the preparation for preaching is properly carried out. The chances are that its intrinsic nature is not easily amenable to the style of the textbook, just as it is difficult to reduce the intrinsic nature of a work of art to a textbook style. Interpretation always has its individual stigma – it cannot be otherwise. It does not like to be detached from the spoken word. It therefore proceeds from person to person.

Before our theme is developed, there is still this to be said: In preparation for preaching, every problem which agitates theology can, strictly speaking, become actual. For there is nothing that occurs in theology which will not have an effect, whether overtly or covertly, sooner or later, either in preaching or on preaching. That fact makes theologically conscientious and theologically qualified preaching particularly sensitive – indeed, even irritable or touchy. If it preserves and observes this connection with theological endeavor, on the other hand, it can always be infused with new theological energy, even though in popular preaching current theological questions are usually not passed around too quickly. One thing is certain, and from it preaching cannot exempt itself: practical theology is much less the crown of all disciplines than it is the rallying point for all the partial problems. Unless it wishes to lag hopelessly behind, it must at least keep in close contact with the primary subjects and results of all the other disciplines, even if that is a tiresome business. Even in this respect, therefore, the field of endeavor has by no means contracted. Nevertheless, no one can isolate himself from the whole, despite the legitimacy of concentrating on his own specialty. Whether we like it or not, preaching does encompass the whole spectrum: church history and doctrine, Old and New Testament studies, faith as well as conduct, worship as well as its place and order, instruction as well as pastoral administration of the word, the mission of the Church in the world as well as the attempt to understand man in his world. Not that these are or should be allowed to become its factual content, for in that case preaching would indeed become a theological supermarket. But these are the matters which always go hand in hand with preaching, and preaching has no control over which of the theological disciplines will now and again supply it with its incentive or with the embarassing questions.

Therefore, preparation for preaching is by no means an invariable methodology. Rather, it is a watchful, efficient, honest service, not determined – let us hope – by alien interests, assisting the Church today to say *what it has to say* – in the double sense of those words. Both for the congregation and for the world, it is always precisely that which it | has to say. We have arranged what is to be said about preparation for preaching under the following headings:

1. The Problem of Translation – the Text and its Freedom.

2. The Problem of Language *(Sprache)* – Man and his History.

3. The Problem of Secularity *(Profanität)* – the Congregation in the World.

II. Particular Problem Areas

1. The Problem of Translation – the Text and Its Freedom[4]

As a rule, the text which in preaching we have to expound as the word of God encountering us today comes to us as part of a larger context. We will have to admit that already in selecting a text, exposition of the text is always implied. The fact that a definite theological outlook steers the selection of a definite series of texts has already been noticed by Luther in his *"Formula Missae"* (with not very favorable comments) in connection with the Epistle lessons of the Ancient Church.[5] We will not concern ourselves here with the dispute as to whether it is preferable to preach from a selected portion of scripture or to pursue a running exposition of entire biblical books. That should not be blown up into a major problem. Kliefoth is probably correct when he says that he is convinced that those preachers who are unable to preach satisfactorily on an individual pericope

---

[4] This point, like all the following, is developed with reference to the particular findings concerning the preparation for preaching which have emerged from various homiletical seminars. It should be added that the interrelated exegetical-homiletical problems have become unusually clear and also most exacting, thanks to the willing cooperation of my New Testament colleagues, ERNST FUCHS (Berlin) and HERBERT BRAUN (Mainz), who agreed to conduct joint exegetical-homiletical seminars.

[5] Weimar Edition, vol. 12, p. 209 (Eng. tr. by P. Z. STRODACH, in the Philadelphia Edition of the Works of Martin Luther, vol. 6, p. 87): "Certainly the time has not yet come to attempt revision here (i. e. concerning the daily Epistle lessons), as nothing ungodly is read. But something seems to be needed, since those parts of the Epistles of Paul in which faith is taught are rarely read, but most frequently those parts dealing with morals and exhortations. While the originator of the Epistles (lections) seems to have been a singularly unlearned and superstitious friend of works, the office required rather that, for the greater part, those sections in which faith in Christ is taught, be appointed."

will scarcely be able to preach any better on entire biblical books. The practice of expounding selected portions of the text runs the risk, especially when it is repeated cyclically, of neglecting certain biblical books. (Of the danger and vice of the preacher living out of the sermonic barrel, it is to be hoped that one will only need to speak *per nefas* [in terms of abuse].) On the other hand, following the lectionary relieves us of the agony of having to choose for ourselves. And whoever flees from the assigned text because it was too difficult for him, soon will have discovered that all texts are fundamentally just as difficult, and he could as easily have remained with the first.

But what is much more important for preparation for preaching to know than lectionary problems is the fact that our texts themselves originated as sermonic materials. They once *were* | preaching, they *are* preaching; essentially, therefore, they can again "*become*" preaching today. They do not want to be anything else but preaching – that is, a report by believing men who, through their testimony, wish to convince (not to persuade) other men, so that faith arises through faith. The objection that the word of the biblical witnesses thus expresses an interest from the outset – and indeed, the interest of faith, which is so readily decried as "subjective" – can only be welcomed by us since it immediately points to the correct category. The witnesses of the Bible, whose word we seek to understand and transmit, report events, words, deeds, encounters, experiences, to the degree they are touched by all these experiences. This involvement disturbs only the person who intends to avoid similar involvement by plucking out "objective facts" from the testimony of the witnesses, facts which he supposedly can then view in detachment, judge as to their reasonableness, and accept or reject. The biblical witnesses certainly have said with all the clarity that could be desired that this is *not* what they want to happen. For they could not effect faith in this manner. No one can do it this way. The most that could be accomplished this way is to gain consent to the incontestable formula $A = A$. Luther, by interpreting a scholastic concept in a slightly different way, calls this kind of consent, "*fides historica*," though with the qualification "*fides diabolica*." Faith as God's way of making us sure of himself is indeed critical, alert, and thoroughly sober; but it has neither the obligation nor the inclination to demonstrate its possibility or its reasonableness in the forum of the unconcerned *(der Nichtbetroffenen)*. Nor does it compare itself with the so-called "objective acts of thought and sight" (Schlatter), by temporarily forgetting or acting as though my eyes were not, in fact, *my* eyes. That is hypothetical naiveté, which would be disqualified even if Kant had never lived. Completely neutral conduct, defined in no way whatsoever by any subjectivity, does not exist even in physical experiments – quite apart from the fact that it has no interest for us. Faith does not have any reasonability which can be made intelligible apart from faith, just as the lover would not care to present reasons for why he is so engaged and not otherwise. Faith will gladly bear the suspicion that such conduct may be very close to fanaticism *(Schwärmerei)*. It will reveal its sobriety at a fitting time, for it is involvement *(Betroffenheit)* and not stupefaction *(Benommenheit)*.

It cannot be claimed that this kind of faith speaks with equal strength from all the texts which we use in preaching, but it certainly speaks from those which derive from witnesses who are moved by God. There is no | sense in attempting here to classify passages by chapter and verse according to whether we consider ourselves to be nearer to the central idea of faith or more on the so-called "periphery." There are also some strictly factual reports in the Bible, of course, and occasionally it becomes apparent, to the delight of the historicists, that the Bible can indeed narrate as reliably, from the point of view of profane history, as anyone could expect. But we are not dealing with its own essential concern when we choose to wander around in this field of secular history. There is no need to maintain that the Bible has fallen down from heaven and that faith is an act of magic, if one holds fast to the indisputable claim that faith only arises from faith, just as it is eternally true that love is only understood by love.

But how can faith arise "from faith"? Surely in this way, that we let ourselves become involved in the verses which we have before us at the beginning of our sermon preparation. The kind of expertness which is necessary to be able to hear Paul and John speak in a real voice will not be spelled out here – a great deal is needed, for unfortunately it is not done with syllables and grammar. It is to be noted, however, that already in the first instant – and that is the attempt at translation – the switches are thrown for the future journey. Next to reading, translation is the most difficult art there is. The person who knows what various nuances mean for the spirit of a language, the intonation (which unfortunately can no longer be recovered in the case of dead witnesses), the adaptable tempo of speaking, the whole sensibility of an intellectual product, the logical structure, the rhythmic flow of a sentence, all as means of expressing the inner intentions – to him who knows something of these things, the first, second, and third translation, this constantly renewed attack upon and attempt to achieve a more suitable re-casting and re-molding into his own language, will be an enchanting and inspiring process. And since the immediate comprehension of the verbal context provokes interpretative activity, it is impossible to proceed with excessive precision at the first stage. It is the responsible transaction of having to exchange our coinage without thereby reducing its value.

The one who has to preside over this transaction will be astonished to notice how many particles, which are the delicate shadings of the linguistic landscape, are overlooked or suppressed. And since translation is not just a necessary evil, but is the backbone of the entire textual endeavor – indeed, it is really the nerve-center of all interpretation – it stands at the very beginning in every respect. His amazement is always great when it is proved to the translator that not only "*minima*" (trivialities) but "*praecipua*" (important matters) have eluded him, or that his translation of the wording has been obstructed by his presupposed mental and verbal picture of the text. He always supposes that he already knows how it reads; but it reads differently. Similarly, he always supposes | that he already knows what is implied therein, what probably is meant; and he robs the text of its freedom to celebrate its première *with us*.

With such imprecise translating there already begins – this is easy to demonstrate – the attempt to draw from the text a desired general truth. If I have it in hand, I can spare myself further deliberation and can preach without further ado. Here we are confronted with the symptom of the "frantic impatience of pastors," a symptom which is criticized by K. G. Steck in his study of the meditation.[6] To make it manageable, to make it practicable, to chop homiletical kindling wood: such are the methods which destroy the freedom of the text. By this I do not mean that one should pretend to be dealing with an unfamiliar passage, when it is in fact well known – who will dispute the fact that many pericopes are retained in our memory word for word (although one will be amazed when he reads them in the original) – but what is really important is to recognize the text's unique form, its historical particularity. The latter is what we fear, for if the text has its own time, its own place, its own address, in addition to its own particular conditions, what "general truth" can I still squeeze from it for my sermon? None, I hope. What is left is only its particular, that is, concrete truth, which only in rare instances can be brought over from there to here without being translated.

Translating does not mean simply to substitute one word for another, but to seek and find at once the new place at which this text, without detriment to its historical individuality, meets us. The short cut by which I picture myself as a listener in the skin of Moses or of Paul is certainly popular, but it is not satisfactory, for I am neither the one nor the other. The historical situation which distinguishes me from them is not submerged so easily. The way to overcome it is not by treating the particular details with indifference, thus effacing the personal profile of the text, but by becoming aware of the involvement *(Betroffenheit)* which is the same for them as for me, but which is described in a particular way in each instance. "The preacher must himself be clear on this point, that his listeners are not the same men to whom the gospel was first proclaimed. If he understands this (because he has noted it in the text), then scripture says to him: 'Your

---

[6] Göttinger Predigtmeditationen, Beiheft 1, 1954, p. 28.

listeners are, notwithstanding, the same men to whom the gospel went forth!' The angelic message, 'Behold, I proclaim to you great joy!' has the strange power to make all men equal.'"[7] True enough! But it is only by precise translation that I appropriate the example of the concrete situation and with it also there always comes the imperative obligation to concretize it anew today. But what presupposition permits me to believe that the words of Isaiah or of Matthew | can have any relationship to me? It is the presupposition that what they say or write has not come *from* them, but *to* them. I have no way of knowing beforehand whether this presupposition is valid. I must take my chances on it today. And the continuity of the faith-producing testimony which I ought to exposit and speak anew today does not consist solely in the fact that they were men such as I am, but also in the fact that their daring assertion, "God spoke to me in this way," is confirmed for me today through its being repeated by my becoming involved – in a way which cannot be fully explained by these words alone.

The persistence in the task of strict, controlled translation is demanded because recognition of the given, concrete textual form guards against hasty appropriation of what is supposed to be the "essential substance" *(Gehalt)* of the text, to which every part and parcel of the text is sacrificed with careless dispatch. Here, in the work of translation, is to be practised what is often critically noted, but which is rarely if ever heeded and which has been completely obscured by false slogans: interpretation is not elimination. It operates neither by selection nor by reduction. It never, at any stage, associates with the following categories which are wrongheaded all along the line: essential substance *(Gehalt)* and external complexity *(Gestalt)*, form and content, tree and bark – and whatever similarly inappropriate distinctions may exist. The discussion, which at this point has run aground on false shibboleths (for example, concerning "demythologizing"), cannot sensibly be advanced if we lump together translation with principle of selection, much less with a subjective and arbitrary principle of selection. Furthermore, nothing can be gained by allegory, which is again being unscrupulously used in contemporary homiletical practice, that notorious "most convenient way for one to avoid the critical question by allowing everything to retain its literal meaning, while dispensing with having to consider it binding, and thus escaping into the psychical sphere."[8]

Thus, freedom of the text is not merely that it does not permit itself to be domesticated by us, that it does not permit itself to be overpowered by

---

[7] E. FUCHS, Was ist Theologie? (Sammlung gemeinverständlicher Vorträge, 203/04), Tübingen, 1953, pp. 20f.

[8] R. BULTMANN, "Neues Testament und Mythologie," in: Kerygma und Mythos, ed. by H.W.BARTSCH, Hamburg, 1951, p. 24; cf. the English translation by R.H.FULLER, in: Kerygma and Myth, I, London, 1953, p. 13.

us – for that would take place at the cost of understanding it. But above all, freedom of the text means that one represents the assertion which is discernible in it intact (an assertion is a movement, and not an "essential substance" [Gehalt]!), not trimming it down because it raises difficulties, not using trickery because it forces us to come clean, and not expounding it in a deceitful manner because fidelity to the text compels us to acknowledge that "I can in no way appropriate this way of speaking about the world, nature, and man for myself." All the better. The text has spoken in its own way; | you translate in your own way. And if the whole point (Gegenstand) of the text is by no means translatable (that also happens), don't try to work magic, but keep within the limits of your understanding and within the measure of your faith. There is a measure to faith (Rom. 12:3). And the two ways of treating the text would both be presumptuous: in defiance of the text's own assertion, to foist upon it what it does not say but what we want it to say; and also, to renounce my present, God-given perspective – which always means, "Here is how I understand time, world, and man" – and to transmute myself back, as it were, by force, into the understanding and speech of men who had an entirely different perspective from mine. Freedom of the text means, make it your aim that the text becomes transparent for yourself and for the listeners – not that your homiletical opinion becomes transparent. Luther has concluded sermons with the observation that he has not succeeded in coming to grips with this text, indeed, that he has only partially understood it. Often we hear him say: "We will hear more of this at another time. May God grant that others after me do better." This praiseworthy practice has gone out of style.

In order that we may see what is meant by the freedom of the text – freedom which we should not curb nor suffocate even where it is (however unnecessarily) embarrassing for us – I have selected two precarious passages over which the allegorical arts have triumphed to the present day. First, Acts 1:9 – "As they were looking on, he was lifted up, and a cloud took him out of their sight." One may, of course, if he so desires (but we would rather not), speak on this text as a 1959 Ascension Day essay (from a catholic pen) has:

". . . Christ is now trans-spatial. This concept of trans-spatiality is well known to modern science. In simple words, the report of the ascension expresses nothing more and nothing less than this when it speaks of the glorified body of the resurrected Lord. The Lord elevates himself slightly from the earth, as though he were exhibiting to his Apostles his freedom from the powers of nature (!). Then a cloud envelops him, providing a visible means for the astonished Apostles to understand that the body of their Master still remains in existence, but has been removed from their sight and touch – and indeed, from the grasp of every material power whatsoever. He is no longer spatial, but trans-spatial; he is no longer on the earth, no longer in this world, but in heaven."[9]

This sort of translation really is passé, although it seems to remain close to the text throughout.

Evangelical preaching, however, hardly fares better when we make a brief synopsis of contemporary sermons on the words of John 20: | 6f.: "He (Peter) went into the tomb; he saw the linen cloths lying, and the napkin, which had been on his (Jesus') head, not lying with the linen cloths but rolled up in a place by itself." Of course, one can say: "What value do these funerary details have for us? None at all. I will ignore them and preach quite simply on the theme, 'Jesus lives.'" (This, as we know, is always correct.) If only I could be so sure that there is also nothing of importance for the text and for its witness in these details . . . Why then has the text reported them? And where do the "non-essential" details leave off? And where do the so-called "central issues" begin? Is the stone a "detail"? Is the *angelus interpres* (angelic interpreter) a "central issue"? When we allow for complete and unobstructed recognition of the text's complexity and of its freedom, the assertion which the text is making is *only* translatable for us today if we adopt a mode of assertion the movement of which is *radically contrary* to that of the text. Symbolism is not the answer, nor is allegory. It is precisely because of the message, which in this text has such an overwhelmingly miraculous form, that every attempt at illustrating Easter falls short. And the question as to whether it is "then still" possible to proclaim the act of God in Jesus Christ must be answered: "*Only* then and just in that way, because it is liberated from the completely inadequate evidence which encumbers its testimony." In preaching, the measure of joy and of evangelical power increases strictly in relation to one's recognition of the freedom of the text – freedom which it has and which it gives to us to understand its assertion today. Every other attempt ends in a shadowy historical "somehow something happened," in the sacrifice of veracity, or (most frequently) in covering the problem over. We are speaking of the task of translation which we first of all have to accomplish in every instance for *ourselves*.

In terms of method, this is not to be understood in such a way that in our sermons on miracle texts we inevitably have to deal with questions of introduction or hermeneutics in the presence of the congregation. But neither is it to be understood in such a way that we do nothing at all, and, from cunning or from fear, throughout our ministry leave the congregation in the dark as to what sort of freedom of an understanding faith it is, in which the text not only places us, but calls us. Preparation for preaching does not mean to spare the student the vexation of the text, nor to teach

---

[9] Mainzer Allgemeine Zeitung, May 7–8, 1959.

him some tricks by which he can circumvent these questions which have
long been open and have continually been brushed aside. Rather, it means
to encourage him and to lay upon him the obligation to confide completely
in the text, in such a way that in attempting a true translation he will find
that the text preserves and perseveres in what it intends to assert, precisely
at those places where we must repeat for the sake of the faith-creating
testimony the assertion of the text *in completely different language*, and
sometimes even *contra versionem explicatam* (contrary to its express
statement). |

2. The Problem of Language – Man and his History

What language, then, should we use? We know what is demanded and
expected of preaching, especially with regard to its language. One needs
only to browse around in the collected essays, "Kritik an der Kirche"
(see n. 12), to notice how severely so-called "ecclesiastical" and "sermonic"
language is condemned; but also with what urgency – indeed, with what
astonishing hopes – the message necessary for man today is expected to
issue from the Church through the rightly spoken gospel. Now terms like
"sermonic language, ecclesiastical language, cultic language," are much
too general, as though one could thereby imagine something concrete.
That there *are* all these things as a mixture of slightly obsolete clichés,
sonorous pomposity, and many unexplained theological concepts, no one
can doubt. Unfortunately, the judgment of Trillhaas probably still holds
true that in the pulpit, many preachers avail themselves of a language
which would, "if used in everyday discourse, produce gales of laughter."[10]
In this case, however, we are not dealing with the problem of language as
such, but only with the problem of diction.

If we ask the usual homiletics methodology where it deals with language,
it would reply, almost without exception, "under formal homiletics" –
that is, under the *modus praedicandi*. Thus language would form a chapter
of the formal aspects, not of the principles of systematic homiletics. This
may appear to be quite reasonable in that the language of preaching,
according to traditional homiletics, is a question dealing with the "how?"
of proclamation, not with the "what?" and certainly not with the "where?"
But we could only proceed along these lines if we were to separate "preaching" from "language," and leave nothing at all to "language" except the
modus loquendi or even "*loquentis*" – the so-called "style of speaking."
Then there would be appended a chapter on so-called "religious eloquence"
which, admittedly, it must *also* include. But this cannot be considered as
an independent subject, for it is self-evident that in preaching, one is

---

[10] Evangelische Predigtlehre, München, 3rd ed., 1948, p. 204.

speaking. "*Rem tene, verba sequentur*" (Hold on to the subject matter; the words will follow). We have been that perceptive for quite a while!

But language is not solely and simply that by means of which the sermon is conveyed. It is rather the way in which preaching *comes to pass*. What is to be proclaimed as the intention and assertion of the text requires to be encountered nowhere else except just *in* the proclamation. It demands to be heard, for faith must come by hearing. But how else could it be heard except by being spoken? It is there, in what is spoken, that it is met. Thus language is not simply a means of conveying the proclamation in the sense of "language of preaching." This would only mean subordination of language, as the genitive clearly indicates. | In that language is an act of communicating, it is much more accurate to say that it is the place and the time for the message of preaching – or perhaps even better, it is the "occasion." Preaching speaks – that is, it "has something to say" – or it is just mute. Unfortunately, there is more mute preaching today than that which "says something." But preaching which "has something to say" is just that place and occasion in which the intention of the text becomes language for every listener, proclaiming that "God is your God in Jesus Christ." Consequently, if preaching is language which has something to say, *what is* emerges through it. We hear *where* we really stand and who is really "at bat." It is said to us in such a way that we unde rstandit, and again are made aware of where we belong.

Why must that be said to us? Because otherwise we cannot understand the world, men, and ourselves. Preaching as language is the very occasion where there is room and time to bring to expression what things really are and what man is. If that is not done, neither the world nor the things have anything to say to us. Everything is blurred, man is without direction. But where the proclamation becomes our language, there we can tarry, listen, understand. And insofar as language is an event which takes time, it also *gives* time and assembles us at *the* place where we hear the language of a quite distinct, unmistakable voice, breaking through in human speech. On the occasion in which preaching takes place as language, place and time are together for us, that is what is signified and embodied in the word *kairos*. "That is why *occasio* (Luther means nothing other than *kairos*) is a great thing . . . The young lads in school do not understand that, for those are *seniles et imperatoriae voces* (old and regal words) . . . One cannot express what *occasio* means, thus one does not understand it. In German, there is no adequate equivalent, for the word "*Gelegenheit*" *est magis alligatum loco et personis quam tempori* (relates more to place and persons than to time). *Occasio* ought to have *plus temporis* (more of the temporal element). Neither do the *latini* have any synonym by which they can fully express it; the word *tempus* (time) is too general. I hold that the etymology is, as one says, *a cadendo* – accidental. The *graeci* also have but one word which means *tempus*, and it may also be expressed by saying, 'Make good use of the momemt, and what the moment brings' . . . That means, 'Grab it, while there is time – *nunc* (now), *nunc*, while the *nunc* is still here.' The Germans have some marvelous proverbs which express this, as they say: 'If someone offers you a young pig, you should open the bag'; and again: 'If our Lord greets you, you should thank him.' That is a very pious way of saying that our Lord God sends the *occasionem* . . . But it is *donum Dei* (a gift of God) to whomever would understand it. . . ."[11]

Thus, as Luther recognized, we are concerned immediately with *time* when it comes to language. Language is the | copula uniting the proclamation with time. Why? Because it announces the time as a time of salvation. That is an event, not a concept. And one of the most difficult tasks of preparation for preaching is to make the text's intention, which has been obtained through translation and which we are accustomed to express conceptually as an aid to ourselves, once again liquescent, and that means to make the concept, which is always abstract, *expressible*. If it is not expressible, if it cannot become an event in language, it is not understood. Luther's test question, which must be incessantly repeated at this point, is "What does that mean? How does that come about?" Many contemporary sermons are not immune to the charge that they have not been able to transform the ciphers of the doctrinal systems into events of life; on the contrary, refuge has been sought in conceptual ciphers. Language sits in judgment upon the contents of doctrine, upon the so-called *fides quae*. And language exercises a just and merciless judgment in that it refuses itself to everything that has not actually become my own. There is no room for deception. It simply is and remains not understood or not understandable. Language as criterion means that you must be able to say it, and say it in such a way that it first becomes transparent for you, and then also for others. He who is unable to make it transparent for others, shows that it has not become so for him. If that is the task, then the sermon must be concerned with matters that can be expressed, and not with ideas or conceptions! God is no conception, for he is not conceivable. Are the concepts of ecclesiastical doctrine really expressible today? We would hope so, but it does not always sound like it. Apart from language, there is no life. Words in themselves do not constitute language. Recitation of formulas does not constitute preaching, for we ourselves are not present in these formulas: we do not find ourselves there, nor do we find our way into them. The expressibility of what is proclaimed by me, as an event today, is the evidence of its vital energy. The moving power of preaching is not any

---

[11] Weimar Edition, Tischreden, vol. 6, p. 359f. (no. 7050). See the English translation, extremely abridged, in W. HAZLITT, The Table-Talk of Martin Luther, London, 1884, p. 363f. (= p. 448 in the later Philadelphia Edition).

so-called "objective validity" *(das "an sich Richtige")*, not truth left over from the day before yesterday, nor that which has long since become speechless, but that which is summoned forth by understanding and understandable language, that which now, through preaching, is brought to life, spoken, and *in that way* is "present" *(anwesend)* – in other respects, let it "be" *(wesen)* where it will! Time after time it seems, says Heinz Zahrnt, that the man in the pulpit does not lower "his bucket deep enough to draw water for our time also, though preaching has probably never yet been so correct and proper – one is almost tempted to say, so alarmingly correct and so boringly proper – as it is in our pulpits today."[12]

What is so startling about preparation for preaching at the point where the intention of the text | – this intention of the text for today – ought to become language, is this: the students suppose that they have a definite, dogmatic "norm" to fulfill in the sermon. Thus it would not be enough to say today with Jeremiah, "God is consumed with concern for his Israel." Nor would it be enough to say today with Matthew, "God does not sell his heaven but gives it away." Rather, some sort of formal dogmatic "extra" must appear here, in order to satisfy somebody's demands. *One* sort of such an "extra" is forced christological interpretation as a purely formal procedure. According to this procedure, preaching achieves its proper goal only when an artificial christological product is produced. Were it not so disastrous, it would be interesting to observe: One always arrives at christology by this approach whether he preaches on Joshua's "national assembly" or on Solomon's concubines. It is a remarkable practice by which Christ is, as it were, simply imposed on everything without ever asking him whether that is what he wants. Indeed, does the text, as a text of scripture, not have a secret center of its own? Do the lines of the whole have no common vanishing point? Must there always be over-interpretation, so that one may exhibit the testimony of formal orthodoxy for himself and for others?

A second kind of false, would-be obligation is that the students (and not they alone!) suppose that they must preach their way right through the entire text, not only with respect to its central intention, but in exact verbal completeness! At the end of such a sermon, the preacher is finished with the text; unfortunately, so is the congregation. We should burden neither the text, nor ourselves, nor our hearers with such a yoke. As dangerous and as objectionable as arbitrary selection may be, the law of strict numerical perfection is an outrage. In contrast to this practice, one would like to advise the preacher to say just one thing today (that does not necessarily mean topical preaching!), and this one thing, confirmed and strenghtened by the entire text, will be more than enough.

---

[12] Kritik an der Kirche, ed. by H. J. Schultz, Stuttgart: Kreuzverlag, 1958, p. 176.

A third kind of obligation which supposedly is to be fulfilled in preaching is the demand to delve into the paradoxical. In that case faith proves itself in that it considers certain things to be possible which have no place in man's natural and historical world of reality, things which everybody would reject as completely irrelevant or absurd anywhere else but in the pulpit. But in church everything is possible. There the absolutely incomprehensible becomes as self-evident as a fairy in a fairy-tale. "Surely what I understand cannot be true." And it is here that the problem of language becomes the problem of man and his history: preaching means proclaiming that God has descended to *us*, not that we ascend to him; and proclaiming that he | has become a real man, flesh and blood, as proof that he understands us and we him. All of this intersects *our* plane, not another or a higher plane, to which I must first elevate myself by faith.

Without any attempt at evading the issues, then, the situation is twofold. First, that history has taken place between God and us in the person of Jesus Christ, and it has occurred on the soil of this earth. And where else should it take place? What has occurred and is occurring, was history and is history – nothing besides, nothing beyond, and nothing but history. The extraordinary thing which occurred in Jesus (and it *was* most extraordinary!) is just this, that temporal, inner worldly events were believed and understood, through the word which proclaimed them, as God speaking and acting, that is, as events which had entered into the world, and not as events which originated there. This includes everything, positively everything. For nothing but that which has come to be historical and accordingly can again become for me my own history today through preaching, is accessible to me at all. Even if I so desired, I could not agree to the two-fold, split concept of history which is found in so many contemporary sermons – split in the sense that the usual concept of history is not considered adequate for dealing with revelation, that is, with God's speaking and acting. Such a view holds that a separate sphere of some sort must be reserved, a kind of historical nature-preserve in which everything may be included that cannot be subsumed under the realm of history, where it would have to be accounted for strictly and candidly. It experiments with the question, "Why shouldn't it be so? It is entirely conceivable or imaginable!"[13] True enough. But we may compare this to an imaginary 100 dollars, which, nevertheless, has no reality. It is not earning interest. The idea that God could, if he wished, perform the most unlikely acts in the realm of nature and history, has long been a pleasant thought. But God has not thought it.

---

[13] Cf. the unanswered questions which CH. HARTLICH and W. SACHS have asked concerning K. BARTH's concept of history: Kerygma und Mythos, ed. H. W. BARTSCH, II, Hamburg, 1952, pp. 117–121.

On the contrary, then, everything that cannot become our own presently occurring history through the word which is preached and believed is untenable as a required or an expected *credendum* (item to be believed), because it is completely irrelevant. Such an item may appear in our discourse as a statement or as a declaration, but it is not a testimony on which, when it is obediently received, life and death hinges. All of these detours of preaching end in *fides historica*. And the demonstration that such thoughts are futile is the fact that they are not expressible, that they cannot become concrete – except as conceptions *(Vorstellungen)*. But we do not preach conceptions. They cannot, therefore, take up their dwelling among us. The controlling | question for theological concepts is not simply "Who?" or "What?" but always "Where?" Whoever fails to take this into account is in the difficult position of having to force upon the free word of the text a language certified ecclesiastically, traditionally or otherwise, but which has no reference to history and thus remains lifeless, incomprehensible because it is obsolete stock, worn out, unhistorical, dead. It is impossible that what ought to be proclaimed can reach us in this way. To "reach us" *(ankommen)* means something entirely concrete (and only the concrete brings salvation!), namely, to find a place to dwell with us in faith which understands, and thus to become personal (not general) truth by coalescing with my existence. That is incarnation. If that is not what it means, we do not know what else it could be. Now, to be sure, the text always exists prior to my faith; I have not fabricated it. But what is the nature of this priority? Does it mean that this faith requires absolute value in itself, for itself, and by itself? Or, that it wants to come *to* us and dwell with us? The very way in which the question is put indicates the answer. The formula for what God has to say to us in Jesus Christ is, in the form of the first commandment: "I am the Lord your God – not *a* God, but *your* God!" *Deus tuus*. For Luther, the *"tuus"* is the most difficult word in the whole of holy scripture.[14] Thus, to the question of man, "Where can I dwell?" God gives his answer, "with me." And the formula for what Jesus said and did is expressed in the words, "You are *my* God forever. Therefore I am not afraid." Preaching cannot "draw Christ close enough into the flesh." There God and faith are together. No one can separate them. And the narratives *(Geschichten)* of scripture become, for the hearing and believing man, his own history. Otherwise they have nothing at all to do with me.

---

[14] Weimar Edition, Tischreden, vol. 2, p. 303 (no. 2047): "And I know one word which is the most difficult of all the words in Scripture, namely 'your' in the first commandment."

3. The Problem of Secularity (Profanität) – the Congregation in the World

The statement that the congregation is born in preaching[15] proves to be pertinent not only with respect to preaching, but also with respect to the congregation, by virtue of the fact that it can be reversed: preaching is born in the congregation. Preparation for preaching has ample opportunity to feel the absence of the congregation, for in proceeding from translation to the language of the sermon where a distinct "you" ought to be addressed, there easily arises a discontinuity. To what congregation should the practice sermon be addressed? Many a student knows what to do. He simply speaks to his fellow students. That is by no means the | worst thing that could happen, for he knows their problems and their questions. His dialogue with them thus does not proceed entirely in a vacuum. Others think of their home congregation, with which they are familiar to some degree. Neither is such a procedure as this to be despised. It is certain that preaching increases in color, comprehensibility, and significance as soon as the congregation is no longer only theoretically present, but actually present – encouraging and irritating, assisting and opposing. Thus it can happen that the congregation becomes the permanent partner in reflection on and drafting of the sermon. Moreover, with the delivery of the sermon, those who are now listening to what they helped produce, to be sure, may take very different attitudes towards the product.

But more important than this, even for students, is the fact that preaching is only learned *from* preaching, and thus basically *in* preaching. The significance of this is always two-fold: first, that a good example provides incentive and good ideas; but also, as Goethe said, that the "inadequate" makes "fruitful." Someone has said rather pointedly, "That which is essential does not occur *along with* preaching, but *after* preaching." That is to say, the congregation ought to be able to live by the word of preaching. The listeners should expect that this word will go with them into the place where they live, work, and spend their days in joy and vexation, in sin and faith. With that in mind, one should not demand too much from his preaching – for the benefit of the congregation. But neither should one expect too little from it.

Building a bridge from preaching to the life of the congregation, from the congregation at worship to the congregation in the world, will succeed more easily the more naturally we bring both areas together in our word. It would be most false and fatal, in terms of language as well as in actuality, to think here of two totally distinct and separate spheres. There is already much too great a gulf between worship and life. We certainly should not

---

[15] H. DIEM, "Die Geburt der Gemeinde in der Predigt," Evangelische Theologie, 9, 1949–50, pp. 193 ff.

assist in widening it. This does not mean that we forcibly and nonchalantly secularize what is "ecclesiastical" – if this expression may be momentarily permitted – for the result will always be that the secular becomes "clericalized." But it does mean that we abandon the wall of separation from the world which, by means of preaching, has already become all too high; that we do not take advantage of the custom of exaggerated solemnity; that when the congregation is assembled for word and communion, everything does not suddenly become "entirely different," with sonorous liturgical countenances and Sunday manners. To be sure, the service God is rendering to us in our worship – which consists of listening, receiving, thanking, praying, and singing – has a style of its own; and lack of style is by no means a bold act of secularity. But in terms of attitude, one should always stand in the pulpit *without* a robe, and many times it would be a real blessing if one stood there in his shirtsleeves. | Still, that is not crucial.

Again at this point, however, what is of primary importance is the freedom of the text to become unencumbered secular language – not pompous, not with a tremolo, not burning incense; rather, with a breath of fresh air and an unaffected naturalness. It should be simple (not ostentatious), concrete (not pallid), completely understandable (not professionally scientific – theology belongs in the study, and not in the pulpit), vigorous (not sluggish), in every respect intent that the congregation should be a *real* partner in the dialogue, without pretense and speculations – or one might prefer to say that the congregation should be superbly "entertained" (for that is the secular meaning of *homilein*). Thus the language of the sermon should be full of life and exciting, as a child relates his adventure, and therefore always a little bit like a good story. At this point there is no regimentation of language. Insofar as the language of preaching maintains strong ties with its content, there is no chance that just everything can insinuate itself into it or find room for play. But nothing is prescribed, and nothing – absolutely nothing – in heaven or on earth is withheld from or forbidden to preaching. Everything is permitted, although not everything is beneficial! But that which determines the freedom or the limitation of the riches and abundance of language is not what is "said," but what truly "says something." Let no one suppose that a fashionable jargon is a new language; it is just a lot of old rot. Neither should anyone think that he can add a cubit to his height in this regard. *"Le style, c'est l'homme."* Language shelters us. But it also betrays us. It can become transparent for us; but it can also remain frightfully inaccessible to us.

What we mean when we speak, on the basis of the text, of genuine secularity, secularity in the sense of the possibility for a man to become God's beloved in the midst of the world through the gospel, may be illustrated from the passages in which Jesus makes the secular comparable to the heavenly, to the kingdom of God; and the opposite also is said, that the kingdom of Heaven is similar to some sort of earthly thing or action. It is unnecessary to be overly concerned and to object that "I cannot say that in so secular a manner, for if I do there is no longer any difference between the New Testament and legendary wisdom." Why should there be special reservations? And who would be served by them? Our texts, it is true, come from scripture, and not from the fairy-tales. Nevertheless, it is also true that sagacity is always sage, whether it is found in the Koran or comes from Isaiah; and foolishness is always foolish, whether it is found in the Vedas or in the Psalms. Not only the most beautiful stories, but also those with the most forceful language and those which are most pregnant with truth begin everywhere with such words as "There was a king...," "A man had two sons...," "A man had a vineyard...." This familiarity and simplicity at the very beginning marks the advent of that which is unheard of. Where there is narration and preaching of this sort, the Spirit is at work. |

But, to be sure, one must begin! And he must begin at the beginning; that is, at once, with the matter at hand, with the text, with the intention of the message. Introductions are the death of the sermon. First, because they usually beat around the bush, or lead away from the matter at hand rather than to it. We have listened to the chimes, we have sung, we have prayed, we have heard the scripture lesson; what should we wait for? Introductions are mostly a product of embarrassment – "One cannot approach the congregation so directly. One must lead them slowly to the matters at hand." Are we to think of a *praedispositio ad verbum*? Well, the preacher's efforts usually end here! Secondly, introductions are perhaps intended to defend or justify the text, as it were. But that is entirely irrelevant. It is a reflection of our false, self-defensive attitude towards faith (or rather, little faith) before the world.

And the genuine secularity which we gain from the text is this, that with the gospel we are ahead of everything in *all* situations. The most necessary and beneficial piece of political advice, which the congregation ought to gain from the sermon, is this: "Never let your theme be given you by your opponent. If your opponent dictates the theme to you, he is steering the preaching, the attitudes, and the conduct from the start – and he will never let go of the reins." The gospel has already overtaken everything from the very start. Against this power and wisdom of the gospel, criticism and opposition always come too late. Thus we are always able to say the essential things we have to say positively, and that means, evangelically.

In genuine secularity, moreover, we also gain this, that under no circumstances do we retreat from the world into a storm-free zone of sacred ritual. This is one of the most important things that we must say today, for example, to the oppressed church in middle and east Germany, *viz.*, that it should not lapse into an unjustified reliance on liturgy which is, as is well known, quite objective and thus not subject to persecution or prohibition. When we say this, we are not concerned with false antitheses as they are often drawn between homiletics and liturgy. Rather, we are concerned with the danger of taking flight, whether because of understandable fear or because of resignation, with regard to the power and promise of preaching. This danger seeks its prey in the *whole* scope of preaching, and also everywhere in the congregation. If we seek an "unassailable scope" for preaching, or even if we hold ourselves entirely aloof from preaching, then we are trying to do the same thing with regard to life – admittedly, entirely in vain. The congregation, which receives its mandate through preaching, is sent back into the world, not released from it. It distinguishes itself from the world not through external evidences of self-authoritative sanctity, but through *the* faith which without despair says what it has to say in the right place because it understands its baptism, seizes hold of it, and rejoices in it. |

"Preparation for preaching," as it must be presented to the future preacher, has not been treated here as a discussion of technical methodological or formal practices. Such practices, which must *also* be discussed in *their* appropriate place, are almost self-understood. Rather, we have sought to understand preparation for preaching in such a way that we tried to demonstrate – in relation to a few major categories – the continuity of the movement, with deference to its freedom, which proceeds from the text: from the translation, into language, to the world-centered actions of the congregation. We find these three steps, which form a close-knit unity in the whole matter, also mentioned in Luther's formulation: "To the event, therefore, there also belongs the right use of the event, so that it is made evident through the word, held fast through faith, and thus man is made whole." "*Ad factum ergo requiritur etiam usus facti, ut per verbum declaretur et per fidem teneatur et sic homo (credens) salvetur.*"

Revised October 31, 1965

haRpeR ✦ coRchbooks

HUMANITIES AND SOCIAL SCIENCES

American Studies: General

THOMAS C. COCHRAN: The Inner Revolution: *Essays on the Social Sciences in History*　TB/1140

EDWARD S. CORWIN: American Constitutional History. *Essays edited by Alpheus T. Mason and Gerald Garvey*　TB/1136

A. HUNTER DUPREE: Science in the Federal Government: *A History of Policies and Activities to 1940*　TB/573

OSCAR HANDLIN, Ed.: This Was America: *As Recorded by European Travelers in the Eighteenth, Nineteenth and Twentieth Centuries. Illus.*　TB/1119

MARCUS LEE HANSEN: The Atlantic Migration: 1607-1860. *Edited by Arthur M. Schlesinger; Introduction by Oscar Handlin*　TB/1052

MARCUS LEE HANSEN: The Immigrant in American History. *Edited with a Foreword by Arthur M. Schlesinger*　TB/1120

JOHN HIGHAM, Ed.: The Reconstruction of American History　TB/1068

ROBERT H. JACKSON: The Supreme Court in the American System of Government　TB/1106

JOHN F. KENNEDY: A Nation of Immigrants. *Illus. Revised and Enlarged. Introduction by Robert F. Kennedy*　TB/1118

RALPH BARTON PERRY: Puritanism and Democracy　TB/1138

ARNOLD ROSE: The Negro in America: *The Condensed Version of Gunnar Myrdal's An American Dilemma*　TB/3048

MAURICE R. STEIN: The Eclipse of Community: *An Interpretation of American Studies*　TB/1128

W. LLOYD WARNER and Associates: Democracy in Jonesville: *A Study in Quality and Inequality* ‖　TB/1129

W. LLOYD WARNER: Social Class in America: *The Evaluation of Status*　TB/1013

American Studies: Colonial

BERNARD BAILYN, Ed.: The Apologia of Robert Keayne: *Self-Portrait of a Puritan Merchant*　TB/1201

BERNARD BAILYN: The New England Merchants in the Seventeenth Century　TB/1149

JOSEPH CHARLES: The Origins of the American Party System　TB/1049

LAWRENCE HENRY GIPSON: The Coming of the Revolution: 1763-1775. † *Illus.*　TB/3007

LEONARD W. LEVY: Freedom of Speech and Press in Early American History: *Legacy of Suppression*　TB/1109

PERRY MILLER: Errand Into the Wilderness　TB/1139

PERRY MILLER & T. H. JOHNSON, Eds.: The Puritans: *A Sourcebook of Their Writings*
Vol. I TB/1093; Vol. II TB/1094

KENNETH B. MURDOCK: Literature and Theology in Colonial New England　TB/99

WALLACE NOTESTEIN: The English People on the Eve of Colonization: 1603-1630. † *Illus.*　TB/3006

LOUIS B. WRIGHT: The Cultural Life of the American Colonies: 1607-1763. † *Illus.*　TB/3005

American Studies: From the Revolution to the Civil War

JOHN R. ALDEN: The American Revolution: 1775-1783. † *Illus.*　TB/3011

RAY A. BILLINGTON: The Far Western Frontier: 1830-1860. † *Illus.*　TB/3012

GEORGE DANGERFIELD: The Awakening of American Nationalism: 1815-1828. † *Illus.*　TB/3061

CLEMENT EATON: The Freedom-of-Thought Struggle in the Old South. *Revised and Enlarged. Illus.*　TB/1150

CLEMENT EATON: The Growth of Southern Civilization: 1790-1860. † *Illus.*　TB/3040

LOUIS FILLER: The Crusade Against Slavery: 1830-1860. † *Illus.*　TB/3029

DIXON RYAN FOX: The Decline of Aristocracy in the Politics of New York: 1801-1840. ‡ *Edited by Robert V. Remini*　TB/3064

FELIX GILBERT: The Beginnings of American Foreign Policy: *To the Farewell Address*　TB/1200

FRANCIS J. GRUND: Aristocracy in America: *Social Class in the Formative Years of the New Nation*　TB/1001

ALEXANDER HAMILTON: The Reports of Alexander Hamilton. ‡ *Edited by Jacob E. Cooke*　TB/3060

THOMAS JEFFERSON: Notes on the State of Virginia. ‡ *Edited by Thomas P. Abernethy*　TB/3052

BERNARD MAYO: Myths and Men: *Patrick Henry, George Washington, Thomas Jefferson*　TB/1108

JOHN C. MILLER: Alexander Hamilton and the Growth of the New Nation　TB/3057

RICHARD B. MORRIS, Ed.: The Era of the American Revolution　TB/1180

R. B. NYE: The Cultural Life of the New Nation: 1776-1801. † *Illus.*　TB/3026

† The New American Nation Series, edited by Henry Steele Commager and Richard B. Morris.

‡ American Perspectives series, edited by Bernard Wishy and William E. Leuchtenburg.

* The Rise of Modern Europe series, edited by William L. Langer.

‖ Researches in the Social, Cultural, and Behavioral Sciences, edited by Benjamin Nelson.

§ The Library of Religion and Culture, edited by Benjamin Nelson.

ᵘ Not for sale in Canada.

Σ Harper Modern Science Series, edited by James R. Newman.

FRANK THISTLETHWAITE: America and the Atlantic Community: *Anglo-American Aspects, 1790-1850* TB/1107

A. F. TYLER: Freedom's Ferment: *Phases of American Social History from the Revolution to the Outbreak of the Civil War. 31 illus.* TB/1074

GLYNDON G. VAN DEUSEN: The Jacksonian Era: 1828-1848. † *Illus.* TB/3028

LOUIS B. WRIGHT: Culture on the Moving Frontier TB/1053

American Studies: Since the Civil War

RAY STANNARD BAKER: Following the Color Line: *American Negro Citizenship in Progressive Era.* ‡ *Illus. Edited by Dewey W. Grantham, Jr.* TB/3053

RANDOLPH S. BOURNE: War and the Intellectuals: *Collected Essays, 1915-1919.* ‡ *Ed. by Carl Resek* TB/3043

A. RUSSELL BUCHANAN: The United States and World War II. † *Illus.* Vol. I TB/3044; Vol. II TB/3045

ABRAHAM CAHAN: The Rise of David Levinsky: *a documentary novel of social mobility in early twentieth century America. Intro. by John Higham* TB/1028

THOMAS C. COCHRAN: The American Business System: *A Historical Perspective, 1900-1955* TB/1080

THOMAS C. COCHRAN & WILLIAM MILLER: The Age of Enterprise: *A Social History of Industrial America* TB/1054

FOSTER RHEA DULLES: America's Rise to World Power: *1898-1954.* † *Illus.* TB/3021

W. A. DUNNING: Essays on the Civil War and Reconstruction. *Introduction by David Donald* TB/1181

W. A. DUNNING: Reconstruction, Political and Economic: *1865-1877* TB/1073

HAROLD U. FAULKNER: Politics, Reform and Expansion: *1890-1900.* † *Illus.* TB/3020

JOHN D. HICKS: Republican Ascendancy: *1921-1933.* † *Illus.* TB/3041

ROBERT HUNTER: Poverty: *Social Conscience in the Progressive Era.* ‡ *Edited by Peter d'A. Jones* TB/3065

HELEN HUNT JACKSON: A Century of Dishonor: *The Early Crusade for Indian Reform.* ‡ *Edited by Andrew F. Rolle* TB/3063

ALBERT D. KIRWAN: Revolt of the Rednecks: *Mississippi Politics, 1876-1925* TB/1199

WILLIAM L. LANGER & S. EVERETT GLEASON: The Challenge to Isolation: *The World Crisis of 1937-1940 and American Foreign Policy* Vol. I TB/3054; Vol. II TB/3055

WILLIAM E. LEUCHTENBURG: Franklin D. Roosevelt and the New Deal: *1932-1940.* † *Illus.* TB/3025

ARTHUR S. LINK: Woodrow Wilson and the Progressive Era: *1910-1917.* † *Illus.* TB/3023

ROBERT GREEN MCCLOSKEY: American Conservatism in the Age of Enterprise: *1865-1910* TB/1137

GEORGE E. MOWRY: The Era of Theodore Roosevelt and the Birth of Modern America: *1900-1912.* † *Illus.* TB/3022

RUSSEL B. NYE: Midwestern Progressive Politics: *A Historical Study of its Origins and Development, 1870-1958* TB/1202

WALTER RAUSCHENBUSCH: Christianity and the Social Crisis. ‡ *Edited by Robert D. Cross* TB/3059

WHITELAW REID: After the War: *A Tour of the Southern States, 1865-1866.* ‡ *Edited by C. Vann Woodward* TB/3066

CHARLES H. SHINN: Mining Camps: *A Study in American Frontier Government.* ‡ *Edited by Rodman W. Paul* TB/3062

TWELVE SOUTHERNERS: I'll Take My Stand: *The South and the Agrarian Tradition. Intro. by Louis D. Rubin, Jr.; Biographical Essays by Virginia Rock* TB/1072

WALTER E. WEYL: The New Democracy: *An Essay on Certain Political Tendencies in the United States.* ‡ *Edited by Charles B. Forcey* TB/3042

VERNON LANE WHARTON: The Negro in Mississippi: *1865-1890* TB/1178

Anthropology

JACQUES BARZUN: Race: *A Study in Superstition. Revised Edition* TB/1172

JOSEPH B. CASAGRANDE, Ed.: In the Company of Man: *Twenty Portraits of Anthropological Informants. Illus.* TB/3047

W. E. LE GROS CLARK: The Antecedents of Man: *Intro. to Evolution of the Primates.* ° *Illus.* TB/559

CORA DU BOIS: The People of Alor. *New Preface by the author. Illus.* Vol. I TB/1042; Vol. II TB/1043

RAYMOND FIRTH, Ed.: Man and Culture: *An Evaluation of the Work of Bronislaw Malinowski* ‖ ° TB/1133

L. S. B. LEAKEY: Adam's Ancestors: *The Evolution of Man and His Culture. Illus.* TB/1019

ROBERT H. LOWIE: Primitive Society. *Introduction by Fred Eggan* TB/1056

SIR EDWARD TYLOR: The Origins of Culture. *Part I of "Primitive Culture."* § *Intro. by Paul Radin* TB/33

SIR EDWARD TYLOR: Religion in Primitive Culture. *Part II of "Primitive Culture."* § *Intro. by Paul Radin* TB/34

W. LLOYD WARNER: A Black Civilization: *A Study of an Australian Tribe.* ‖ *Illus.* TB/3056

Art and Art History

WALTER LOWRIE: Art in the Early Church. *Revised Edition. 452 illus.* TB/124

EMILE MÂLE: The Gothic Image: *Religious Art in France of the Thirteenth Century.* § *190 illus.* TB/44

MILLARD MEISS: Painting in Florence and Siena after the Black Death: *The Arts, Religion and Society in the Mid-Fourteenth Century. 169 illus.* TB/1148

ERICH NEUMANN: The Archetypal World of Henry Moore. *107 illus.* TB/2020

DORA & ERWIN PANOFSKY: Pandora's Box: *The Changing Aspects of a Mythical Symbol. Revised Edition. Illus.* TB/2021

ERWIN PANOFSKY: Studies in Iconology: *Humanistic Themes in the Art of the Renaissance. 180 illustrations* TB/1077

ALEXANDRE PIANKOFF: The Shrines of Tut-Ankh-Amon. *Edited by N. Rambova. 117 illus.* TB/2011

JEAN SEZNEC: The Survival of the Pagan Gods: *The Mythological Tradition and Its Place in Renaissance Humanism and Art. 108 illustrations* TB/2004

OTTO VON SIMSON: The Gothic Cathedral: *Origins of Gothic Architecture and the Medieval Concept of Order. 58 illus.* TB/2018

HEINRICH ZIMMER: Myth and Symbols in Indian Art and Civilization. *70 illustrations* TB/2005

Business, Economics & Economic History

REINHARD BENDIX: Work and Authority in Industry: *Ideologies of Management in the Course of Industrialization* TB/3035

GILBERT BURCK & EDITORS OF FORTUNE: The Computer Age: *And Its Potential for Management* TB/1179

THOMAS C. COCHRAN: The American Business System: *A Historical Perspective, 1900-1955* TB/1080

THOMAS C. COCHRAN: The Inner Revolution: *Essays on the Social Sciences in History* TB/1140

History: Modern European

4

Political Science & Government

Psychology

Christianity: General

Christianity: Origins & Early Development

Christianity: The Middle Ages and The Reformation

Christianity: The Protestant Tradition

NATURAL SCIENCES AND MATHEMATICS

Biological Sciences